H. A. Wheeler.

Eastleigh.

May 18 . 1915.

Martin

WILLIAM COBBETT

WILLIAM COBBETT

A Study of His Life as Shown in His Writings

BY E. I. CARLYLE, F.R.Hist.S.

FELLOW OF MERTON COLLEGE, OXFORD

ILLUSTRATED

LONDON

ARCHIBALD CONSTABLE AND COMPANY

LIMITED

1904

Edinburgh: T. and A. Constable, Printers to His Majesty

PREFACE

THE object of this work, as has been set forth in the title, is to portray the life and character of William Cobbett, with the assistance chiefly of the materials to be found in his writings. Besides writing several fragmentary autobiographies, Cobbett had the habit of illustrating his disquisitions on politics, on finance, or on agriculture, with personal references and reminiscences which, collected together, would fill several volumes. These autobiographical treasures are to be found in all of his works, though not everywhere in equal abundance. Moreover, they are usually sudden excursions with little in the context to indicate their presence to the seeker. His *Political Register*, for instance, is particularly rich in references to his past life, but in order to discover them it is necessary to examine more than seventy volumes page by page. As much the same process is necessary in regard to his other works the task is one of some magnitude, for Cobbett was probably the most prolific writer whom England has known, with the exception of Defoe.

Perhaps the number of Cobbett's writings, in addition to the ephemeral interest of many of them, is a reason why they are now so little read. With a view of bringing some of his less known pieces to the notice of the public, I have selected passages for quotation which, though not directly autobiographical, yet seem to illustrate his political and social opinions, or to afford good examples of his literary style. But I have endeavoured to avoid extracts which are recommended only by their beauty of form and to choose those in preference whose context is in direct connection with the narrative.

While necessarily basing this study chiefly on Cobbett's own writings, I have also availed myself of the statements and opinions of his contemporaries in regard to him. But to collect these together is a task which would require many years to perform with any approach to completeness. Not only is the literary output of the first forty years of the nineteenth century immeasurably greater than that of any similar preceding period, but it has also been much less worked over. Thus while its extraordinary volume renders an exhaustive examination impossible, its unorganised condition makes it very difficult to proceed on any satisfactory process of selection. It is certain that much material of importance must still lie hidden amid the immense mass of contemporary newspapers, periodicals, and books, which have neither been analysed nor indexed.

I have, however, always where possible, applied independent tests to Cobbett's statements of fact, and in general I have found them accurate, except where he has meant to mislead. Almost all his writings were intended for immediate publication, and were composed with the knowledge that they would be jealously scrutinised by his political antagonists. If he made a serious mis-statement, he was liable to be confuted at once and to incur corresponding discredit. In two or three instances where he has undoubtedly made false assertions, he made them either under the influence of strong feeling or because he believed that the actual facts could not become known. In general his statements in regard to occur-rences or events may be relied on. Where facts seemed to discredit him, he took refuge in silence or in vehement utterance on a different topic.

Only two serious biographies of Cobbett are in existence. The first was published in two large volumes in 1836 immediately after his death. Its author, Robert Huish, at one time held a commission in the army and afterwards made his living by the compilation of books. In the same year in which his *Memoirs of Cobbett* appeared he published lives of Henry Hunt and O'Connell, so that his rate of writing must have been prodigious. Although a strong opponent of the Tory party he had also a great dislike to Cobbett, and he lost no opportunity of present-ing him at a disadvantage. The chief value of his work indeed consists in the collection of hostile passages concerning Cobbett which he made from contemporary publications. In most respects it is worthless, filled with ridiculous blunders and void of any particulars concerning some of the most important passages in Cobbett's life.

The other biography of Cobbett is entirely different in

character : it is that published in 1878 by Mr. Edward Smith. Mr. Smith had a profound admiration for Cobbett and a great knowledge of the literature that grew up around his hero. He has devoted considerable attention to ascertaining the particulars of Cobbett's biography. To any one interested in Cobbett's career his work must always be valuable.

In conclusion I should like to say that I am very much indebted to Mr. Thomas Seccombe for his advice and assistance, and that I shall always be grateful to him for the interest he has taken. I have also to thank Mr. Sidney Lee and the Rev. R. C. Gillie, of Eastbourne, for calling my attention to references to Cobbett which otherwise I might have overlooked.

CONTENTS

NOTES ON THE ILLUSTRATIONS

CARICATURES OF COBBETT

[*The first eight of these are by* GILLRAY, *and the remainder by* 'H. B.' (JOHN DOYLE)]

WILLIAM COBBETT

CHAPTER I

COBBETT'S EARLY LIFE

THE parish of Farnham, Cobbett's birthplace, is situated in the extreme west of Surrey, within a short distance of the Hampshire border. The chalk ridges of the North Downs, running east and west, cut Surrey in two and extend far into Hampshire. In western Surrey they consist for the most part of a succession of rolling downs, covered with short turf or with heather or gorse and sparsely dotted with pine-trees, while the line of high ground is broken in two places by the streams of the Wey and the Mole. Farnham lies in the valley of the Wey, and Guildford to the eastward in that of the Mole, with the ridge of the Hog's Back running between them. The district of Farnham, both in Cobbett's time and now, is chiefly devoted to the cultivation of hops, and to him it seemed the 'neatest' spot in England, and perhaps in the whole world. He loved to dwell on its well-ordered appearance, on its lines of close-clipped hedges extending in every direction and becoming fainter to the eye as they receded in the distance, and on the thousand indications of rustic prosperity which the neighbourhood afforded. Three miles east of Farnham rises Crookesbury Hill, a pine-clad height, which forms the most

A

conspicuous landmark in that direction, and half-way between the hill and the town is Moor Park, the last retreat of Sir William Temple, famous as the abode of Swift and Stella. Overhanging the town to the north-west is Hungry Hill, close under which runs the London road. At the present day Farnham is a scene of bustle and activity owing to the nearness of the military camp at Aldershot. It has far outgrown its former limits and has extended itself eastward across the Wey. In Cobbett's time, however, the town only reached the western border of that stream, although there were a few isolated buildings on the other bank. It was then a peculiarly retired country town with a long main street, overlooked on the north by Farnham Castle, a favourite residence of the Bishops of Winchester. Among the few houses existing at that time on the other side of the Wey was that in which Cobbett was born. It was an inn called the 'Jolly Farmer,' and still stands unaltered, facing a bridge over the stream at a point where a lane from Weydon Mill runs into Abbey Street. It is a long low building with pretty casement windows, and a big plastered gable showing towards the road. Though now part of a long street running parallel with the river, it then stood alone, forming an outpost of the town in the south-eastern side towards Millbridge and Frensham. In this house Cobbett spent the first twenty years of his life.

The story of Cobbett's earlier years is only preserved in his own writings, chiefly in a fragment of autobio-graphy, published at Philadelphia in 1796, under the title of *The Life and Adventures of Peter Porcupine*. The motto prefixed to this pamphlet, 'Now, you lying varlets, you shall see how a plain tale will put you down,' is an incorrect quotation from Shakespeare's *Henry IV*. While its inaccuracy shows haste, its purport indicates that the book was written in the heat of controversy. In composing this autobiographical fragment Cobbett had two objects in view — first, to justify his Tory principles to the Americans by showing that they were not aristocratic prejudices acquired by birth and education, and secondly, to indicate delicately that though he had the misfortune to differ from many of his neighbours on political questions, yet as a self-taught, self-made man, he was really akin to the majority of Americans in the disposition of his mind.

'To be descended from an illustrious family,' he observes, 'certainly reflects honour on any man, in spite of the sans-culotte principles of the present day. This is however an honour that I have no pretension to. All that I can boast of in my birth, is, that I was born in England; the country from whence came the men who explored and settled North America; the country of Penn, and of the father and mother of George Washington.'

He goes on to say that his grandfather, George Cobbett, was a day-labourer in the neighbourhood of Farnham.

'I have heard my father say, that he worked for one farmer from the day of his marriage to that of his death, upwards of forty years. He died before I was born,[1] but I have often slept beneath the same roof that had sheltered him, and where his widow dwelt for several years after his death. It was a little thatched cottage with a garden before the door. It had but two windows; a damson-tree shaded one, and a clump of filberts the other. Here I and my brothers went every

---

[1] George Cobbett died on 13th December 1760, at the age of fifty-nine.

Christmas and Whitsuntide to spend a week or two, and
torment the poor old woman with our noise and dilapidations.
She used to give us milk and bread for breakfast, an apple-
pudding for our dinner, and a piece of bread and cheese for
supper. Her fire was made of turf, cut from the neighbouring
heath, and her evening light was a rush dipped in grease.'

Cobbett's father, George Cobbett, was a farmer and
also landlord of the 'Jolly Farmer.'

'The reader will easily believe, from the poverty of his
parents, that he had received no very brilliant education; he
was, however, learned, for a man in his rank of life. When a
little boy, he drove plough for twopence a day; and these his
earnings were appropriated to the expenses of an evening
school. What a village schoolmaster could be expected to teach,
he had learnt; and had, besides, considerably improved himself
in several branches of mathematics; he understood land-
surveying well, and was often chosen to draw the plans of a
disputed territory: in short, he had the reputation of possessing
experience and understanding, which never fails in England, to
give a man in a country place, some little weight with his neighbours. He was honest, industrious, and frugal; it was not therefore wonderful, that he should be situated in a good farm, and
happy in a wife of his own rank, like him, beloved and respected.'

On 12th October 1759 George Cobbett married Ann
Vincent, of whom her son William always spoke with
tenderness. She was unable to write, for her mark may
still be seen in the Farnham marriage register. William
was born in his father's house on 9th March. The year
of his birth is not quite certain. He himself has said
that it was 1766, but this is impossible, for he was
baptized on 1st April 1763. At the time of his death
his son, John M. Cobbett, had an extract made from
the Farnham register which he thought fixed his father's
birth in 1762. But an examination of the register shows

that John M. Cobbett quoted it incorrectly, and that
though the date 9th March 1762 is not impossible, it is
more probable that Cobbett was born on 9th March 1763.[1]

Cobbett was the third of four sons, George, Thomas,
William, and Anthony. Of his brothers the eldest
became a shopkeeper, the second a farmer, and the
youngest entered the service of the East India Company as a private soldier. He himself began work at
an early age.

'I do not remember the time when I did not earn my living.
My first occupation was, driving the small birds from the turnip-
seed, and the rooks from the pease. When I first trudged a-field,
with my wooden bottle and my satchel swung over my shoulders,
I was hardly able to climb the gates and stiles; and, at the close
of the day, to reach home, was a task of infinite difficulty. My
next employment was weeding wheat, and leading a single horse
at harrowing barley. Hoeing pease followed, and hence I
arrived at the honour of joining the reapers in harvest, driving
the team, and holding plough. We were all of us strong and
laborious, and my father used to boast, that he had four boys,
the eldest of whom was but fifteen years old, who did as much
work as any three men in the parish of Farnham. Honest pride
and happy days!'[2]

In his *English Gardener* he says that Waverley Abbey,
an estate some two miles south-east of Farnham, was a
haunt of his childhood. It belonged to Sir Robert Rich,
a lieutenant-general, who had been severely wounded at
Culloden. The Abbey, which had been the earliest
foundation of the Cistercians in England, had a beautiful
kitchen-garden—

'The spot,' says Cobbett, 'where I first began to learn to
work, or, rather, where I first began to eat fine fruit in a garden;

---

[1] For date of Cobbett's birth see Appendix A.
[2] *Life and Adventures of Peter Porcupine.*

and, though I have now seen and observed upon as many fine gardens as any man in England, I have never seen a garden equal to that of Waverley. Ten families, large as they might be, including troops of servants (who are no churls in this way), could not have consumed the fruit produced in that garden. The peaches, nectarines, apricots, fine plums, never failed; and if the workmen had not lent a hand, a fourth part of the produce never could have been got rid of.'

Cobbett's early education was slender.

'I have some faint recollection of going to school to an old woman, who, I believe, did not succeed in learning me my letters. In the winter evenings my father learnt us all to read and write, and gave us a pretty tolerable knowledge of arithmetic. Grammar he did not perfectly understand himself, and therefore his endeavours to learn us that necessarily failed; for though he thought he understood it, and though he made us get the rules by heart, we learnt nothing at all of the principles.'[1]

Slight though this education was, it was sufficient to enable him to gratify that love of literature which was a notable feature of his earlier years. Many years later he narrated how he first became acquainted with Swift, an author who afterwards strongly influenced the form and style of his own writings.

'At eleven years of age[2] my employment was clipping of box-edgings and weeding beds of flowers in the garden of the Bishop of Winchester,[3] at the Castle of Farnham, my native town. I had always been fond of beautiful gardens; and, a gardener, who had just come from the King's gardens at Kew, gave such a description of them as made me instantly resolve to work in

---

[1] *Life and Adventures of Peter Porcupine.*

[2] Cobbett was probably older when this incident occurred. He goes on to say that he entered the army at sixteen, fixing the year of his birth erroneously at 1766.

[3] John Thomas. He had two contemporaries of the same name, at Salisbury and Rochester.

AN APOCRYPHAL INCIDENT IN COBBETT'S CHILDHOOD.

those gardens. The next morning, without saying a word to any one, off I set, with no clothes except those upon my back, and with thirteen half-pence in my pocket. I found that I must go to Richmond, and I accordingly went on, from place to place, inquiring my way thither. A long day (it was in June) brought me to Richmond in the afternoon. Two penny-worth of bread and cheese and a penny-worth of small beer, which I had on the road, and one half-penny that I had lost somehow or other, left three pence in my pocket. With this for my whole fortune, I was trudging through Richmond, in my blue smock-frock and my red garters tied under my knees, when, staring about me, my eye fell upon a little book in a bookseller's window, on the outside of which was written: "TALE OF A TUB; price 3d." The title was so odd, that my curiosity was excited. I had the three pence, but, then, I could have *no supper*. In I went, and got the little book, which I was so impatient to read, that I got over into a field at the upper corner of Kew Gardens, where there stood a *haystack*. On the shady side of this, I sat down to read. The book was so different from any-thing that I had ever read before: it was something so *new* to my mind, that, though I could not at all understand some of it, it delighted me beyond description; and it produced what I have always considered a sort of birth of intellect. I read on till it was dark, without any thought about supper or bed. When I could see no longer, I put my little book in my pocket, and tumbled down by the side of the stack, where I slept till the birds in Kew Gardens awaked me in the morning; when off I started to Kew, reading my little book. The singularity of my dress, the simplicity of my manner, my confident and lively air, and, doubtless, his own compassion besides, induced the gardener, who was a Scotsman, I remember, to give me victuals, find me lodging, and set me to work. And it was during the period that I was at Kew that the present king[1] and two of his brothers laughed at the oddness of my dress, while I was sweeping the grass plat round the foot of the Pagoda. The gardener, seeing me fond of books, lent me some gardening books to read; but these I could not relish after my *Tale of a*

[1] George IV.

Tub, which I carried about with me wherever I went, and when I, at about twenty years old, lost it in a box that fell overboard in the Bay of Fundy in North America, the loss gave me greater pain than I have ever felt at losing thousands of pounds.'[1]

While the perusal of Swift's satire was the beginning of Cobbett's delight in literature, his interest in politics, which absorbed so much of his life, was first awakened by the American War of Independence.

'As to politics,' he says, 'we were like the rest of the country people in England; that is to say, we neither knew or thought anything of the matter. The shouts of victory, or the murmurs at a defeat, would now and then break in upon our tranquillity for a moment; but I do not remember ever having seen a newspaper in the house. . . . After, however, the American war had continued for some time, and the cause and nature of it began to be understood, or rather misunderstood, by the lower classes of the people in England, we became a little better acquainted with subjects of this kind. . . . My father was a partizan of the Americans: he used frequently to dispute on the subject with the gardener of a nobleman who lived near us. This was generally done with good humour over a pot of our best ale; yet the disputants sometimes grew warm, and gave way to language that could not fail to attract our attention. My father was worsted no doubt, as he had for antagonist a shrewd and sensible old Scotchman, far his superior in political knowledge; but he pleaded before a partial audience: we thought there was but one wise man in the world, and that that one was our father. He who pleaded the cause of the Americans had an advantage, too, with young minds: he had only to represent the king's troops as sent to cut the throats of a people, our friends and relations, merely because they would not submit to oppression; and his cause was gained. Speaking to the passions is ever sure to succeed on the uninformed.

'Men of integrity are generally pretty obstinate in adhering to

---

[1] *Cobbett's Evening Post*, 5th February 1820.

an opinion once adopted. Whether it was owing to this, or to the weakness of Mr. Martin's arguments, I will not pretend to say; but he never could make a convert of my father: he continued an American, and so staunch a one, that he would not have suffered his best friend to drink success to the King's arms at his table. I cannot give the reader a better idea of his obstinacy in this respect, and of the length to which this difference in sentiment was carried in England, than by relating the following instance.

'My father used to take one of us with him every year to the great hop-fair at Wey-hill. The fair was held at Old Michaelmas-tide, and the journey was, to us, a sort of reward for the labours of the summer. It happened to be my turn to go thither, the very year that Long Island was taken by the British.[1] A great company of hop-merchants and farmers were just sitting down to supper as the post arrived, bringing in the Extraordinary Gazette, which announced the victory. A hop-factor from London took the paper, placed his chair upon the table, and began to read with an audible voice. He was opposed, a dispute ensued, and my father retired, taking me by the hand, to another apartment where we supped with about a dozen others of the same sentiments. Here Washington's health, and success to the Americans, were repeatedly toasted, and this was the first time, as far as I can recollect, that I ever heard the General's name mentioned.'[2]

Cobbett's life was passed amid the trivial incidents of a country village until he had reached his twenty-first year. He has related inimitably the occasion of his entry on a larger life.

'Towards the autumn of 1782, I went to visit a relation who lived in the neighbourhood of Portsmouth. From the top of Portsdown, I, for the first time, beheld the sea, and no sooner did I behold it, than I wished to be a sailor. I could never

[1] Long Island was captured late in August 1776, when Cobbett was probably thirteen years old.
[2] *Life and Adventures of Peter Porcupine.*

account for this sudden impulse, nor can I now. Almost all English boys feel the same inclination: it would seem that, like young ducks, instinct leads them to rush upon the bosom of the water.

'But it was not the sea alone that I saw; the grand fleet was riding at anchor at Spithead.[1] I had heard of the Wooden Walls of Old England: I had formed my ideas of a ship and of a fleet; but, what I now beheld, so far surpassed what I had ever been able to form a conception of, that I stood lost between astonishment and admiration. I had heard talk of the glorious deeds of our admirals and sailors, of the defeat of the Spanish Armada, and of all those memorable combats, that good and true Englishmen never fail to relate to their children about a hundred times a year. The brave Rodney's victories over our natural enemies, the French and Spaniards, had long been the theme of our praise, and the burden of our songs. The sight of the fleet brought all these into my mind; in confused order, it is true, but with irresistible force. My heart was inflated with national pride. The sailors were my countrymen; the fleet belonged to my country, and surely I had my part in it and in all its honours: yet, these honours I had not earned; I took to myself a sort of reproach, for possessing what I had no right to, and resolved to have a just claim, by sharing in the hardships and the dangers.

'I arrived at my uncle's late in the evening, with my mind full of my seafaring project. Though I had walked thirty miles during the day, and consequently was well wearied, I slept not a moment. It was no sooner daylight, than I arose and walked down towards the old castle, on the beach at Spithead. For a sixpence given to an invalid, I got permission to go upon the battlements: here I had a closer view of the fleet, and at every look my impatience to be on board increased. In short, I went from the castle to Portsmouth, got into a boat, and was in a few minutes on board the *Pegasus* man-of-war.'

---

[1] Lord Howe's fleet of one hundred and eighty-three sail, comprising thirty-four ships of the line, which lay at Spithead refitting from 15th August to 11th September before proceeding to the relief of Gibraltar. It was during this stay that the loss of the *Royal George* occurred.

The *Pegasus* was a seventy-four, captured in that very
year from the French. She was commanded by the
Hon. George Cranfield Berkeley, brother of the fifth
Earl of Berkeley. Cobbett was brought before him,
but met with a discouraging reception. Berkeley drew
a gloomy picture of the common sailor's life, and plainly
showed him his opinion of his motive in volunteering, by
telling him that it was better to be led to church in a
halter to be tied to a girl he did not like, than to be
tied to the gangway, or, as the sailors called it, married
to Miss Roper. Cobbett earnestly disclaimed the insinuation that he had eloped on account of a bastard, but his
blushes confirmed the captain's suspicions and he refused
to take him. An application to the port admiral to have
his name enrolled was equally unsuccessful.

'I returned once more to the plough,' says Cobbett, 'but I
was spoiled for a farmer. I had, before my Portsmouth adventure, never known any other ambition than that of surpassing
my brothers in the different labours of the field: but it was
quite otherwise now; I sighed for a sight of the world; the
little Island of Britain seemed too small a compass for me.
The things in which I had taken most delight were neglected ;
the singing of the birds grew insipid, and even the heart-cheering
cry of the hounds, after which I formerly used to fly from my
work, bound o'er the fields, and dash through the brakes and
coppices, was heard with the most torpid indifference. Still,
however, I remained at home till the following spring, when I
quitted it, perhaps for ever.[1]

'It was on the 6th May 1783, that I, like Don Quixote, sallied
forth to seek adventures. I was dressed in my holiday clothes,
in order to accompany two or three lasses to Guildford fair.
They were to assemble at a house about three miles from my
home, where I was to attend them ; but, unfortunately for me,
I had to cross the London turnpike road. The stage-coach had

[1] Written in 1796, four years before his return to England.

just turned the summit of a hill, and was rattling down towards me at a merry rate. The notion of going to London never entered my mind till this very moment, yet the step was completely determined on before the coach came to the spot where I stood. Up I got, and was in London about nine o'clock in the evening.'

Seventeen years passed before Cobbett revisited his native village. He has left a picture of his return extraordinarily charged with pathetic emotion. It may well be given here for it abounds in touches of description which make his early life more real:

'I had to cross in my post-chaise, the long and dreary heath of Bagshot. Then at the end of it to mount a hill called Hungry Hill; and from that hill I knew that I should look down into the beautiful and fertile vale of Farnham. My heart fluttered with impatience, mixed with a sort of fear, to see all the scenes of my childhood; for I had learned before of the death of my father and mother.[1] There is a hill, not far from the town, called *Crooksbury Hill*, which rises up out of a flat, in the form of a *cone*, and is planted with Scotch fir-trees. Here I used to take the eggs and young ones of crows and magpies. This hill was a famous object in the neighbourhood. It served as the superlative degree of height. *As high as Crooksbury Hill* meant with us the utmost degree of height. Therefore, the first object that my eyes sought was this hill. *I could not believe my eyes!* Literally speaking, I, for a moment, thought the famous hill removed, and a little heap put in its stead; for I had seen in New Brunswick a single rock or hill of solid rock, ten times as big, and four or five times as high! The post-boy, going down hill, and not a bad road, whisked me, in a few minutes, to the Bush Inn, from the garden of which I could see the prodigious *sand hill*, where I had began my gardening works. What a *nothing!* But now came rushing into my mind all at once, my pretty little garden, my little blue smock-frock, my little nailed shoes, my pretty pigeons, that I used to feed out of my hands, the last kind words and tears of my gentle and tender-

[1] His father died in July 1792.

hearted and affectionate mother! I hastened back into the room. If I had looked a moment longer, I should have dropped. When I came to reflect, *what a change!* I looked down at my dress. What a change! What scenes I had gone through! How altered my state! I had dined the day before at the Secretary of State's [1] in company with *Mr. Pitt*, and had been waited on by men in gaudy liveries. I had had no one to assist me in the world. No teachers of any sort. Nobody to shelter me from the consequences of bad, and no one to counsel me to good, behaviour. I felt proud. The distinctions of rank, birth, and wealth, all became nothing in my eyes; and from that moment I resolved never to bend before them.' [2]

On his departure from home, however, the greatness which Cobbett felt that he had reached in 1800, had still to be attained. He started in the world modestly enough.

'It was by mere accident that I had money enough to defray the expenses of this day. Being rigged out for the fair, I had three or four crown and half crown pieces (which most certainly I did not intend to spend), besides a few shillings and half-pence. This, my little all, which I had been years in amassing, melted away like snow before the sun, when touched by the fingers of the inn-keepers and their waiters. In short, when I arrived at Ludgate Hill, and had paid my fare, I had but half-a-crown in my pocket.

'By a commencement of that good luck, which has hitherto attended me, through all the situations in which fortune has placed me, I was preserved from ruin. A gentleman, who was one of the passengers in the stage, fell into conversation with me at dinner, and he soon learned that I was going, I knew not whither, nor for what. This gentleman was a hop merchant in the Borough of Southwark, and, upon closer inquiry, it appeared that he had often dealt with my father at Weyhill. He knew

---

[1] William Windham, who was not at that time a Secretary of State, but Secretary at War. He was, however, a member of the cabinet, an honour never before conferred on the holder of that office.

[2] Cobbett's *Year's Residence in the United States*, ed. 1828, pp. 34-5.

the danger I was in; he was himself a father, and he felt for my parents. His house became my home; he wrote to my father and endeavoured to prevail on me to obey his orders, which were to return immediately home. I am ashamed to say that I was disobedient. It was the first time that I had ever been so, and I have repented of it from that moment to this. Willingly would I have returned; but pride would not suffer me to do it. I feared the scoffs of my acquaintances more than the real evils that threatened me.

'My generous preserver finding my obstinacy not to be overcome, began to look out for an employment for me. He was preparing an advertisement for the newspaper, when an acquaintance of his, an attorney, called in to see him. He related my adventure to this gentleman, whose name was Holland, and who, happening to want an understrapping quill-driver, did me the honour to take me into his service, and the next day saw me perched upon a great high stool, in an obscure chamber in Gray's Inn, endeavouring to decypher the crabbed draughts of my employer.

'I could write a good plain hand, but I could not read the pot-hooks and hangers of Mr. Holland. He was a month in learning me to copy without almost continual assistance, and even then I was of but little use to him; for, besides that I wrote a snail's pace, my want of knowledge in orthography gave him infinite trouble; so that for the first two months I was a dead weight upon his hands. Time, however, rendered me useful; and Mr. Holland was pleased to tell me, that he was very well satisfied with me, just at the very moment when I began to grow extremely dissatisfied with him.

'No part of my life has been totally unattended with pleasure, except the eight or nine months I passed in Gray's Inn. The office (for so the dungeon where I wrote was called) was so dark, that on cloudy days we were obliged to burn candle. I worked like a galley slave from five in the morning till eight or nine at night, and sometimes all night long. How many quarrels have I assisted to foment and perpetuate between those poor innocent fellows, John Doe and Richard Roe! How many times (God forgive me!) have I set them to assault each other with guns, swords, staves, and pitchforks, and then brought them to answer for their misdeeds before our Sovereign Lord the King, seated in his Court of Westminster! When I think of the *saids* and *so forths*, and the counts of tautology that I scribbled over; when I think of those sheets of seventy-two words, and those lines two inches apart my brain turns. Gracious heaven, if I am doomed to be wretched, bury me beneath Iceland snows, and let me feed on blubber; stretch me under the burning line, and deny me thy propitious dews; nay, if it be thy will, suffocate me with the infected and pestilential air of a democratic club-room,[1] but save me from the desk of an attorney!

'Mr. Holland was but little in chambers himself. He always went out to dinner, while I was left to be provided for by the *laundress*, as he called her. Those gentlemen of the law, who have resided in the Inns of Court in London, know very well what a *laundress* means. Ours was, I believe, the oldest and ugliest of the sisterhood. She had age and experience enough to be Lady Abbess of all the Nuns in all the convents in Irish-town. It would be wronging the Witch of Endor to compare her to this hag, who was the only creature that deigned to enter into conversation with me. All except the name, I was in prison, and this weird sister was my keeper. Our chambers were to me, what the subterraneous cavern was to Gil Blas; his description of the Dame Leonardo exactly suited my laundress; nor were the professions, or rather the practice, of our masters altogether dissimilar.'[2]

To one of his brothers he wrote at the time in a similar strain:

'I am in an earthly hell, if you feel that you have any roguery in you, and have a disposition to exercise it to its full extent, put yourself at the top of a coach, as I did, and make the best of your way to London. I could point out to you many places where you could practice roguery to perfection, but stop no where, get into an attorney's office as soon as you can, and you will have plenty of scope for your abilities. You may have

---

[1] When he wrote this Cobbett was a Tory.
[2] *Life and Adventures of Peter Porcupine.*

now and then some thing to do with *wit*, but it is only writing Surrey to wit, Middlesex to wit. If you think that you have any tenderness of conscience about you, for God's sake leave it behind you, it is of no use at all to you in an attorney's office ; and try as much as you can to obliterate from your mind all the fusty, antiquated notions about the responsibility of an oath, it is the most easy and convenient method of getting over a difficulty or mistake, for perjury is not the only dirty place which attorneys wade through to obtain their unhallowed gains.'[1]

Cobbett thus narrates the tale of his deliverance from Holland's office:

'I never quitted this gloomy recess except on Sundays, when I usually took a walk to St. James's Park, to feast my eyes with the sight of the trees, the grass, and the water. In one of these walks, I happened to cast my eyes upon an advertisement inviting all loyal young men, who had a mind to gain riches and glory, to repair to a certain rendezvous, where they might enter into His Majesty's Marine Service, and have the peculiar happiness and honour of being enrolled in the Chatham division. I was not ignorant enough to be the dupe of this morsel of military bombast; but a change was what I wanted; besides, I knew that marines went to sea, and my desire to be on that element had rather increased than diminished by my being penned up in London. In short, I resolved to join this glorious corps; and to avoid all possibility of being discovered by my friends, I went down to Chatham and enlisted into the marines as I thought, but the next morning I found myself before the captain of a marching regiment. There was no retreating; I had taken a shilling to drink his majesty's health, and his further bounty was ready for my reception.

'When I told the captain (who was an Irishman and who has since been an excellent friend to me) that I thought myself en-

---

[1] Cobbett to a brother, quoted in Huish's *Memoirs of Cobbett*, 1836, i. 18. The original is not extant. The only difficulty about accepting this letter as genuinely written at this time is that the style seems too mature for so early a period. Huish, writing immediately after Cobbett's death, had access to documents which have since disappeared.

The recruiting of Cobbett.

gaged in the marines: "By Jases, my lad," said he, "and you have had a narrow escape."'

He further consoled Cobbett by informing him that the 54th regiment, into which he had enlisted, was one of the oldest and boldest in the whole army, 'and that it was at that moment serving in that fine, flourishing, and plentiful country, Nova Scotia.' After dwelling on the beauties and riches of that terrestrial paradise he dismissed Cobbett enchanted with his good fortune.[1]

Cobbett enlisted early in 1784, and remained for more than a year at Chatham, before joining his regiment, engaged in learning his duties. He avoided the dissipations of his comrades.

'When in the army I was often tempted to take up the cards. But the words of my father came into my mind and rescued me from the peril. . . . During this part of my life I lived amongst, and was compelled to associate with, the most beastly of drunkards, where liquor was so cheap that even a soldier might be drunk any day ; yet I never, during the whole time, even *tasted* of that liquor ; my father's and especially my mother's precepts were always at hand to protect me.'[2]

While living a life of temperance he neglected no opportunity of improving his understanding. On this subject he received good advice from a friend. During his short residence in London he had made the acquaintance of Benjamin Garlike, afterwards British envoy at Copenhagen. On enlisting, Cobbett immediately informed him of what he had done, and, says Cobbett, he

'began his answer to me in somewhat these words: "Now, then, my dear Bill, it is for you to determine, whether you shall,

---

[1] *Life and Adventures of Peter Porcupine.*
[2] *Cobbett's Evening Post*, 5th February 1820.

B

all your life, yield an abject submission to others, or whether you yourself shall be a guider and leader of men. Nature has done her part towards you most generously; but her favours will be of no avail without a knowledge of grammar. Without that knowledge you will be laughed at by blockheads: with it, you may laugh at thousands who think themselves learned men." [1]

Cobbett acted in accordance with that advice.

'I learned grammar when I was a private soldier on the pay of sixpence a day. The edge of my berth, or that of the guard-bed, was my seat to study in; my knapsack was my bookcase; a bit of board lying on my lap was my writing-table; and the task did not demand any thing like a year of my life. I had no money to purchase candle or oil; in winter time it was rarely that I could get any evening-light but that of *the fire*, and only my *turn* even of that. And if I, under such circumstances, and without parent or friend to advise or encourage me, accomplished this undertaking, what excuse can there be for *any youth*, however poor, however pressed with business, or however circumstanced as to room or other conveniences? To buy a pen or a sheet of paper I was compelled to forego some portion of food, though in a state of half-starvation! I had no moment of time that I could call my own; and I had to read and to write amidst the talking, laughing, singing, whistling, and brawling of at least half a score of the most thoughtless of men, and that, too, in the hours of their freedom from all control. Think not lightly of the *farthing* that I had to give, now and then, for ink, pen, or paper! That farthing was, alas! a *great sum* to me! I was as tall as I am now; I had great health and great exercise. The whole of the money, not expended for us at market, was *twopence* a week for each man. I remember, and well I may! that, upon one occasion, I, after all absolutely necessary expenses, had, on a Friday, made shift to have a half-penny in reserve, which I had destined for the purchase of a *red herring* in the morning; but, when I pulled off my clothes at night, so hungry then as to be hardly able to endure life, I found that I had *lost*

[1] *Political Register*, 6th December 1817.

my half-penny ! I buried my head under the miserable sheet and rug, and cried like a child.' [1]

In spite of these privations Cobbett persevered in his self-education, spending his leisure in reading and study. He joined a circulating library at Brompton, fell in love with the librarian's pretty daughter, and read more than once the greater part of the books it contained. He became copyist to Colonel Debbieg, the commandant of the garrison, for whom he transcribed his famous correspondence with the Duke of Richmond, for which the Colonel was twice court-martialled, and on account of which he lost most of the rewards due to his long service.[2] He did not long endure, to their full extent, the hardships of a private soldier. While still at Chatham he was raised to the rank of a corporal, and his promotion rendered him the more impatient to join his regiment. Early in 1785 he was sent with a detachment to the headquarters of the 54th in Nova Scotia. In spite of the eulogies of the Irish captain, who had enlisted him, Cobbett did not find that colony particularly attractive.

'Nova Scotia had no other charm for me than that of novelty. Everything I saw was new : bogs, rocks, and stumps, mosquitoes and bull-frogs. Thousands of captains and colonels without soldiers, and of 'squires without stockings or shoes. In England I had never thought of approaching a 'squire without a most respectful bow ; but, in this new world, though I was but a corporal, I often ordered a 'squire to bring me a glass of grog, and even to take care of my knapsack.' [3]

---

[1] *Advice to Young Men*, 1837, pp. 39-41.
[2] See *Correspondence between the Duke of Richmond and Colonel Debbieg*, 1784, and *A Copy of the Proceedings of a general Court-Martial, held at the Horse Guards for the trial of Colonel Hugh Debbieg*, 1789.
[3] *Life and Adventures of Peter Porcupine.*

After a few weeks in Nova Scotia, the regiment was ordered to St. John's in New Brunswick, and it remained in that province until it was relieved and sent home in September 1791. Cobbett soon raised himself by his knowledge and capacity to a post of importance. Shortly after his arrival, he became clerk to the regiment, and within two years he was promoted sergeant-major. He ascribed his advancement to his habit of never wasting his time.

'To this, more than to any other thing, I owed my very extra-ordinary promotion in the army. I was *always ready* : if I had to mount guard at *ten*, I was ready at *nine* : never did any man, or any thing, wait one moment for me. Being at an age *under twenty years*,[1] raised from corporal to sergeant-major *at once*, over the heads of thirty sergeants,[2] I naturally should have been an object of envy and hatred ; but this habit of early rising and of rigid adherence to the precepts which I have given you really subdued these passions, because every one felt that what I did he had never done, and never could do. Before my promotion, a clerk was wanted to make out the morning report of the regiment. I rendered the clerk unnecessary ; and long before any other man was dressed for the parade, my work for the morning was all done, and I myself was on the parade, walking, in fine weather, for an hour perhaps. My custom was this : to get up in summer at day-light, and in winter at four o'clock ; shave, dress, even to the putting of my sword-belt over my shoulder, and having my sword lying on the table before me, ready to hang by my side. Then I ate a bit of cheese, or pork and bread. Then I prepared my report, which was filled up as fast as the companies brought me in the materials. After this I had an hour or two to read, before the time came for any duty out of doors, unless when the regiment, or part of it, went out to exercise in the morning. When this was the case, and the

[1] Cobbett again erroneously fixes 1766 as the year of his birth.

[2] In another place he gives their number as 'nearly fifty.' See *Cobbett's Evening Post*, 5th February 1820.

COBBETT INSTRUCTING HIS OFFICERS.

matter was left to me, I always had it on the ground in such
time as that the bayonets glistened in the *rising sun*, a sight
which gave me delight, of which I often think, but which I
should in vain endeavour to describe.   If the *officers* were to go
out, eight or ten o'clock was the hour, sweating the men in the
heat of the day, breaking in upon the time for cooking their
dinner, putting all things out of order and all men out of humour.
When I was commander, the men had a long day of leisure
before them ; they could ramble into the town or into the woods ;
go to get raspberries, to catch birds, to catch fish, or to pursue
any other recreation, and such of them as chose, and were
qualified, to work at their trades.   So that here, arising solely
from the early habits of one very young man, were pleasant and
happy days given to hundreds.'[1]

After attaining the rank of sergeant-major, Cobbett
was rewarded to some extent for his assiduous study,
not indeed by any considerable pecuniary recompense,
but by that sense of power, which is dear to any man
with a capacity for affairs.

'Then I became the sergeant-major to the regiment,' he says,
'which brought me in close contact at every hour with the whole
of the *Epaulet* gentry, whose profound and surprising ignorance
I discovered in a twinkling.   But I had a very delicate part to
act with these gentry ; for, while I despised them for their gross
ignorance and their vanity, and hated them for their drunkenness and rapacity, I was fully sensible of *their power*, and I knew
also the envy which my sudden rise over the heads of so many
old sergeants had created.   My path was full of rocks and pit-
falls ; and, as I never disguised my dislikes or restrained my
tongue, I should have been broken or flogged for fifty different
offences, given to my superior jackasses, had they not been kept
in awe by my inflexible sobriety, impartiality, and integrity, by
the consciousness of their inferiority to me, and by the real and
almost indispensable necessity for the use of my talents.   First,
I had by my skill and by my everlasting vigilance, eased them

[1] *Advice to Young Men*, pp. 32-34.

all of the trouble of even *thinking* about their duty; and this made me their master, a situation in which, however, I acted with so much prudence, that it was impossible for them, with any show of justice, to find fault. They, in fact, resigned all the discipline of the regiment to me, and I very freely left them to swagger about, and to get roaring drunk out of the profits of their pillage, though I was at the same time making preparations for bringing them to justice for that pillage, in which I was finally defeated by the protection which they received at home.

'To describe the various instances of their ignorance, and the various tricks they played to disguise it from me, would fill a volume. It is the custom in regiments to give out *orders* every day from the officer commanding. These are written by the adjutant, to whom the sergeant-major is a sort of deputy. The man whom I had to do with was a keen fellow, but wholly illiterate. The orders, which he wrote, most cruelly murdered our mother tongue. But, in his absence, or, during a severe drunken fit, it fell to my lot to write orders. As we both wrote in the same book, he used to look at these. He saw *commas*, *semicolons*, *colons*, *full points*, and *paragraphs*. The questions he used to put to me, in an obscure sort of way, in order to know *why* I made these divisions, and yet, at the same time, his attempts to disguise his object, have made me laugh a thousand times. As I often had to draw up statements of considerable length, and as these were so much in the style and manner of a *book*, and so much unlike anything he had ever seen before in man's handwriting, he at last fell upon this device : he made *me* write, while he pretended to *dictate !* Imagine to yourself me sitting, pen in hand, to put upon paper the precious offspring of the mind of this stupid curmudgeon ! But, here a greater difficulty than any former arose. He that could not *write* good grammar, could not, of course, *dictate* good grammar. Out would come some gross error, such as I was ashamed to see in my handwriting. I would stop; suggest another arrangement; but this I was at first obliged to do in a very indirect and deli-cate manner. I dared not let him perceive that I saw, or suspected, his ignorance; and, though we made sad work of it, we got along without any very sanguinary assaults upon mere

grammar.   But this course could not continue long ; and he put
an end to it in this way : he used to tell me *his story*, and leave
me to put it upon paper ; and thus we continued to the end of
our connection.

'He played me a trick upon one occasion, which was more
ridiculous than anything else, but which will serve to show how
his ignorance placed him at my mercy.   It will also serve to
show a little about Commissioners sent out by the Government.
There were three or four Commissioners sent out to examine
into the state of the Provinces of Nova Scotia and New
Brunswick.   Their business was of a very extensive nature.
They were to inquire into the number of the people, the extent
of their settlements, the provisions expended on them, and a
great variety of other matters.   Upon all these several heads
they were to make a *Report*, and to subjoin to it a detail in
figures.   It required great ingenuity to frame these tables of
figures, to bring the rude and undigested materials under general
heads, dividing themselves into more particular sections, and
then again subdividing themselves, and so on, and showing at
last, a sort of total, or result of the whole.   To frame this
Appendix to the Report, and to execute it in any moderate space
of paper required a *head*, an *eye*, and a *hand* ; and to *draw up
the Report itself* was a task of a still superior order.   The Commissioners, the name of one of whom was *Dundas* . . . who or
what he was besides, I know not ; and I have forgotten the
names of the rest.   But they closed their work at Fredericton
in New Brunswick, where I was with my regiment.   As the
arrival of every stranger was an excuse for a roaring drunk with
our heroes, so this ceremony now took place.   But, the Commissioners had their *Report* to make.   And, what did my ass of
an Adjutant do, *but offer to do it for them!*   They, who, in all
likelihood, did not know how to do it themselves took him at
his word ; and, there was he in the sweetest mess that ever vain
pretender was placed in.   He wanted to get some favour from
the Commissioners, and relied upon me, not only to perform the
task, but to keep the secret.   But, then, the part he had to act
now was full of difficulty.   The Report of these fellows was no
concern of mine.   It could not, by any contrivance, be hooked

in among my *duties*. He therefore talked to me at first in a sort of ambiguous manner. He said that the Commissioners wanted him to do it, and d——n them, he would not do it for them. Then, when I saw him again, he *asked* me something about it, showing me their rude mass of papers at the same time. I now began to find what he would be at; but I affected not to understand him, turned the matter as soon as I could, and so we parted. At this time I had long been wanting to go and see an old farmer and his family and to shoot wild pigeons in his woods; and, as the distance was great, and a companion on the journey necessary, I wanted a sergeant to go with me. The leave to do this had been put off for a good while, and the Adjutant knew that I had the thing at heart. What does he do now, but come to me and after talking about the Report again, affect to lament that he should be so much engaged with it, that there was no hope of my being permitted to go on my *frolic* till *he had finished the Report*. I, who knew very well what this meant, began to be very anxious for this *finishing*, to effect which I knew there was but one way. Tacked on to the pigeon-shooting the Report became an object of importance, and I said, "*perhaps I could do something*, Sir, in putting the papers in order for you." That was enough. Away he went, brought me the whole mass, and, tossing them down upon the table: "There," said he, "do what you like with them; for d——n the rubbish, I have no patience with it." Rubbish it really was, if we looked only at the rude manner of the papers; but the matter would to me, at this day, have been very interesting. I d——d the papers as heartily as he did, and with better reason; but, they were to bring me my week's frolic, and, as I entered into everything with ardour, this pigeon-shooting frolic, at the age of about twenty-three, was more than a compensation for all the toil of this Report and its Appendix. To work I went, and with the assistance of my shooting companion sergeant, who called over the figures to me, I had the Appendix completed in rough draft in two days and one night. Having the detail before me the Report was a short work, and the whole was soon completed. But, before a *neat copy* was made out, the thing had to be shown to the Commissioners. It would not do to show it them *in my handwriting*. The Adjutant got over this difficulty by *copying the Report*; and having shown it; and had it highly applauded, "well then," said he, "here, sergeant-major, *go and make a fair copy*." This was the most shameless thing that I ever witnessed. This Report and Appendix, though I hated the job, were, such was my habit of doing everything well, executed with so much neatness and accuracy, that the Duke of Kent, who afterwards became Commander-in-Chief in those Provinces, and who was told of this Report which was in his office at Halifax, had a copy of it made to be kept in the office, and carried the original with him to England as a curiosity, and of this fact he informed me himself. The Duke, from some source or other, had heard that it was I who had been the penman upon this occasion, though I had never mentioned it to anybody. It drew forth a great deal of admiration at Fredericton, and the Lieutenant-Governor, General Carleton, asked me in plain terms *whether it was I* who had drawn up the Report. The Adjutant had told me that *I need not say* but it was he, *because* he had promised to do it himself. I was not satisfied with his logic; but the pigeon-shooting made me say that I certainly would say it was done by him, if any one should ask me. And I kept my word with him ; for, as I could not give the question of the Governor the *go by*, I told him a lie at once, and said it was the Adjutant. However, I lied in vain; for when I came to Halifax, in my way from the United States to England, *ten years* afterwards, I found that the real truth was known to a number of persons, though the thing had wholly gone out of my mind.'[1]

In this passage as well as in many others Cobbett shows that he had a small opinion of the officers of his regiment. For many of the rank and file on the other hand he had a great regard, and he claimed for some of them considerable powers of mind.

'The most witty man I ever knew was a private soldier. He was not only the most witty, but *far* the most witty. He was a Staffordshire man, he came from Walsall, and his name was

[1] *Political Register*, 6th December 1817.

John Fletcher. I have heard from that man more bright thoughts of a witty character than I ever heard from all other men, and than I have ever read in all the books that I have read in my whole life. No coarse jokes, no puns, no conundrums, no made-up jests, nothing of the *college* kind,[1] but real sterling, sprightly wit. When I have heard people repeat the profligate sayings of Sheridan, and have heard the House of Commons roaring at his green-room trash, I have always thought of poor Jack Fletcher, who, if he could have put his thoughts on paper, would have been more renowned than Butler or Swift.'

Of another comrade, Cobbett writes with strong feeling :

'There was one of our own sergeants, whose name was Smaller, and who was a Yorkshireman, who began learning his A B C and who, at the end of a year, was as *correct* a writer as I ever saw in my life. He was about my own age ; he was promoted as soon as he could write and read : and well he deserved it, for he was more fit to command a Regiment than any Colonel or Major that I ever saw. He was strong in body, but still stronger in mind. He had capacity to dive into all subjects. Clean in his person, an early riser, punctual in all his duties, sober, good-tempered, honest, brave, and generous to the last degree. He was once with me in the dreary woods, amongst the melting snows, when I was exhausted at nightfall, and fell down, unable to go farther, just as a torrent of rain began to pour upon us. Having first torn off his shirt and rent it in the vain hope of kindling fire by the help of his pistol, he took me upon his back, carried me five miles to the first dwelling of human being, and at the end of his journey, having previously pulled off his coat and thrown it away, he had neither shoe, nor stocking, nor gaiter left ; his feet and legs were cut to pieces, and covered with blood ; and the moment he had put me down and saw that I was still alive, he bursted into a flood of tears that probably saved his own life : which, however, was then saved only to be lost in Holland, under the Duke of York.

---

[1] Cobbett had a great contempt for English university training.

How often has my blood boiled with indignation at seeing this fine, this gallant, this honest, this true-hearted and intelligent young man, standing with his hand to his hat before some worthless and stupid sot of an officer, whom nature seemed to have designed to black his shoes!'[1]

These extracts sufficiently show Cobbett's estimate of the merits of his officers. Other causes besides their illiteracy and drunkenness led him to look on them with aversion. When raised to a position of comparative importance in the regiment he did not forget the hardships from which he had suffered while a private soldier, and as his knowledge of regimental affairs became greater, he was convinced that those hardships were principally caused by the peculations and the connivance of the officers.

'One suffers injustice,' he says, 'from men of great endowments of mind with much less of heartburning than from men whom one cannot help despising; and if my officers had been men of manifest superiority of mind, I should, perhaps, not have so soon conceived the project of bringing them, or some of them at least, to shame and punishment for the divers flagrant breaches of the law committed by them, and for their manifold, their endless wrongs against the soldiers, and against the public.—The project was conceived so early as the year 1787, when an affair happened that first gave me a full insight into regimental justice. It was shortly this: that the Quarter-Master, who had the issuing of the men's provision to them, *kept about a fourth part of it to himself.* This, the old sergeants told me, had been the case *for many years*; and they were quite astonished and terrified at the idea of my complaining of it. This I did, however; but, the reception I met with convinced me, that I must never make another complaint, 'till I got safe to England, and safe out of the reach of that most curious of courts, a *Court-Martial.*— From this time forward, I began to collect materials for an

[1] *Political Register*, 6th December 1817.

exposure, upon my return to England. I had ample opportunities for this, being the keeper of all the books, of every sort, in the regiment, and knowing the whole of its affairs better than any other man. But, the winter previous to our return to England, I thought it necessary to make extracts from books, lest the books themselves should be destroyed. . . . In order to be able to *prove* that these extracts were correct, it was necessary that I should have a *witness* as to their being *true copies*. This was a very ticklish point. One foolish step here, would have sent me down to the ranks with a pair of bloody shoulders. Yet, it was necessary to have the witness. I hesitated many months. At one time, I had given the thing up. I dreamt twenty times, I dare say, of my papers being discovered, and of my being tried and flogged half to death. At last, however, some fresh act of injustice towards us made me set all danger at defiance. I opened my project to a corporal, whose name was *William Bestland*, who wrote in the office under me, who was a very honest fellow, who was very much bound to me for my goodness to him, and who was, with the sole exception of myself, the only sober man in the *whole regiment*.[1]

'To work we went, and during a long winter, while the rest were boosing and snoring, we gutted no small part of the regimental books, rolls, and other documents. Our way was this : to take a copy, sign it with our names, and clap the regimental seal to it, so that we might be able to swear to it, when produced in court.'[2]

The regiment returned to England in 1791, landing at Portsmouth in November. Cobbett, in spite of the fact that he had a good prospect of obtaining a commission, immediately applied for his discharge. This he obtained on 19th December, together with a most favourable testimonial from his major, Lord Edward Fitzgerald, afterwards famous for his share in the Irish rising in

[1] When Cobbett wrote this he forgot Sergeant Smaller.
[2] *Political Register*, 17th June 1809.

Cobbett copying the Regimental Accounts.

1798 and for his unhappy fate. On 14th January 1792 he wrote to the Secretary at War, Sir George Yonge, making grave charges of malversation against certain officers in his regiment and enclosing a letter of petition to the King. The officers accused were Captain Richard Powell and two lieutenants—Christopher Seton and John Hall. Lieutenant-Colonel Andrew Bruce, who had been originally included in the charges, died at Naples on 13th December 1791, before they were finally preferred.

On 24th January Cobbett was requested to call on Yonge at the War Office. He had an interview, told his story, and was promised a reply in a day or two.

After waiting until 10th February he wrote again, urging that his means were small, and that to detain him in London was to ruin him. On 15th February he was told that it was intended to try the accused only on a part of the charges preferred, and when he received the remodelled list sent him by the Judge Advocate, he says that he perceived that 'even of those charges that were suffered to remain, the parts the most material were omitted.' He was also notified that the court-martial was to be held at Portsmouth or Hilsea, in spite of the fact that he had always maintained that at those places he and his witnesses would not be safe from violence. Finding a remonstrance against this resolution disregarded by the Judge Advocate, he appealed on 7th March directly to Pitt, and succeeded in getting the court-martial removed to London.

By this time Cobbett was seriously discouraged. He had imagined that the peculation he was prepared to unmask was something peculiar to the regiment. He had no idea that it was part of a system of plunder that extended through the whole service. But the constant hindrances and discouragements that he met with showed that powerful interests were arrayed against him. He began to fear that he would be unable to establish his charges to the satisfaction of an unfriendly court. Eight days after his first communication with Sir George Yonge he had written to him urging that the regimental books should be secured to prevent their being tampered with. He had received several assurances that this should be done, but on 20th March, four days before the court-martial, he went to Portsmouth, and ascertained that the books had never been secured at all. He might have produced his certified extracts, but his witness, Bestland, could not obtain his discharge on account of some suspicion of a connection between them, and Cobbett was pledged both by a promise and by ordinary humanity not to implicate him while he remained subject to military discipline. On the same day that he learned that the regimental books had not been secured, he wrote from Fratton, near Portsmouth, to the Judge Advocate, complaining that these documents had been left in the hands of the accused contrary to the assurances of the Secretary at War, and demanding the discharge of a man, whom he should name, as the only condition on which he would attend the court-martial. To this letter he received no reply. Other circumstances increased his apprehensions.

'As I was going down to Portsmouth,' he says, 'I met several of the sergeants coming up, together with the music-master; and, as they had none of them been in America, I wondered what they could be going to London for; but, upon my return,

If my Accusation is without foundation the authors of cruelty have not yet devised the tortures I ought to endure Hell itself, as painted by the most fiery bigot, is too mild a punishment for me!

BEELZEBUB, PAWNBROKER
Utmost Value for Souls taken in Pawn

Cobbett accusing his Officers.

I was told by a *Captain Lane*, who had been in the regiment, that they had been brought up to swear that, at an entertainment given to them by me before my departure from the regiment, I had drunk "*the destruction of the House of Brunswick.*" This was false; but I knew that that was no reason why it should not be *sworn* by such persons and in such a case.'[1]

Convinced that he was in serious danger, Cobbett resolved to abandon the prosecution, and to disappear. When the court-martial met on 24th March he was not present. It was adjourned until the 27th, but as he still remained hidden, the case was proceeded with, and the three officers were declared honourably acquitted. Cobbett in the meanwhile remained in retirement, and took an early opportunity of proceeding to France. A circumstantial tale is told by Robert Huish, Cobbett's biographer, to the effect that Cobbett retired to Farnham, where he was recognised by a soldier of his former regiment, a spy of the accused officers, and only escaped denunciation by having the presence of mind to give the man into custody as a deserter, and promptly fleeing to France.[2] But Huish gives no authority for his story, and it is impossible to reconcile it with Cobbett's statement that he did not revisit Farnham after his departure in 1782, until his second return to England in 1800. It must therefore be rejected for lack of corroboration.

Cobbett's conduct in this affair was at a later time made the occasion of serious attacks by his enemies, whilst it has been condemned even by less hostile critics. Among others, Lord Brougham, while considering that Sir George Yonge had failed to act 'with tolerable fair-

[1] *Political Register*, 17th June 1809.   [2] *Memoirs of Cobbett*, i. 84-7.

ness and prudence,' thought that the revival of the story in 1817 seriously injured Cobbett's reputation.[1] In order to pronounce a final verdict, it would be necessary to possess a much more intimate knowledge of the details of the business than can be attained at the present day. Perhaps it is impossible completely to justify Cobbett's conduct, after bringing such serious charges, in declining to support them at all hazards. On the other hand, there is a strong probability that, had he persisted, he would have failed to gain an impartial hearing, and there can be no doubt that if he had not established his accusations, the consequences to himself would have been very serious. It would be ridiculous to suspect Cobbett of actual want of courage, but he was not of the temperament of which martyrs are made. When he thought he had a reasonable prospect of victory, he was ready to encounter great dangers, but to risk ruin without that prospect, in order to preserve his integrity, was beyond him, and, indeed, he would have condemned such conduct as an act of folly.[2]

[1] Brougham's *Life and Times* (1871), i. 438.
[2] The chief sources of information in regard to the affair of the court-martial are a pamphlet issued in 1809 by Cobbett's political opponents, and Cobbett's reply in the *Political Register* for 17th June 1809. The pamphlet is entitled ' Proceedings of a Court-Martial held at the Horse-Guards on the 24th and 27th of March 1792, for the trial of Capt. Richard Powell, Lieut. Christopher Seton, and Lieut. John Hall on several charges preferred against them respectively by William Cobbett.' It was distributed broadcast through England by his opponents. Cobbett, in his reply, complained that it entirely perverted the affair by publishing only part of the correspondence between him and the authorities. He did not, however, himself supply the rest of the correspondence, but contented himself with the general narrative of the circumstances which I have quoted.

COBBETT FLEEING FROM THE COURT MARTIAL.

JUDGE : "Call William Cobbett into court to make good his charges."
COBBETT (*in boat*): "Call away and be d——d.   I'm off."

CHAPTER II

COBBETT'S short stay in London was not entirely occupied with the business of the court-martial. At that
time he was a disciple of Tom Paine, and had embraced
republican principles. In these beliefs he remained
rooted until he took up his abode at Philadelphia about
a year later, when he found that the republican doctrines
of the Americans were not to his taste.[1] Under these
influences, and burning with indignation at the abuses
which he had witnessed in the army, he began his career
as an author by writing a small pamphlet entitled *The
Soldier's Friend; or, Considerations on the late pretended
Augmentation of the Subsistence of the Private Soldier.*
It was published before July 1792 by Ridgway, at York
Street, St. James's Square, without the author's name,
and offered to the public at sixpence. In the following
year it was reprinted without the publisher's name, with
the description, 'written by a subaltern,' and sold for
twopence. The pamphlet was chiefly occupied with an
admission made by the Secretary at War in the House
of Commons on 15th February 1792 that unauthorised
deductions had lately been made from the soldier's pay.

[1] *Political Register*, 5th October 1805.

C

A strong attack was made on the conduct of the officers in this respect.

'The world is often deceived in these jovial, honest-looking fellows, the officers of the army; I have known very few of them but perfectly well knew how to take care of themselves, either in peace or war; and I could mention characters in this *honourable* profession that would shine among the *Seed of Abraham*, or do honour to the Society of Stock-Jobbers.'

The writer concluded by pointing out that, while soldiers were taught to believe that they were supported by a gift from the Crown, they were in reality paid from the public funds by Act of Parliament, and that their pay ought to be regarded as their rightful property.

At the time of the mutiny at the Nore in 1797 copies of this pamphlet were distributed among the sailors, and in 1805, when Cobbett was troubling the Government by his attacks on Lord Melville, he was reproached with having caused the mutiny by means of his pamphlet. This charge was expressly made on 27th July in a periodical entitled *A Review of the Reports made by the Naval Commissioners: by a Society of Gentlemen.* Cobbett stated in reply that, though he had given information on the subject in a general manner to the person who wrote the pamphlet, he was not himself the author and had nothing to do with either the printing or publishing of it. The latter part of this statement may be true, but the pamphlet bears unmistakable traces of his style. At a much later date he claimed the authorship, and stated that he gave it in manuscript to Captain Thomas Morris, brother of Charles Morris, the songwriter and boon companion of the Prince of Wales, and that Morris took it to Ridgway. At a still later period he included it among his works, and gave such particulars about its appearance as indicate that he must have been intimately concerned in it.[1]

But Cobbett's sojourn in London was also the period of a more important event in his life than the writing of a pamphlet. Before the final fiasco of the court-martial he entered on marriage. On 5th February 1792 he was married at Woolwich to Ann, the daughter of Thomas and Ann Reid. He had made her acquaintance in America.

'When I first saw my wife she was *thirteen years old*,[2] and I was within about a month of *twenty-one*.[3] She was the daughter of a Sergeant of Artillery, and I was the Sergeant-Major of a regiment of Foot, both stationed in forts near the city of St. John, in the province of New Brunswick. I sat in the same room with her for about an hour, in the company of others, and I made up my mind that she was the very girl for me. That I thought her beautiful is certain, for that I had always said should be an indispensable qualification ; but I saw in her what I deemed marks of that sobriety of *conduct* . . . which has been by far the greatest blessing of my life. It was now dead of winter, and, of course, the snow several feet deep on the ground, and the weather piercing cold. It was my habit, when I had done my morning's writing, to go out at break of day to take a walk on a hill at the foot of which our barracks lay. In about three mornings after I had first seen her, I had, by an invitation to breakfast with me, got up two young men to join me in my walk; and our road lay by the house of her father and mother. It was hardly light, but she was out on the snow, scrubbing out a washing-tub. "That's the girl for me," said I, when we had got out of her hearing. One of these young men came to England soon afterwards; and he, who keeps an inn in Yorkshire, came over to Preston at the time of the election [in

---

[1] *Political Register*, 28th December 1833.
[2] She was born at Chatham on 28th March 1774.
[3] Probably he was nearly twenty-four.

1826] to verify whether I were the same man. When he found that I was he appeared surprised; but what was his surprise when I told him that those tall young men whom he saw around me were the *sons* of that pretty little girl that he and I saw scrubbing out the washing-tub on the snow in New Brunswick at day-break in the morning!

'From the day that I first spoke to her, I never had a thought of her ever being the wife of any other man, more than I had a thought of her being transformed into a chest of drawers; and I formed my resolution at once, to marry her as soon as we could get permission, and to get out of the army as soon as I could. So that this matter was at once settled as firmly as if written in the book of fate. At the end of about six months my regiment, and I along with it, were removed to Fredericton, a distance of *a hundred miles* up the river of St. John; and, which was worse, the artillery was expected to go off to England a year or two before our regiment! The artillery went, and she along with them; and now it was that I acted a part becoming a real and sensible lover. I was aware that, when she got to that gay place Woolwich, the house of her father and mother, necessarily visited by numerous persons not the most select, might become unpleasant to her, and I did not like, besides, that she should continue to *work hard*. I had saved a *hundred and fifty guineas*, the earnings of my early hours, in writing for the paymaster, the quartermaster, and others, in addition to the savings of my own pay. *I sent her all my money* before she sailed, and wrote to her to beg of her, if she found her home uncomfortable, to hire a lodging with respectable people: and, at any rate, not to spare the money by any means, but to buy herself good clothes, and to live without hard work, until I arrived in England; and I, in order to induce her to lay out the money, told her that I should get plenty more before I came home.

'As the malignity of the devil would have it, we were kept abroad *two years longer* than our time, Mr. Pitt (England not being so tame then as she is now[1]) having knocked up a dust with Spain about Nootka Sound. Oh, how I cursed Nootka Sound, and poor bawling Pitt too, I am afraid! At the end of

[1] Written in 1829.

four years, however, home I came, landed at Portsmouth, and got my discharge from the army by the great kindness of poor Lord Edward Fitzgerald, who was then the major of my regiment. I found my little girl *a servant of all work* (and hard work it was) *at five pounds a year*, in the house of a Captain Brisac; and, without hardly saying a word about the matter, she put into my hands *the whole of my hundred and fifty guineas unbroken !*' [1]

The marriage was a happy one, and Cobbett's family life was the only part of his career unruffled by continual storms. It is therefore interesting to learn that the engagement was nearly broken off by an incident as romantic as the courtship itself. The story is rather a long one, but it is inimitably, if somewhat complacently, told by Cobbett himself:

'The Province of New Brunswick, in North America, in which I passed my years from the age of eighteen to that of twenty-six, consists in general of heaps of rocks, in the interstices of which grow the pine, the spruce, and various sorts of fir-trees, or, where the woods have been burnt down, the bushes of the raspberry or those of the huckleberry. The province is cut asunder lengthwise by a great river, called the St. John, about two hundred miles in length, and at half-way from the mouth full a mile wide. Into this main river run innumerable smaller rivers, there called *creeks*. On the sides of these creeks the land is, in places, clear of rocks ; it is, in these places, generally good and productive ; the trees that grow here are the birch, the maple, and others of the deciduous class ; natural meadows here and there present themselves, and some of these spots far surpass in rural beauty any other that my eyes ever beheld ; the creeks, abounding towards their sources in waterfalls of endless variety, as well in form as in magnitude, and always teeming with fish, while water-fowl enliven their surface, and while wild pigeons of the gayest plumage flutter, in thousands upon thousands amongst the branches of the beautiful trees, which sometimes for miles together form an arch over the creeks.

[1] *Advice to Young Men*, pp. 97-9.

'I, in one of my rambles in the woods, in which I took great delight, came to a spot at a very short distance from the source of one of these creeks. Here was everything to delight the eye, and especially of one like me, who seem to have been born to love rural life, and trees and plants of all sorts. Here were about two hundred acres of natural meadow, interspersed with patches of maple trees in various forms and of various extent; the creek (there about thirty miles from its point of joining the St. John) ran down the middle of the spot, which formed a sort of dish, the high and rocky hills rising all round it except at the outlet of the creek, and these hills crowned with lofty pines: in the hills were the sources of the creek, the waters of which came down in cascades, for any one of which many a nobleman in England would, if he could transfer it, give a good slice of his fertile estate; and in the creek, at the foot of the cascades, there were, in the season, salmon, the finest in the world, and so abundant, and so easily taken, as to be used for manuring the land.

'If nature in her very best humour, had made a spot for the express purpose of captivating me, she could not have exceeded the efforts which she had here made. But I found something here besides these rude works of nature; I found something in the fashioning of which *man* had had something to do. I found a large and well-built log dwelling-house, standing (in the month of September) on the edge of a very good field of Indian corn, by the side of which there was a piece of buckwheat just then mowed. I found a homestead, and some very pretty cows. I found all the things by which an easy and happy farmer is surrounded: and I found still something besides all these; something that was destined to give me a great deal of pleasure and also a great deal of pain, both in their extreme degree; and both of which, in spite of the lapse of forty years, now make an attempt to rush back into my heart.

'Partly from misinformation, and partly from miscalculation, I had lost my way; and, quite alone, but armed with my sword and a brace of pistols, to defend myself against the bears, I arrived at the log-house in the middle of a moonlight night, the hoar frost covering the trees and grass. A stout and clamorous dog, kept off by the gleaming of my sword, waked the master of the house, who got up, received me with great hospitality, got me something to eat, and put me into a feather-bed, a thing that I had been a stranger to for some years. I, being very tired, had tried to pass the night in the woods between the trunks of two large trees, which had fallen side by side, and within a yard of each other. I had made a nest for myself of dry fern, and had made a covering by laying boughs of spruce across the trunks of the trees. But, unable to sleep on account of the cold; becoming sick from the great quantity of water that I had drunk during the heat of the day, and being, moreover, alarmed at the noise of the bears, and lest one of them should find me in a defenceless state, I had roused myself up, and had crept along as well as I could. So that no hero of eastern romance ever experienced a more enchanting change.

'I had got into the house of one of those YANKEE LOYALISTS, who, at the close of the revolutionary war, had accepted of grants of land in the King's Province of New Brunswick; and who, to the great honour of England, had been furnished with all the means of making new and comfortable settlements. I was suffered to sleep till breakfast-time, when I found a table, the like of which I have since seen so many in the United States, loaded with good things. The master and mistress of the house, aged about fifty, were like what an English farmer and his wife were half a century ago. There were two sons, tall and stout, who appeared to have come in from work, and the youngest of whom was about my age, then twenty-three. But there was *another member* of the family, aged nineteen, who (dressed according to the neat and simple fashion of New England, whence she had come with her parents five or six years before) had her long, light-brown hair twisted nicely up, and fastened on the top of her head, in which head were a pair of lively blue eyes, associated with features of which that softness and that sweetness so characteristic of American girls, were the predominant expressions, the whole being set off by an expression indicative of glowing health, and forming, figure, movements, and all taken together, an assemblage of beauties, far surpassing any that I had ever seen but *once* in my life. That *once* was, too, *two years agone*; and, in such a case and at such an age, two years, two whole years, is a long, long while! It was a space as long as the eleventh part of my then life! Here was the *present* against the *absent*: here was the power of the *eyes* pitted against that of the *memory*: here were all the senses up in arms to subdue the influence of the thoughts; here was vanity, here was passion, here was the spot of all spots in the world, and here were also the life and the manners and the habits and the pursuits that I delighted in: here was everything that imagination can conceive, united in a conspiracy against the poor little brunette in England! What then, did I fall in love at once with this bouquet of lilies and roses? Oh! by no means. I was, however, so enchanted with *the place*, I so much enjoyed its tranquillity, the shade of the maple trees, the business of the farm, the sports of the water and of the woods, that I stayed at it to the last possible minute, promising, at my departure, to come again as often as I possibly could; a promise which I most punctually fulfilled.

'Winter is the great season for jaunting and *dancing* (called *frolicking*) in America. In this Province the river and the creeks were the only *roads* from settlement to settlement. In summer we travelled in *canoes*; in winter in *sleighs* on the ice or snow. During more than two years I spent all the time I could with my Yankee friends: they were all fond of me: I talked to them about country affairs, my evident delight in which they took as a compliment to themselves: the father and mother treated me as one of their children; the sons as a brother; and the daughter, who was as modest and as full of sensibility as she was beautiful, in a way to which a chap much less sanguine than I was would have given the tenderest interpretation: which treatment I, especially in the last-mentioned case, most cordially repaid.

'It is when you meet in company with others of your own age that you are, in love matters, put most frequently to the test, and exposed to detection. The next-door neighbour might, in that country, be ten miles off. We used to have a frolic, sometimes at one house, and sometimes at another. Here, where female eyes are very much on the alert, no secret can long be kept; and very soon father, mother, brothers, and the whole neighbourhood looked upon the thing as certain, not excepting herself, to whom I, however, had never once even talked of marriage, and had never even told her that I *loved* her. But I had a thousand times done these by *implication*, taking into view the interpretation that she would naturally put upon my looks, appellations, and acts; and it was of this, that I had to accuse myself. Yet I was not a *deceiver*; for my affection for her was very great: I spent no really pleasant hours but with her: I was uneasy if she showed the slightest regard for any other young man: I was unhappy if the smallest matter affected her health and spirits: I quitted her in dejection, and returned to her with eager delight: many a time, when I would get leave but for a day, I paddled in a canoe two whole succeeding nights in order to pass that day with her. If this was not love, it was first cousin to it; for as to any *criminal* intention, I no more thought of it, in her case, than if she had been my sister. Many times I put to myself the questions: "What am I at? Is not this wrong? *Why do I go?*" But still I went.

'Then further in my excuse, my *prior engagement*, though carefully left unalluded to by both parties, was, in that thin population, and owing to the singular circumstances of it, and to the great talk that there always was about me, *perfectly well known* to her and all her family. . . . So that here was no *deception* on my part: but still I ought not to have suffered even the most distant hope to be entertained by a person so innocent, so amiable, for whom I had so much affection, and to whose heart I had no right to give a single twinge. I ought, from the very first, to have prevented the possibility of her ever feeling pain on my account. I was young, to be sure; but I was old enough to know what was my duty in this case, and I ought, dismissing my own feelings, to have had the resolution to perform it.

'The *last parting* came; and now came my just punishment! The time was known to everybody, and was irrevocably fixed; for I had to move with a regiment, and the embarkation of a regiment is an *epoch* in a thinly settled province. To describe the parting would be too painful even at this distant day, and with this frost of age upon my head. The kind and virtuous father came forty miles to see me just as I was going on board in the river. *His* looks and words I have never forgotten. As the vessel descended, she passed the mouth of *that creek*, which I had so often entered with delight; and though England, and all that England contained, were before me, I lost sight of this . creek with an aching heart.

'On what trifles turn the great events in the life of man! If I had received a *cool* letter from my intended wife; if I had only heard a rumour of anything from which fickleness in her might have been inferred; if I had found in her any, even the smallest abatement of affection; if she had but let go even one of the hundred strings by which she held my heart: if any of these, never would the world have heard of me. Young as I was; able as I was as a soldier; proud as I was of the admiration and commendations of which I was the object; fond as I was, too, of the command, which, at so early an age, my rare conduct and great natural talents had given me; sanguine as was my mind, and brilliant as were my prospects, yet I had seen so much of the meannesses, the unjust partialities, the insolent pomposity, the disgusting dissipations of that way of life, that I was weary of it: I longed, exchanging my fine laced coat for the Yankee farmer's homespun, to be where I should never behold the subtle crouch of servility, and never hear the hectoring voice of authority again; and on the lonely banks of this branch-covered creek, which contained (she out of the question) every thing congenial to my taste and dear to my heart, I, unapplauded, unfeared, un-envied, and uncalumniated, should have lived and died.'[1]

Cobbett was not destined to so tranquil an existence. From the first days of his marriage he was beset with care and anxiety. In less than two months he was a fugitive from his native country to which he had returned, only a few weeks before, after six years of exile. It is

---

[1] *Advice to Young Men*, ed. 1837, pp. 136-44.

possible that solicitude for his wife made him more reluctant to face the consequences of sustaining his charges at the court - martial. Towards the end of March 1792, he landed at Calais and took up his residence at Tilques, a village in the neighbourhood of St. Omer.

'I should be the most ungrateful monster that ever existed,' he says, ' were I to speak ill of the French people in general. I went to that country full of all those prejudices that Englishmen suck in with their mother's milk, against the French and against their religion : a few weeks convinced me that I had been deceived with respect to both. I met everywhere with civility, and even with hospitality, in a degree that I never had been accustomed to. I found the people among whom I lived, excepting those who were already blasted with the principles of the accursed revolution, honest, pious, and kind to excess.' [1]

He had intended to stay in France till the spring of 1793, to perfect himself in the language, and then to proceed to the United States. But, as the storm of the Revolution grew to a height, he saw that war with England was inevitable, and resolved to hasten his departure. In August he hired a coach to convey him to Paris, but when he had reached Abbeville he heard of the successful attack on the King's Swiss guards at the Tuileries and the subsequent deposition of Louis XVI. In consequence he turned off towards Le Havre and embarked for America.

He landed at Philadelphia in October and for a short time lived at Wilmington, then a little port on the Delaware, about twenty-eight miles below Philadelphia. Soon after his arrival he was joined by his wife, who

---

[1] *Life and Adventures of Peter Porcupine.* This passage was written while Cobbett was a Tory.

had not shared his hurried flight to France. He earned a livelihood by teaching English at six dollars a month to French refugees, most of them moderate republicans, large numbers of whom came over to America after the overthrow of the Girondists. To aid in their instruction he drew up his *Tuteur Anglais*, published at Philadelphia in 1795. A good deal of this work was probably written by his French pupils, for it is impossible that Cobbett should have acquired a sufficient knowledge of the French language during his short stay at Tilques to have composed the work without assistance. The book possessed considerable merits. In 1800 it was adopted by the Prytanée Français, who published a new edition at Paris under the title of *Le Maître Anglais*. It had a great vogue in France and Belgium for many years, reaching a thirty-fifth edition in 1861.

But before this grammar was in print Cobbett had commenced to write on more congenial subjects. He still retained the beliefs and prejudices of his childhood, and with Cobbett throughout life every belief *was* a prejudice. He had an intense detestation for the French Revolution, which extended to all who sympathised with its principles. Under these circumstances he was filled with indignation when he learned that Dr. Priestley, whose property at Birmingham had been destroyed by a mob on account of his revolutionary leanings, had been received in New York with ovations. An accident led him to express his sentiments publicly.

'At the memorable epoch of Dr. Priestley's emigration to America, I followed, in the city of Philadelphia, the profession of teacher of the English language to Frenchmen. Newspapers were a luxury for which I had little relish, and which, if I had been ever so fond of, I had not time to enjoy. The manifestoes, therefore, of the Doctor, upon his landing in that country, and the malicious attacks upon the monarchy and the monarch of England which certain societies in America thereupon issued through the press, would, had it not been for a circumstance, purely accidental, have escaped, probably for ever, not only my animadversion, but my knowledge of their existence. One of my scholars, who was a person that we in England should call a Coffee-house Politician, chose, for once, to read his newspaper by way of lesson ; and, it happened to be the very paper which contained the addresses presented to Dr. Priestley at New York, together with his replies. My scholar, who was a sort of republican, or, at best, but half a monarchist, appeared delighted with the invectives against England, to which he was very much disposed to add. Those Englishmen who have been abroad, particularly if they have had time to make a comparison between the country they are in and that which they have left, well know how difficult it is, upon occasions such as I have been describing, to refrain from expressing their indignation and resentment ; and there is not, I trust, much reason to suppose that I should, in this respect, experience less difficulty than another. The dispute was as warm as might reasonably be expected between a Frenchman, uncommonly violent even for a Frenchman, and an Englishman not remarkable for *sang froid* ; and, the result was, a declared resolution, on my part, to write and publish a pamphlet in defence of my country, which pamphlet he pledged himself to answer : his pledge was forfeited ; it is known that mine was not.' [1]

In fulfilment of this pledge Cobbett's *Observations on the Emigration of Dr. Joseph Priestley*, appeared shortly after Priestley's landing at New York in June 1794. It was published anonymously in Philadelphia by Thomas Bradford.[2] It was brought out, says Cobbett, with con-

[1] *Political Register*, 29th September 1804.
[2] For an account of Bradford and his family see Appleton's *Cyclopædia of American Biography*, 1887, i. 350-51.

siderable trepidation on behalf of the booksellers, for Priestley was very popular. The first publisher to whom he offered it was an Irishman named Mathew Carey.

'Mr. Carey received me as booksellers generally receive authors (I mean authors whom they hope to get but little by); he looked at the title from top to bottom, and then at me from head to foot. "No, *my lad*," says he, "I don't think it will suit." My *lad*! God in heaven forgive me! I believe that at that moment I wished for another yellow fever to strike the city; not to destroy the inhabitants, but to furnish me too with *the subject of a pamphlet* that might make me rich.[1] . . . From Mr. Carey I went to Mr. Bradford, and left the pamphlet for his perusal. The next day I went to him to know his determination. He hesitated, wanted to know if I could not make it a little *more popular*, adding that unless I could, he feared that the publishing of it would endanger *his windows*. *More popular* I could not make it. I never was of an accommodating disposition in my life, the only alteration I would consent to was in the title. I had given the pamphlet the double title of "The Tartuffe Detected; or, Observations, etc." The former was suppressed, though had I not been pretty certain that every press in the city was as little free as that to which I was sending it, the *Tartuffe Detected* should have remained; for the person on whom it was bestowed merited it much better than the person so named by Molière.'[2]

The pamphlet is a violent assault on Priestley and the French Revolution. It shows little knowledge of either, but possesses considerable controversial power of a rough kind. A couple of extracts will show the quality of the piece. Speaking of the destruction of Priestley's property Cobbett says:

[1] Carey laid the foundation of his fortune by publishing an account of the ravages of the yellow fever in Philadelphia in 1793. For some account of Carey, see *One Hundred Years of Publishing*, Lea Brothers and Co., Philadelphia, 1885. [2] *Life and Adventures of Peter Porcupine.*

'The Doctor laid his damages at £4122, 11s. 9d. sterling, of which sum £420, 15s. was for works in manuscript, which he said had been consumed in the flames. The trial of this cause took up nine hours; the jury gave a verdict in his favour, but curtailed the damages to £2502, 18s. It was rightly considered that the imaginary value of the manuscript works ought not to have been included in the damages; because the Doctor being the author of them, he in fact possessed them still, and the loss could be little more than a few sheets of dirty paper. . . . This sum, then, of £420, 15s. being deducted, the damages stood at £3701, 16s. 9d., and it should not be forgotten that even a great part of this sum was charged for an apparatus of philosophical instruments, which in spite of the most unpardonable gasconade of the Philosopher, can be looked upon as a thing of imaginary value only; and ought not to be estimated at its cost any more than a collection of shells or insects, or any other of the *frivola* of a virtuoso.'

The next quotation is a rather clever piece of eristic :

'Either Priestley foresaw the consequences of the French Revolution or he did not foresee them. If he did not, he must confess that his penetration was far inferior to that of his antagonists, and even to that of the multitude of his countrymen; for they all foresaw them. If he did foresee them, he ought to blush at being called the "friend of human happiness"; for to foresee such dreadful calamities, and to form a deliberate plan for bringing them upon his country, he must have a disposition truly diabolical. If he did not foresee them, he must have an understanding little superior to that of an idiot : if he did, he must have the heart of a Marat. Let him choose.'

The way in which Cobbett begs the whole question in the phrase 'consequences of the French Revolution' is worthy the attention of controversial writers who aspire to fame.

The attack on Priestley was immediately reprinted in London, where it was loudly praised, but in America its reception was of a more mingled kind. The two great political parties in the United States, the Federalists and the Democrats, looked with very different feelings on the contest which had commenced between England and France. While the Federals, among whose leaders were Washington, Adams, and Hamilton, desired alliance with England, or at least the observance of strict neutrality in the European struggle, the Democrats, who numbered among them Jefferson, Madison, and Monroe, were in thorough sympathy with the French Revolution, and desired to assist the French with arms. On this account Cobbett's attack on Priestley infuriated the Democrats, who held that philosopher in veneration, but it gained him approbation and support from a powerful and energetic section among the Ultra-Federalists, who were strongly imbued with admiration for English opinions and institutions. Although Cobbett ultimately injured this party by the extreme violence of his opinions and especially by his refusal to become naturalised, which enabled the Democrats to assert that the most powerful advocate of the English cause was a foreign adventurer, yet during an earlier period he rendered it numerous and important services. Until that time the Democrats had been pre-eminently the popular party, noted for the dexterity with which they employed the popular weapons of violence and invective : they had been accustomed to shout down their opponents with clamour and abuse. In Cobbett, how-ever, they met an adversary with a voice more powerful than their own, and one whom no threat could terrify and no slander destroy. Protected at first by his obscurity,

and writing anonymously or under the shelter of a pseudonym, he emerged at a later time into the full light of
publicity and bore without shrinking the utmost efforts
of party hate.[1]

In point of literary ability it was not difficult for
Cobbett to hold his own against any champion whom the
Democrats could produce. Indeed he was capable of
far more. His powers would have earned him fame in
the best days of English pamphleteering—in the time of
Swift and Defoe, or in the later period when Dr. Johnson
and John Wesley did not consider writing political pamphlets beneath the dignity of their pen. It is often
said that Cobbett modelled himself on Swift, whose *Tale
of a Tub* had fascinated him at an early age. Certainly
he makes frequent references to Swift's writings, and
there can be little doubt that he studied them, especially
the *Drapier Letters*, with considerable profit. He was
inferior to Swift in power of sustained satire, nor did he
possess Swift's trained and scholarly mind. Like Swift,
he used a plain vernacular style, never employing trite
phrases and carrying bluntness of diction to the verge of
vulgarity. But the thought, though often coarse, was
never vulgar, and he had the power, under apparent carelessness of expression, of saying exactly what he meant,
and of influencing his readers precisely as he intended.
And, with that marvellous power of expression, he had
the mind of a poet and could describe rural life and
country people in a way that has never been surpassed.
As an advocate he had an appearance of honest bluntness which powerfully influenced public opinion. He

---

[1] For an account of Cobbett's relations with the American parties, see
H. C. Lodge's *Studies in History*, Boston, 1884.

D

knew how to seem a plain, downright man, indifferent whether his statements offended his hearers. And yet all the time he was carefully turning every phrase and sentence to appeal to those whom he was addressing. There was no hypocrisy in this. Cobbett possessed the supreme qualification for successful controversy, an unfaltering belief in the entire truth of his own views and opinions. It served him in two ways. In the first place, he was so entirely convinced that he was right, and that those who opposed him were mentally incapable of reasoning justly, that he frequently persuaded his readers. And in the second place, having infallible certainty on his side, he had no need to make too careful an inquiry into evidence. Errors in fact are possible, but there is no room for error in theories founded on the intuitive promptings of common sense. Therefore, if facts appeared hostile, they had to be manipulated, and in the art of manipulation Cobbett was an adept.

The *Observations on Priestley's Emigration* had originally been prompted by love of England. The pamphlet, however, had drawn Cobbett into American politics, and in his next work he definitely attacked an American political party. On 8th January 1795 he published *A Bone to Gnaw for the Democrats*. It was an answer to *The Political Progress of Britain*, a brochure by James Thomson Callender. Callender originally published his treatise anonymously at Edinburgh and London in 1792. It was, according to its second title, ' An impartial History of Abuses in the Government of the British Empire, in Europe, Asia, and America. From the Revolution in 1688 to the present time: the whole tending to prove the ruinous consequences of the popular system of

Taxation, War, and Conquest.' Attacks on church and state were then dealt with summarily, and in January 1793, Callender, having been identified as the author, was arrested. He escaped from prison and established himself in Philadelphia, where he republished his treatise. As Cobbett knew little or nothing concerning the subject of the pamphlet he was reduced to rely chiefly upon personal abuse of Callender, whom he rechristened with gentle pleasantry, 'Tom the Tinker,' and 'Newgate Callender,' a delicate allusion to the unfortunate man's imprisonment, at the same time insinuating that the British had so many of his stamp that they were sending them to Botany Bay in shiploads.

The best thing in the pamphlet is a clever description of the feelings of William Penn on witnessing one of those fêtes in celebration of the triumphs of the French Revolutionary party, in which the Philadelphians at that time delighted to indulge :

'I thought I was walking up Market Street, by the side of old William Penn, the founder of the city; who told me, I thought, that he was come upon earth again to see if his descendants, and those of his companions, continued to walk in the paths of peace and integrity. I thought I asked him with a kind of sneer, whether he had not found things surpassing his expectation; upon which the old man, after a heavy sigh, told me a long deal about freeing blacks with one hand, and buying whites with the other, about godly malice and maple sugar, . . . etc., etc., etc., to the end of the chapter.

'Before the good man had finished his story, which, by the by, was a pretty tough one, we were, I thought, got to the upper end of Market Street, where we were stopped by a monstrous crowd of people, that not only blocked up the way, but filled all the fields for a great way out. I thought, how-ever, that we wedged along among the crowd for a good while,

till at last we could penetrate no further.   Our ears were assailed
from all quarters with the firing of cannon, sounding of trumpets,
beating of drums, ringing of bells, singing, whooping, hallooing,
and blaspheming, as if hell itself had been broken loose.   Yet,
the crowd seemed not to express the least fear: joy seemed
seated on every countenance, and expectation in every eye.   We
had not waited long in this situation, when two banners at some
little distance, announced the approach of a procession, at once
the most ludicrous and the most idolatrous that ever eyes beheld.
I thought, there was a sort of pyramid, made of paper, with a red
night cap upon the top of it, and carried by two Americans and
two foreigners, all of whom, like the pyramid, were dressed in
red night caps.   Round the pyramid marched, I thought, a bevy
of virgins in white robes, each wearing a crown and cestus
tricolor, and bearing a garland in her hand ; and (what stuff do
we dream of !) I thought these nymphs were ushered by nine or
ten priests, whose only mark of distinction was a *nosegay of straw*
tied round with a ribbon.   I thought that behind these, came a
company of artillery with their cannon, and that they were
followed by a gang of music. . . .

 '"After this I beheld, and, lo, a great multitude that no man
could number, of all nations, and kindreds, and peoples, and
tongues," and *colours*.   I thought, however, I could distinguish
amongst them (but it is all a dream) the *Chiefs* of the *State of
Pennsylvania* !

 'I thought, we followed this antick show into a spacious enclosure, where, on an altar, not of burnished gold, but of deal
boards, stood *The Goddess*, the object of the Feast.   She was
dressed like the Cyprian Queen when she received the prize
from the Idalian Shepherd ; that is to say,—in her skin : in her
right hand she held a staff mounted with a nightcap, and in
her left, a dagger ; on her head she had a cap, decorated, in
appearance, with pendent lilies, but, upon closer examination, I
thought I found them to be real bells.   This discovery led me
to perceive, that I had committed an error with respect to the
identity of her person; for hearing that her worshippers were
called *cunnus*, I had concluded she was the goddess *Cloacina*,
and in this opinion I was in some measure confirmed by seeing

her worshipped with *nosegays of straw*; but the cap and bells set me right at once. In short, I saw plainly it was the *Goddess of Folly*; which, I thought, was besides fully proved by the behaviour of the crowd. But, still, the dagger remained unexplained; for, we all know, that that weapon is not among the insignia of this goddess. In this perplexity I happened to cast my eyes downwards, and, on the front of the altar, I thought I saw the following phrase from Voltaire: "*Sous ma tutelle, les singes agacent les tigres.*"

'The priests I thought were ranged round the altar, offering up their nosegays, and invoking the assistance of the Goddess, while the air rang with Hallelujahs. The invocation was no sooner ended and the benediction given by the High-Priest, than the whole (not excepting the *Chiefs*, I thought, of the *State of Pennsylvania*) began dancing and capering *à la cannibale* round the altar, at the same time deafening the very firmament with their cries.

'Here my venerable companion, who had been very uneasy during the whole scene, would absolutely stop no longer; and to confess a truth, I began to feel a good deal uneasy myself. I thought we got with some difficulty to the outside, and seeing a young fellow of milder aspect than the rest, the old man ventured to ask him, *how long these people had been Pagans*. I thought the fellow gave him a look of infinite contempt and answered: "I see you are a superstitious old fool, that knows nothing of the luminous close of the Eighteenth Century. Why, you stupid old dog, we are all Christians yet: What you have seen to-day is only a jubilee, to celebrate the downfall of *our best friend*,[1] and the massacre of *nine hundred* of our neighbours by the hands of *forty thousand* two-legged monsters!"

'As he spoke these last words, I thought his person, which was that of a genteel and gentle American, assumed the hideous form of the terrific *Medusa*; his fingers were transformed into the claws of a Tiger, the fangs of a boar hung down his foaming jaws, his eyes became a glaring ball, and his hair a bed of snakes, curling round his scull and hissing destruction. The poor old

---

[1] Louis XVI., who assured American Independence by assisting the colonies against England.

man, though immortal, was appalled, and rushed into the grave
to hide himself from the petrifying sight.   I uttered a shriek,
and awaked; but awaking was very far from putting an end to
my fright ; still the noise continued and still was I stiffened with
horror, unable to determine whether it was a dream or not.   My
voice, however, had alarmed the family, and Oh ! how glad was I
to find, that the noise I heard was nothing but that of the French
and "our own *citizens*" assembled to celebrate the "*Holy* Insur-
rection" of the 23rd Thermidor.'

A Bone to Gnaw was unfavourably reviewed in the
American Monthly Review by the editor, Smith.   The
criticism drew from Cobbett a caustic rejoinder, entitled
A Kick for a Bite, in which he paid especial attention to
Smith's grammatical inaccuracies.   This was followed in
March 1795 by the second part of *A Bone to Gnaw*, notable
as the first pamphlet issued under the famous pseudonym,
Peter Porcupine.   The name was originated by some reviewer of the first part of *A Bone to Gnaw*, who likened
Cobbett to a porcupine, chiefly on account of the popular
belief that that animal uses its quills as weapons of
offence by discharging them at its adversaries.   Cobbett
took up the nickname and in *A Kick for a Bite* referred to
himself as Peter Porcupine.   He employed the pseudonym
for almost all his future publications in America.

In the second part of *A Bone to Gnaw*, Cobbett
occupied himself with the 'Proceedings' of the United
Irishmen, a democratic club in Dublin.   After incurring
his displeasure by criticising the Government of Ireland
and alleging that the interests of the Irish people were
neglected, they roused him to anger by a florid address to
Priestley :

'"Farewell," continue the *United Irishmen*, "Farewell, great
and good man; but before you go, we beseech a portion of your

parting prayer" (down upon your marrow-bones, reader), "for Archibald Hamilton Rowan, Muir, Palmer, Margarot, and Gerald, who are now, like you, preparing to cross the bleak ocean —Farewell! soon will you embrace your sons on the American shore; Washington will *take you by the hand*, and the *shade* of Franklin look *down*, with calm delight, on the first statesman of the age extending his *protection* to its first philosopher." Here is certainly some mistake in the close of this farewell. What do they mean by the *shade* of Franklin's looking *down*? To look *down* on a person one must be in an elevated situation, and, I fancy, it is pretty generally believed, by those who understand the geography of the invisible world, that Franklin's *shade*, as it is here termed, has taken a different route. Indeed, this must be a *bull*; they certainly meant to say, that Washington *would look down upon him*, and Franklin *take him by the hand*; at least, this would be nearer the truth, for sure I am, that Franklin will take him by the hand before the President of the United States will.' [1]

The latter part of the pamphlet is taken up with accounts of the cruelties committed at Lyon under the orders of the French Convention, and with reflections on the conquest of Holland by France.

'Patriot Paine, the heathen philosopher, has observed, that republics never marry. There is more humour than truth in this observation; for though one would imagine, that the name of *sister* which they give to each other, would be an insuperable bar to such an union, yet experience proves the contrary; for the French republic does not only marry, but is guilty of polygamy. She has already espoused the republic of Batavia (commonly called Holland) and the poor little Geneva, and she is now swaggering about like a Jack Wh—re with a couple of under punks at her heels. She wanted to make love to the cheek of John Bull; but John, beast as he is, had too much grace to be seduced by her. "No," said John, "you heathenish cannibal, I will not touch you; you reek with blood; get from my sight,

---

[1] *Porcupine's Works*, 1801, ii. 111.

you stabbing strumpet!" John was half right; for she is indeed a cruel spouse; something like the brazen image, formerly made use of in Hungary, that cracked the bones, and squeezed out the blood and guts of those who were condemned to its embraces.

'How happy were we [Americans] in escaping a marriage with a termagant like this! We were, indeed, within an inch of it. Brissot and his crew sent out one of their citizens (who had been employed with so much success in negotiating the marriage with Geneva) to marry us by proxy, and the democrats were beginning to sing "Come, haste to the wedding"; when the President, who had not burnt his Bible, saw that the laws of consanguinity did not allow of a marriage between two sisters, and therefore, like a good old father of his country, he peremptorily forbade the banns. Heavens bless him for it! if he had not done this, we might long ago have seen the *citizen inviting* the Congress, as Pichegru does the Dutch assembly, to send him five hundred oxen for breakfast.'[1]

During the course of 1795 negotiations were carried on between the United States and England, with a view to the settlement, among other matters, of various questions concerning the duty of the United States Government as a neutral, which had become pressing since the outbreak of war between France and England. A treaty was signed on 19th November. Popular opinion in the States, however, was so strongly on the side of France that the negotiations were very much disliked, and a flood of pamphlets appeared, attacking the conduct of the Government, which was in the hands of the Federal party, with Washington as President. In reply to these attacks, and especially to some spurious *Letters of Franklin* (Philadelphia, 1795), Cobbett, in August, before the conclusion of the treaty, wrote a treatise

---

[1] *Porcupine's Works*, 1801, ii. 147-8.

entitled *A Little Plain English addressed to the People of the United States on the Treaty negotiated with his Britannic Majesty, and on the Conduct of the President relative thereto.* In this pamphlet, which shows a considerable advance on his previous productions in treatment of political questions, Cobbett strenuously defended the Federal Government for their conduct, and showed with great force how necessary was a good understanding with Great Britain for the commercial interests of the United States. The pamphlet was immediately reprinted in London, and was welcomed as a powerful presentation of the British case.

Towards the close of the year Cobbett again used his pen in defence of the Government. The interception of a despatch of the French envoy, M. Fauchet, had given rise to the belief that Edmund Randolph, the American Secretary of State, was in French pay. Randolph had strong French sympathies, and was ardently opposed to the English treaty, but the charge of corruption rested on a misunderstanding of Fauchet's statements, and is now generally regarded as baseless.[1] But Randolph's conduct had certainly been imprudent, and he was compelled to resign his office. In defence of his conduct, he published *A Vindication of Mr. Randolph's Resignation* (Philadelphia, 1795), and this pamphlet formed the text for Cobbett's reply, which appeared on 1st January 1796, and was entitled *A New Year's Gift to the Democrats; or, Observations on a Pamphlet entitled 'A Vindication of Mr. Randolph's Resignation.'* It is almost unnecessary to say that Cobbett took the blackest view of Randolph's conduct, and represented him as a greedy

[1] See M. D. Conway's *Omitted Chapters of History*, 1888.

dependant on the wages of France. He showed ability, however, in indicating the weak points of the *Vindication*, and his conduct won him the gratitude of the Federal officials.

In January 1796 Cobbett quarrelled violently with Thomas Bradford, who hitherto had acted as his publisher. He had undertaken to edit some of the debates in Congress in periodical form, under the title *A Prospect from the Congress Gallery*. After the successful publication of the first number early in 1796, Bradford proposed a new arrangement, and a vehement dispute ensued.

'His son offered me,' says Cobbett, 'I believe, a hundred dollars a number, in place of eighteen; and I should have accepted his offer, had it not been for a word that escaped him during the conversation. He observed, that their customers would be much disappointed, for that his *father had promised* a continuation, and *that it should be made very interesting*. This slip of the tongue opened my eyes at once. What! a bookseller undertake to promise that I should write, and that I should write to please his customers too! no! if all his *customers*, if all the Congress with the President at their head, had come and solicited me; nay, had my salvation depended on a compliance, I would not have written another line.'[1]

The squabble that followed reflected little credit on either party. Bradford represented Cobbett as a needy hireling, whom he had taken from the gutter, and on whose back he had put a decent coat. Cobbett rebutted these statements with unnecessary earnestness, and then proceeded to a violent personal attack on Thomas Bradford and his son, Samuel F. Bradford. The father he accused of longings after aristocratic connections, un-

[1] *Life and Adventures of Peter Porcupine.*

worthy in a republican, while the son was treated to pure Billingsgate.

'That lump of tallow streaked with lampblack,' and 'this hatter turned printer, this sooty-fisted son of ink and urine, whose heart is as black and as foul as the liquid in which he dabbles,'

may serve as specimens of Cobbett's art of controversy.

The chief interest of the *Prospect from the Congress Gallery* lies in the fact that it was probably the germ of Cobbett's later production, the *Parliamentary Debates*. In the *Prospect*, however, he did not confine himself to reporting the proceedings of Congress, but interspersed a vigorous commentary, supporting the Federal party, and vehemently assailing the Democrats.

Within a month the *Prospect* was re-issued as the first number of the *Political Censor*, which continued to appear at intervals until January 1797. Eight numbers were published in all. These, however, were not confined to the proceedings of Congress, but dealt with a variety of topics, chiefly of a political and social character.

In February 1796 Cobbett brought out *The Bloody Buoy thrown out as a warning to the Political Pilots of America*, which consisted of a collection of atrocities committed by the French revolutionaries, especially by the notorious Jean Baptiste Carrier. This compilation, a sensational record of horrors selected for the most part from various French authors, had considerable vogue. It was reprinted in London in 1797, and in 1798 an abridgment appeared, which reached a seventh edition within the year.

Early in 1796 the growth of Cobbett's fame led to a curious interview between him and Talleyrand, the diplomatist. At that time Talleyrand was living in Philadelphia. He had fled from France at the fall of the monarchy and was proscribed by the Revolutionary Government. After failing to find an asylum in England he came to New York, whence he removed to Philadelphia. At the beginning of 1796 he was still a refugee, but he was strongly suspected of being a secret agent of the French Government, and later in the year he actually made his peace and returned to Paris. His attention was excited by Cobbett's onslaught on the French party, and he sought an interview for the purpose, as Cobbett believed, of ascertaining whether the new writer could be purchased. Cobbett has given an account of the meeting in *Porcupine's Gazette* for 6th May 1797 :

'Some months after his arrival in this city [Talleyrand] left a message with a friend of his, requesting me to meet him at that friend's house. Several days passed away before that meeting took place : I had no business to call me that way, and therefore I did not go. At last this modern Judas and I got seated by the same fireside. I expected that he wanted to expostulate with me on the severe treatment he had met with at my hands : I had called him an apostate, a hypocrite, and every other name of which he was deserving; I therefore leave the reader to imagine my astonishment, when I heard him begin with complimenting me on my *wit* and *learning*. He praised several of my pamphlets, the New Year's Gift in particular, and still spoke of them as mine. I did not acknowledge myself the author, of course, but yet he would insist that I was ; or, at any rate, they reflected, he said, *infinite honour* on the author, let him be who he might. Having carried this species of flattery as far as he judged it safe, he asked me, with a vast deal of apparent seriousness, whether I had received my education at *Oxford*, or at *Cambridge*! Hitherto I had kept my countenance pretty well; but this abominable stretch of hypocrisy, and the placid mien and silver accent with which it was pronounced, would have forced a laugh from a Quaker in the midst of a meeting. I don't recollect what reply I made him; but this I recollect well, I gave him to understand that I was no trout, and consequently was not to be caught by tickling.

'This information led him to something more solid. He began to talk about *business*. I was no *flour merchant*,[1] but I taught English; and as luck would have it, this was the very commodity that Bishop Perigord wanted. If I had taught Thornton's[2] or Webster's[3] language, or sold sand or ashes, or pepper-pot, it would have been just the same to him. He knew the English language as well as I did; but he wanted to have dealings with me in some way or other.

'I knew, that, notwithstanding his being *proscribed* at Paris, he was extremely intimate with Adet,[4] and this circumstance led me to suspect his real business in the United States: I therefore did not care to take him as a scholar. I told him, that being engaged in a translation[5] for the press, I could not possibly quit home. This difficulty the lame fiend hopped over in a moment. He would very gladly come to my house. I cannot say but it would have been a great satisfaction to me to have seen the *ci-devant* Bishop of Autun, the guardian of the holy oil that anointed the heads of the descendants of St. Louis, come trudging through the dirt to receive a lesson from me; but on the other hand I did not want a French spy to take a survey either of my desk or my house. My price for teaching was *six* dollars a month; he offered me *twenty*; but I refused; and before I left him I gave him clearly to understand that I was not to be purchased.'[6]

So far indeed from having any intention of reconsidering his position, Cobbett had resolved to abandon the protection of his pseudonym and publicly to announce himself in his own person as the champion of

---

[1] When Talleyrand came to New York in 1794 he set up as a merchant.

[2] William Thornton, a phonetic reformer.

[3] Noah Webster, author of the *American Dictionary of the English Language*.

[4] The French minister to the United States.

[5] The *Bloody Buoy*. This and the reference to the *New Year's Gift*, almost fixes the interview in January 1796, for the *Bloody Buoy* appeared in February.

[6] *Porcupine's Works*, v. 361-3.

English interests. Either the occasion or the consequence of his quarrel with Bradford was a determination to become a bookseller himself. In the spring of 1796 he took a house in Second Street. On 11th July he opened it as a bookseller's shop and used the occasion for displaying his patriotism and defying American sympathy with France.[1]

'I resolved to put the power and the courage of the democrats to the test, by opening shop with a grand exhibition of the portraits of kings, queens, princes, nobles, and bishops, and, in short, with every portrait, picture, or book, that I could obtain, and that I thought likely to excite rage in the inveterate enemies of Great Britain, particularly a large, coarse, sixpenny representation of Lord Howe's victory over the French. Never since the beginning of the American rebellion had any one before dared to exhibit at his window the portrait of George the Third. . . . At the time when I adopted my measure of defiance, I knew not one British subject in America besides myself, who was not afraid to own, and who, in fact, did not, in some way or other, *deny his country and his king*; who did not call himself *an American citizen*, and who had not formally, and by oath, transferred his allegiance to the United States. On the first morning of my exhibition, I had put up a representation of Lord Howe's victory in a leaf of the *European Magazine*; but, a bookseller, with whom I was acquainted, and who came to see *how I stood it*, whispered me, while the rabble were gazing and growling at my door, that he had two large representations of the same action. They were about four feet long and two wide; the things which are hawked about and sold at the farmhouses in England, and had been crammed, more, perhaps, by way of packing-stuff than otherwise, into a parcel of goods that had been sent out from London. But the letters were large; the mob, ten or twenty deep, could read, and they did read aloud too, "LORD HOWE'S DECISIVE VICTORY OVER THE FRENCH FLEET," and, therefore though the price was augmented from

[1] See *Porcupine's Works*, iv. 3-4.

sixpence to *two dollars* each, I purchased them, and put one up at the window . . . the other . . . was sold to two Englishmen, who were amongst the numbers that went to America about the years 1794 and 1795, misled by the representations of Paine and others, and being, as they frankly acknowledged to me, enemies of their country when they left it. They had mixed amongst the crowd, had taken the part of their country, and had proposed to maintain their words with their fists. After the quarrel had, in some degree, subsided, they, partly, perhaps, by way of defiance, came into the shop to purchase each of them a picture of Lord Howe and his victory. Finding that I had but one for sale, they would have purchased that; but, as it amounted to more money than both of them were possessed of, they went, and, in their phrase, which I shall never forget, *kicked their master*, that is to say, got money in advance upon their labour, which was then engaged in the digging of a cellar. Having thus obtained the two dollars, each of them took an end of the print in his hand, displayed it, and thus carried it away through the mob, who, though they still cursed, could not help giving signs of admiration.'[1]

But some of the more virulent spirits were not moved to admiration so easily as the crowd. Until this time the identity of Cobbett with Peter Porcupine was generally unknown: now it became a matter of notoriety. Anonymous threats were showered upon him; he was menaced with tar and feathers and with the ruin of his property. An unsigned letter sent to his landlord, John Oldden, threatening the destruction of his house if Cobbett was not evicted, drew from the tenant on 22nd July 1796 *The Scare Crow*, a strong protest against his assailants, in which he remarked:

'When William Penn was tracing out his beloved city of Philadelphia, if any one had told him that the time would come, when a man should be threatened with murder for offering to

[1] *Political Register*, 5th Oct. 1805.

sale in one of the streets, a print "indicative of British prowess," I much question if the good man, though a Quaker, would not have said that it was a d——ned lie. Poor old fellow! he little dreamed what was to happen at the close of the "enlightened" eighteenth century.'[1]

The author of the letter to Oldden accused him of exhibiting in his window, 'Courtley' pictures and 'prints indicative of the prowess of our enemies the British, and the disgrace of the French.' Cobbett replied:

'What does the cut-throat mean by "*courtly* prints." I have Ankerstrom the regicide,[2] that can be no courtly print at any rate. I have indeed the portraits of the late king and queen of France, but as they are dead, one would imagine that they could create no alarm. . . . 'Tis true, I have the portraits of Billy Pitt and Lord Grenville, and several other noble personages; but then, I have Marat and Lepelletier, by way of rubbing off as I go. I have a right reverend Father in God in one corner of my window, and if I could procure the right Irreverent Father in the Devil, Tom Paine, I would hoist him in the other; for want of him I have Dr. Priestley, who, upon a shift, is very capable of supplying his place. I have some groups too, executed by order of the French Convention, which I humbly presume will not be called *courtly*. The taking of the Bastile decorates one pane of my window, as it did the Birmingham Club-Room; the French people on their marrow-bones acknowledging the existence of God, by order of Robespierre, decorates another; and a third is ornamented with a representation of the "glorious victory" obtained over the Swiss guards, on the tenth of August 1792. I am promised a print of poor Richard in the arms of a brace of angels, who are carrying him off, God knows whither. I am sure now all these things are republican enough, and if my sovereign Lords will but please to take my whole collection into view, I cannot think that they will find me so criminal as I have been represented.'[3]

---

[1] *Porcupine's Works*, iv. 12.

[2] Ankerstrom shot Gustavus III. of Sweden at a masked ball at Stockholm on 16th March 1792.   [3] *The Scare Crow*, pp. 14-15.

This bantering reply failed to soften democratic resentment. The *Aurora* newspaper was a principal vehicle for attacks upon Cobbett, and for anecdotes, innuendoes, and pretended communications holding him up to ridicule. He was described as a man who had become so inured to the cat-of-nine-tails while in the army that horsewhipping had no terrors for him. A forged advertisement announced that on a certain day he was prepared to give ocular demonstration that he had not suffered the lash for misdemeanours, and an equally imaginative account of his *levée* described the incredulity of his visitors after inspecting his back. The shops were crowded with placards announcing a *Pill for Porcupine*, *The Imposter detected*, *The History of a Porcupine*, *The Little Innocent Porcupine Hornet's Nest*. He was represented in caricature as trampling on *The Rights of Man* and as destroying the statue of Liberty that he might obtain from Satan a bag of money for reward.[1] The notoriety which he had attained was a source of intense pleasure to Cobbett. Intrepid by nature, he did not fear the threats of violence that were constantly launched against him, but he keenly relished the indirect compliment to his talents which those threats implied.

'Dear Father,' he says in an apostrophe to George Cobbett's shade, 'when you used to set me off to work in the morning, dressed in my blue smock frock and woollen spatterdashes, with my bag of bread and cheese and bottle of small beer swung over my shoulder on the little crook that my good old godfather Boxall gave me, little did you imagine that I should become one day so great a man as to have my picture stuck in the windows, and have four whole books published about me in the course of one week.'

---

[1] For a detailed account of the attacks on Cobbett, see Mr. Edward Smith's *Life of William Cobbett*, 1878, i. 171-79.

With cheerful readiness he set about replying to his opponents. In August, in answer to a scurrilous 'History of Peter Porcupine' by Paul Hedgehog which appeared in the *Aurora*, he published *The Life and Adventures of Peter Porcupine*, which is the chief source for details of his early life. He also made more general rejoinders in September and November in his *Censor*, and in October in the *Gros Mousqueton Diplomatique*.

But in the meantime a new occasion of wrath had been afforded to Cobbett by the action of Thomas Paine in attacking Washington. Although in later life, after his change of politics, he celebrated Paine's virtues, at this period he regarded him as the incarnation of evil. Ever since Paine had been rescued from a French prison by the intervention of the American envoy he had been filled with dissatisfaction. He partly relieved his feelings in the May number of the *Censor* by a funeral ode which concluded :

'Tom Paine for the Devil is surely a match,
In hanging Old England he cheated Jack Catch,
In France (the first time such a thing had been seen)
He cheated the watchful and sharp guillotine,
And at last, to the sorrow of all the beholders
He marched out of life with his head on his shoulders.'

In August 1796, feeling that the American Government had neglected him, Paine published in the form of a letter a long and bitter attack on Washington's military career, as well as on his policy while President. This thoroughly roused Cobbett, who devoted the September number of the *Censor* to a 'Life of Thomas Paine, interspersed with Remarks and Reflections.'[1] The Life was

[1] This Life was reprinted in London by John Wright in 1797.

founded on the hostile biography written by George Chalmers in 1791 under the pseudonym of Francis Oldys. Cobbett's 'remarks and reflections' were uncomplimentary in character, but they failed to satisfy his indignation, and in December he published in the *Censor* a direct reply to Paine's letter to Washington, entitled a 'Letter to the infamous Tom Paine.'[1] Washington himself read this reply, and in a letter to David Stuart said that, making allowance for Cobbett's English asperity, for his occasional strong and coarse expressions, and for his want of official information in regard to many matters, he considered it 'not a bad thing.'[2] Apart from the fact that it obtained Washington's approval, the chief interest of this epistle lies in comparing it with Cobbett's later utterances with regard to Paine, when he had become an ardent disciple of that freethinking apostle. With a solicitude for consistency which in later life he would have considered unnecessary, Cobbett contrasted Paine's abuse of Washington in the 'Letter' with his former eulogies of that statesman in *The Rights of Man*, and after triumphantly printing the contradictory passages in parallel columns proceeded to address Paine in an impassioned apostrophe.

'Now atrocious, infamous miscreant, "look on this picture and on this." I would call on you to blush, but the rust of villainy has eaten your cheek to the bone, and dried up the source of suffusion. Are these the proofs of your disinterestedness and consistency? Is it thus that you are always the same, and that "you *preserve through life* the right-angled character of man"?'[3]

---

[1] It was reprinted in London in the same year.
[2] Washington to Stuart 8th January 1797, quoted in Conway's *Life of Paine*, 1892, ii. 175.   [3] *Porcupine's Works*, iv. 331.

With this delicious sentence which has a flavour of the *Eatanswill Gazette*, a biographer of Cobbett has been unkind enough to compare an estimate in the *Political Register* of 1818 :[1]

'Whatever fault may be ascribed to Mr. Paine, *not one can lay inconsistency to his charge.*[2] From his first appearance in the political world, he adopted one uniform mode of opinion, and although I could not go along with him in all the wanderings of his inflamed imagination, yet as an arduous defender of the people's rights, as a strenuous and unflinching advocate for the curtailment of aristocratical power, as the champion of popular power in opposition to the abuses of a monarchical government, Paine will always stand pre-eminent in the world.'

On 4th March 1797, Cobbett brought out the first number of *Porcupine's Gazette and Daily Advertiser*, and this newspaper absorbed much of his attention for the next two years. Some such publication was necessary if he wished to reply to the numerous attacks made on him. It also served as a convenient vehicle for supporting the Federal party and for advocating the cause of an English alliance. Unfortunately it afforded him too ready a means of assailing his opponents and eventually brought on him serious disaster. Even before the final catastrophe he found himself in peril more than once. In August the Spanish minister, Don Carlos Martinez de Yrujo, applied to the Federal Government to prosecute Cobbett for libels on himself and on the King of Spain, who had been depicted in *Porcupine's Gazette* as a tool in the hands of the French republicans. Cobbett was accordingly bound over to appear in the Federal district court in April 1798. This, however, did not satisfy the

---

[1] Huish, *Memoirs of Cobbett*, i. 161-62.   [2] The italics are not Cobbett's.

Spanish envoy who requested that the trial might take place in the state court, where the chief-justice, Thomas M'Kean, was a strong Democrat in politics and was also de Yrujo's father-in-law.   Consent was obtained and the trial was appointed for November 1797.   M'Kean vehemently attacked Cobbett in his charge to the grand jury, but notwithstanding they threw out the bill by a majority of one.   Cobbett improved the occasion in *The Republican Judge*, a pamphlet published in the same month, in which he assailed the authors of the prosecution and the minority of the grand jury with his accustomed vehemence.

The happy result of this action encouraged Cobbett to greater violence, and his vituperation of the French people occasioned so much scandal that early in 1799 the President, John Adams, although himself approving of the observance of neutrality between England and France, resolved to order him to leave the United States under the provisions of the Alien Act, and was only prevented by the remonstrances of the Attorney-General. On learning the intention of the President, Cobbett began to prepare for such an emergency by secretly realising his property.   In the end, however, his departure was not owing to official compulsion, but was the result of a private law-suit.   In 1793 Philadelphia had been subjected to a severe visitation of yellow fever, which carried off four thousand inhabitants in three months.   Naturally so terrible a scourge absorbed the attention of medical men, and several different courses of treatment were advocated with more or less success.   Amongst these systems that of Dr. Benjamin Rush attracted great attention.   It was of the violent character common at that time, consisting of a strong purge followed by copious bleeding. So drastic a treatment no doubt destroyed many, but it is improbable that zeal for medicine would have induced Cobbett to intervene in the professional controversy that arose over Rush's remedy. Benjamin Rush, however, besides being one of the greatest American physicians of the eighteenth century, was also eminent as a politician. Like M'Kean, he had signed the Declaration of Independence, and after the peace of 1782 had become a strong Democrat. Moreover, he was a Quaker and a friend of Thomas Paine. In 1797 the yellow fever revisited Philadelphia, and Rush began to advertise his treatment widely by means of the Democratic press. Under these circumstances Cobbett needed little persuasion to induce him to denounce both Rush and his system. In a short time he had succeeded in making Rush extremely uncomfortable. He drew forcible comparisons between him and another great advocate of bleeding, Dr. Sangrado in *Gil Blas*. He ridiculed the doctor and his remedies alike, with that scurrility in which constant practice had made him an adept, and which would have been contemptible had it been less happily pointed. One remark particularly infuriated Rush. With fatal pride he had termed his remedy the ' Samson of Medicine.' On this Cobbett remarked in *Porcupine's Gazette* that the title was fitting, for in the hands of Rush and his followers it had slain more Americans than ever Samson slew of the Philistines. Rush could not endure this gibe, and so, says Cobbett, like Nicodemus Broadbrim in Foote's play [1] ' he sent for a sinful man in the flesh called an attorney,

[1] *Devil upon Two Sticks.*

to prepare a parchment and carry us unto judgment.'
In October 1797 he commenced his suit in the supreme
court of Pennsylvania. Cobbett, apprehensive, not
without cause, that he might find the State court biased,
applied to have his case removed to the next circuit
court of the Federal Government, on the ground that he
was an alien. His petition was summarily rejected by
M'Kean, but the trial was put off for nearly two years,
on account, as Cobbett insinuates, of the difficulty of
packing a jury. The interval of waiting had been
utilised by Cobbett to make fresh attacks on Rush and
every one connected with the case. The trial came on
on 13th December 1799. Cobbett awaited it with little
confidence. M'Kean was no longer judge, as he had
been appointed governor of the State, but he possessed
great influence. He could hardly be expected to look
on Cobbett kindly, for in September a statement had
appeared in *Porcupine's Gazette* to the effect that at the
time of the war of the Revolution he had been publicly
horsewhipped for malpractices by an American general,
and had afterwards acquired a fortune by cheating the
starving American soldiers.[1] Shippen, the new chief-
justice, was a friend of M'Kean, and equally hostile to
Cobbett's political principles. He summed up strongly
against Cobbett, and the jury found for Rush, assessing
the damages at five thousand dollars. There is indeed
no need to seek for an explanation of the verdict by dis-
paraging the impartiality of the tribunal. The malice
of the libel was so obvious that no adequate defence was
possible. Cobbett himself acknowledged after the event
the weakness of his case, and characteristically imputed

[1] *Porcupine's Works*, xi. 47.

it to the treachery of one of his counsel. But Shippen
in his charge to the jury showed that Cobbett's action
was intrinsically indefensible. Cobbett had made no
attempt to combat Rush's system by argument; he had
not gone into the merits of his method of cure, nor had
he advanced any medical reasons against the remedy.
He had confined himself to gross personal abuse of the
doctor himself. He had styled him repeatedly a quack,
an empiric, a pretender to physic. He had attacked his
private character, made sport of the humbleness of his
origin, and held his personal manners up to ridicule. In
defence, he had urged that there was no indication of
malice, and that the subject of dispute was a matter of
public concern. Cobbett's attacks on Rush's private
character were held a disproof of the former plea, while
they removed the libel from the class of attacks properly
defended by the latter.[1]

There is no doubt that the verdict affected Cobbett
very deeply. In spite of the fact that the damages as well
as the expenses of the suit were ultimately repaid him by
some political sympathisers in Canada,[2] the verdict nearly
ruined him. He had removed to New York before the
decision of the trial, taking with him such of his property
as he had been able to realise. But his effects at
Philadelphia were sold by auction to defray the damages
and costs, and naturally they realised considerably less
than their value. A new edition of *Porcupine's Works*
which he had in hand was disposed of as waste paper,

---

[1] For a strong condemnation of Rush and commendation of Cobbett see
W. Rowley's *Treatise of Putrid, Malignant, Infectious Fevers*, London,
1804; for a high eulogy of Rush and his system see Thacher's *American
Medical Biography*, Boston, 1828.

[2] *Political Register*, 10th April 1830.

and he was not inclined to treat the matter as lightly as he had the destruction of Priestley's manuscripts at Birmingham. Like many people who have been very poor, Cobbett was keenly alive to the value of money. Risk of personal injury never daunted him, but through-out life he was sensitive to pecuniary loss. But he did not lose heart or courage under his reverse.

'To say that I do not feel this stroke, and very sensibly too, would be great affectation, but to repine at it would be folly, and to sink under it cowardice.'[1]

With this stout utterance he commenced the task of repairing his fortunes.

In consequence of his removal to New York, the publication of *Porcupine's Gazette* was suspended on 26th October 1799, and in January 1800 he issued a farewell number, in which he announced that the paper had never yielded him a farthing, that it had only been published for public reasons, and that it would be dis-continued. On 15th February he issued the first number of a new periodical intended to appear at intervals of a fortnight. It was entitled the *Rushlight*, because, he said in the prefatory advertisement, 'as it is intended to assist the public view in the inspecting of various tenebrious objects, it may be called, and not, I presume, improperly, a *Light*; and as the appearance of this light must be attributed wholly to the Philadelphian phlebotomist, gratitude will sanction the propriety of prefixing to it the name of *Rush*.' Only five numbers of this periodical appeared. He found his position in New York far from comfortable, and he was seized with a

[1] *Porcupine's Works*, xi. 212.

great longing to return to England, for he had so long praised that country that he had ended by believing his own eulogies. Numerous invitations were constantly received by him, and on 1st June 1800 he sailed. He issued a farewell address in the Philadelphian papers, in which he remarked, not without dignity :

'To my friends, who are also the real friends of America, I wish that peace and happiness which virtue ought to ensure, but which I greatly fear they will not find ; and as to my enemies, I can wish them no severer scourge, than that which they are preparing for themselves and their country. With this I depart for my native land, where neither the moth of *Democracy* nor the rust of *Federalism* doth corrupt, and where thieves do not, with impunity, break through and steal five thousand dollars at a time.' [1]

[1] *Porcupine's Works*, xii. 110.

CHAPTER III

COBBETT THE TORY

COBBETT was conveyed to England in the post-office packet, *Lady Arabella*. Stopping at Halifax on the way he was very graciously received by the Duke of Kent, at that time Commander-in-Chief in the province.[1] He landed at Falmouth on 4th July 1800, after being chased by a large French vessel, which pressed the *Lady Arabella* so close that the crew were compelled to heave her guns overboard to lighten her. At Falmouth he was lodged and entertained by Pellew, the collector of customs. His chief friend in London was John Wright, a bookseller in Piccadilly, who was intimately associated with Canning, Hookham Frere, William Gifford of the *Anti-Jacobin*, John Gifford of the *Anti-Jacobin Review*, and other lions of the Tory party. Cobbett had employed Wright as his agent, while he was in America. When he came to London he took a lodging near him in St. James's Street, whence he removed in March 1801 to Pall Mall. He had over five hundred pounds with which to begin the world anew, and he received a warm welcome from a crowd of ministerialists and office-holders, besides being noticed by at least one minister, Mr. William Windham, the Secretary at War. Windham was one of the old Whigs,

---

[1] *Political Register*, 10th April 1830.

who had joined Pitt's ministry in 1794. He was a man after Cobbett's own heart, an upright and cultivated country gentleman with a strong taste for sport. He patronised the prize-ring and defended bull-baiting as a means of maintaining the hardihood of the race. On 7th August, a few days after Cobbett's arrival in London, he invited him to dine at his house, with a party of whom Pitt and Canning were two.[1] Pitt, who did not love journalists and was generally haughty with strangers, was unusually affable.

'I was of course,' said Cobbett,[2] 'very proud of this invitation, and I felt more than ever disposed to use my talents in support of the system as it was then going on ; which stood in real need of support, for Bonaparte was making fearful progress, and I resolved in my mind to set up a daily paper. While, however, I was thinking about this, Mr. George Hammond, the Under Secretary of State for Foreign Affairs (Lord Grenville being the Secretary), sent for me to his office, and made me an offer of a Government paper. The Government had two, the *True Briton* and the *Sun*; the former a morning and the latter an evening paper. They were *their property*, office, types, lease of houses, and all; and the former was offered to me as a *gift* with all belonging to it. . . . My answer to Mr. Hammond was conveyed in reminding him of the fable of the *wolf* and the *mastiff*, the latter of which having, one night, when loose, rambled into a wood, met the former all gaunt and shagged, and said to him, "Why do you lead this sort of life? See how fat and sleek I am ! Come home with me and live as I do; dividing your time between eating and sleeping." The ragged friend having accepted the kind offer, they then trotted on together till they got out of the wood, when the wolf, assisted by the light of the moon, the beams of which had been intercepted by the trees, spied a *crease*, a little *mark*, round the neck of the mastiff. "What is your fancy," said he, "for making that mark round

---

[1] *Windham's Diary*, ed. Mrs. Baring, 1866, p. 430.
[2] *Political Register*, 10th April 1830.

your neck?" "Oh," said the other, "it is only the mark of my *collar* that my master ties me up with." " *Ties you up !*" exclaimed the wolf, stopping short at the same time ; "give me my ragged hair, my gaunt belly and my *freedom*," and so saying he trotted back to the wood.

'In short I refused the offer, though worth several thousand pounds. . . . From that moment, all belonging to the Government looked on me with *great suspicion*.'

Resolved to keep his integrity, Cobbett on his own account set up a daily paper, which was to give the ministry independent support. In memory of his American newspaper he named it the *Porcupine*. In September he published a prospectus of his project, with many severe reflections on the Americans and much coarse abuse of the French, and announced his intention of offering an uncompromising support to the war with France and an equally resolute opposition to the emissaries of the republican party, 'still preaching fanaticism and infidelity, still bawling for that change which they have the audacity to call Reform.' Not without thought of past tribulations Cobbett announced his intention of not admitting advertisements of quack medicines. 'I am told by adhering to this resolution, I shall lose five hundred a year, and excite the resentment of the numerous body of empirics, but their money I hope I shall never be so graceless as to covet, and as to their resentment, I have nothing to fear from that, so long as I abstain from their death-dealing nostrums.' In the early conduct of his paper Cobbett found that public taste in England was hardly prepared for such full-flavoured polemic as had served his purpose in America. Although we are not accustomed to regard the end of the eighteenth century as an age of peculiar refinement, yet the standard of literary taste was high, and men who were accustomed to the political writings of Johnson, of John Wesley, of Burke, or of Canning, were likely to be repelled by one who inherited the coarseness of Swift as well as some of his other literary qualities.

'You tell us, Mr. Cobbett,' wrote an indignant and anonymous critic, 'in your Address to the Public, that your paper is read in the best private families, ought you then not to be ashamed of yourself to make use of those expressions so coarse, vulgar, and indelicate, as show you more fit to be the editor of a Billingsgate journal, than that of an English Newspaper; do you forget that you are writing for an English public, and not for a crew of American savages, who can scarcely distinguish between that which is refined. . . . Do you not know that it is the vulgarity of some of our best writers, which expels their works from the tables and bookshelves of the delicate and the refined; and do you hope to succeed with your nauseous trash, or to make a convert to your principles, by defiling your pages with vulgar ribaldry, and coarse invective? Your godfather and your god-mother have not infringed the obligation, which they swore to perform—you have been taught the vulgar tongue with a vengeance; and to quote yourself, I'll be d——d if you be not one of the greatest proficients in it, that I have lately met with.'

In its early days the *Porcupine* was distinguished by its enthusiastic support of Pitt's ministry and of the war party in England. It received contributions from Lord Grenville, under the name of Sulpicius, and from Jeremy Bentham, and it waged relentless warfare against all radical prints and especially against *The Times*. The first question on which Cobbett showed divergence of opinion was in regard to the treatment of the Catholics. Pitt's resignation in February 1801, on account of the refusal of the king to consider any measure of Catholic emancipation, drew from Cobbett a protest against religious concessions on the ground that the repeal of penal laws implied approbation of the offence against which they were directed.

The commencement, however, of the negotiations, which eventually terminated in the Treaty of Amiens, caused a more serious difference between Cobbett and the Government. He opposed the idea of a pacification in the most uncompromising manner. The *Porcupine* was filled with every form of protest, argument, and entreaty against the incredible folly of ending the war. On the other hand peace was at that time very popular with the multitude, who were suffering great hardships owing to the rise in price of several of the necessaries of life. The French envoy, General Law de Lauriston, was received with intense enthusiasm: the horses were taken out of his carriage, and he was dragged in triumph from Oxford Street to Downing Street. Cobbett regarded this manifestation with alarm as indicating the spread of revolutionary sentiments among the lower orders in England. The prospect of a treaty was celebrated with general illuminations in London, but he refused to join in the demonstration. His house in Pall Mall was in consequence attacked on 10th October by the mob, which broke all the windows and nearly forced the front door in spite of the efforts of Mr. Graham, one of the Bow Street magistrates, and his officers. The newspaper office in Southampton Street was also wrecked and the publication of the *Porcupine* was suspended for two days. When it reappeared it contained the first of a series of eight letters to Lord Hawkesbury in reprobation of the peace, which not only are in some ways in advance of any of Cobbett's previous writings, but also show clear indications that Burke's political writings had served as his model. Almost for the first time Cobbett abandoned the extravagance of invective in which ordinarily he delighted and adopted a comparative sobriety of tone. While assailing any idea of peace with France, he devoted the greater part of the letters to a criticism of the actual conditions of the treaty, and in doing so showed a breadth of view which he had rarely manifested in his earlier productions. He was particularly happy in demonstrating how far the treaty had left the rest of Europe at the mercy of France. Although this was not in itself a conclusive argument against making peace, the ministerial party had no wish that the fact should be recognised by the people at large. Cobbett urged forcibly enough that England by accepting the Dutch colony of Ceylon and the Spanish island of Trinidad from France without troubling to obtain the assent of either Holland or Spain, showed that she regarded those states as mere dependencies of France.

These letters were published in book form in November 1801, together with some other extracts from the *Porcupine*, under the title of *A Collection of Facts and Observations, relative to the Peace with Bonaparte*, and they were followed in January 1802 by three *Letters to the Right Honourable Henry Addington*, on the same topic, particularly dealing with the effects of the peace on the Colonies, commerce, manufactures, and constitution of the United Kingdom. The two series of letters were afterwards republished together as a second edition in the same month, under the title of *Letters to the Right Honourable Lord Hawkesbury and to the Right Honour-*

able Henry Addington, with an appendix of documents relating to the peace.

The *Letters to Lord Hawkesbury* were the last publications of importance to appear in the *Porcupine*.

Owing to a variety of causes, the paper was not a success financially. At the very outset Cobbett had an unpleasant experience of English official methods. He placed great dependence on the circulation of the *Porcupine* in the United States, Canada, and the West Indies, where his former customers were very numerous. In fact, he secured beforehand three hundred and ninety-seven orders from America, and expected a sale of at least five hundred copies. In time of war, however, the King's packet-boats were the only regular and sure means of conveyance, and Cobbett found himself compelled to transmit his newspaper by them. He imagined that he could do so on terms similar to those on which periodicals were sent to different parts of Great Britain and Ireland, but on making inquiries, he learned that the exclusive privilege of forwarding newspapers and other periodicals to the West Indies and America had been granted to Francis Freeling,[1] the Secretary and Surveyor of the General Post-Office, as a recompense for public services, and that his charge for transmitting a daily newspaper to these countries was five guineas a year on each copy. Cobbett endeavoured to bargain with Freeling, and offered him two guineas a copy, pointing out that this would bring him in nearly eight hundred guineas a year. At a personal interview Freeling offered to accept three guineas, but insinuated that

---

[1] He was created a baronet in 1828, and was known as a collector of rare books.

F

it would be necessary to keep this agreement secret to prevent the proprietors of other newspapers from thinking themselves aggrieved. He invited Cobbett to think of his proposal.

'I did think of the proposal,' says Cobbett, 'but the more I thought of it, the more I was convinced of the impropriety of acceding to it. Previous to this interview, I might have consented to give even the three guineas a year for each set of papers; but, when, from the conversation of Mr. Freeling, I found that I should, under a promise of secrecy, thereby obtain an unfair, if not an unlawful, advantage over my contemporaries, my mind revolted at the clandestine compact, and I resolved neither to avail myself of the proffered terms, nor to encourage the continuance of what I could not help regarding as an abuse of office, of which His Majesty's Postmaster-General was totally unacquainted.'[1]

The failure to come to an agreement with Freeling destroyed the prospect of a large circulation abroad, for although Cobbett attempted to avail himself of other channels of communication, no efficient ones were to be found. He had also to endure a system of petty persecution from Freeling, who used his official position to annoy him. He was charged exorbitant sums for his packets of American periodicals, and the circulation of the *Porcupine* within Great Britain itself was hindered by discreditable artifices such as irregular delivery and the frequent substitution of other newspapers, the *True Briton*, the *Herald*, or *The Times*, by the Clerks of the Roads, who received the orders from country customers. Against all these abuses Cobbett appealed to the Postmaster-General, Lord Auckland; but he obtained no

---

[1] Cobbett to Lord Auckland, 15th June 1801, in Add. MS. 34455, ff. 395-96 (British Museum).

redress. Lord Auckland replied coldly, justifying Freeling's monopoly, and telling Cobbett that he had mistaken the spirit by which that functionary was actuated.[1]

Had Cobbett obtained a large circulation in England, he might have defied official spite. But he had neither the money requisite to carry on a long struggle, nor the experience necessary for immediate success. He says that he sunk about £750 in the paper.[2]

'I set up my daily paper, but I knew nothing of such a business, which demanded thousands in place of a few hundreds; and, which is very well worth recording, the *advertisements of the Government, which were given even to their opponents*, were *never*, in one single instance, given to me! So strong is their hatred of everything like freedom of mind. They had proof of my zeal and talent; but, they were more afraid of my *disinterested* friendship, than they were of the interested hostility of their most desperate foes.'[3]

In spite of Cobbett's opinion that the Government advertisements were withheld on account of its fear of independent criticism, it is equally probable that they were not bestowed on account of the small circulation which the journal attained. He did, in fact, obtain the Post-Office advertisements for a short time while his negotiation with Freeling was in progress, but on its rupture the Secretary was careful to withdraw them. On 23rd November 1801 Cobbett disposed of the *Porcupine* to John Gifford. In January 1802 it was merged in John Heriot's paper the *True Briton*.

[1] For the whole affair see a memorandum by Cobbett in the *Auckland Papers*, Add. MS. 34455, ff. 393-414, 417.
[2] *Political Register*, 12th October 1805.
[3] *Ibid.*, 10th April 1830.

In March 1801, some time before the *Porcupine* passed out of his hands, Cobbett entered into partnership with John Morgan, an Englishman, formerly resident in Philadelphia, whose patriotic conduct in that city had attracted his regard. They commenced business as booksellers and stationers at the 'Crown and Mitre,' No. 11 Pall Mall. Their first publication of note was a complete collection of Cobbett's writings in America in twelve volumes, under the title of *Porcupine's Works*, which comprised all the pamphlets hitherto mentioned, as well as one or two others and a certain amount of supplementary matter, including a really admirable summary of American politics from the close of the War of Independence to 1794. This collection was issued in May 1801, and dedicated to John Reeves, the king's printer, who had been very kind to Cobbett since his arrival. The list of subscribers, about seven hundred and fifty in number, included the royal princes and many members of the Government. The partnership lasted until March 1803, when the business was made over to J. Harding. Morgan returned to Philadelphia, and Cobbett, who had hitherto lived at the 'Crown and Mitre,' removed to 15 Duke Street, Westminster.

In spite of the failure of the *Porcupine*, it was felt by the opponents of the peace that Cobbett was too valuable an ally to be suffered to remain silent. The leaders of the Opposition, Grenville and Windham, encouraged him to attempt a new literary venture. In consequence, he submitted to Windham the plan of a weekly review, 'something between a newspaper and a magazine,' and Windham and French Laurence, the Regius Professor of Civil Law at Oxford, set on foot a private subscription

in its aid. The *Political Register*, with which Cobbett's
name became so intimately associated, may, in fact, be
regarded as the prototype of such periodicals as the
modern *Spectator* or the *Saturday Review*. It differed
from them in containing intelligence as well as criticism,
but Cobbett's articles on political and social subjects
constituted the real interest of the magazine. The germ
of Cobbett's conception may be found in his American
venture the *Censor*; but that periodical was comparatively slight and ephemeral in character. The *Political
Register* first appeared on 16th January 1802. The first
two numbers were issued fortnightly, the price being
tenpence a number. So great was the success of the
new venture that, after 6th February, it was issued
weekly, and continued to appear until June 1835 with
only a short interruption in 1817. It was entitled at
various times *Cobbett's Weekly Political Register*, *Cobbett's
Weekly Political Pamphlet*, and *Cobbett's Weekly Register*,
and the first four half-yearly volumes were published
with an appendix of State papers under the title of
Cobbett's Annual Register. Although the *Register* became
in later times the great organ of Radical discontent, it
was originally ultra-Tory in its principles.

' I have no intention,' observed Cobbett in a letter addressed
to Addington, 'to range myself in a systematic *opposition* to his
majesty's ministers, or to their measures. Such an opposition I
disclaim. The first object which I have invariably had in view,
is to contribute my mite towards the support of the authority of
that sovereign, whom God has commanded me to honour and
obey, and as the means most likely to effect this object, I have
generally endeavoured to support the measures of those who
have been appointed to exercise that authority. If, therefore, I
do now, or shall in future, openly disapprove of *some* of the

measures of his majesty's present servants, religiously abstaining from every act and word tending to weaken the government, and exerting all my feeble efforts to defend it against its enemies foreign or domestic; I trust that you yourself, if I should happen at all to attract your notice, will have the justice to acquit me of inconsistency of conduct.'

Although he disclaimed the idea of systematic opposition to Government in his new periodical, Cobbett continued his uncompromising hostility to the peace. In fact, he so distinguished himself by his attacks on the French Government that M. Otto, the French Resident at the Court of St. James's, in remonstrating with the English ministers on the licence permitted to the press, designated Cobbett by name as one of those whose attacks were particularly resented by the French Government.[1] On the occasion of the signature of the definite treaty on 27th March 1802, London was again illuminated. Cobbett declined to join in the rejoicings, observing sourly:

'The alliterative words, *peace* and *plenty*, sound well in a song, or make a pretty transparency in the window of an idiot; but the things which these harmonious words represent are not always in unison.'

In consequence, his windows in Pall Mall were again broken. On this occasion the authorities arrested six of the ringleaders of the mob, three of whom were found to be Government clerks. Three of them, one the son of William Beloe, known as a divine and man of letters, were brought up at Bow Street the next morning, committed, and tried at the sessions on 14th July on the

[1] Otto to Hawkesbury, 25th July 1802 (printed in the *Annual Register*, 1803, pp. 659-60).

charge of rioting. They were found guilty, and heavily fined. The counsel for the prisoners asked Cobbett to join in a recommendation to mercy made by the jury, but he replied,

'Certainly not, sir; I came here to ask for justice, and not for mercy.'[1]

The *Political Register* early attracted a large degree of attention. In July 1803 Windham, in replying to an attack on the periodical by Sheridan in Parliament, and to an insinuation that he was among the contributors, took occasion to launch into a panegyric on Cobbett's conduct in America, stating that,

'by his own unaided exertions, he rendered his country services that entitle him to a statue of gold,' and that 'he had resolutely opposed all the bad principles which had been propagated for these ten years in politics.'[2]

This was too much for the journalists on the ministerial side, and Heriot in the *True Briton* raked up the old scandal of Cobbett's earliest publication, *The Soldier's Friend*, which, in 1797, had been distributed, although without Cobbett's sanction, among the seamen previous to the mutiny at the Nore. He suggested that Cobbett, who had formerly moved the soldiery to mutiny, was now endeavouring to excite the navy, and that such services would be more fittingly rewarded with the pillory or the gibbet than with a statue of gold. Cobbett, in reply, categorically denied that he was the author of *The Soldier's Friend*. But not content with verbal retort,

[1] *Political Register*, 31st July 1802.
[2] *Annual Register*, 1803, p. 206; cf. *Cobbett's Political Register*, 20th August 1803.

he proceeded to Heriot's office, and inflicted on him 'personal chastisement in the very apartment where he had fabricated the libel.' Heriot brought an action for assault, but did not appear to prosecute, probably feeling that he would expose himself to ridicule.[1]

In the meantime the short peace of Amiens had been broken and the outbreak of war in May led to a spirited appeal by Cobbett to the people of the kingdom, which was reprinted by the ministry and sent to all the parish clergy with directions that it should be posted on the church doors and distributed in the aisles. It first appeared in the *Political Register* for 30th July 1803, and may be found occasionally in its later form in old collections of pamphlets and broadsides. This official recognition was a source of sardonic satisfaction to Cobbett in later times, when he was regarded as an incendiary by the ruling classes, and he more than once humorously alleged it as a proof he had once been respectable. The peroration is a fine example of Cobbett's popular style of declamation:

'The sun, in his whole course round the globe, shines not on a spot so blessed as this great, and now united Kingdom; gay and productive fields and gardens, lofty and extensive woods, innumerable flocks and herds, rich and inexhaustible mines, a mild and wholesome climate, giving health, activity, and vigour to fourteen millions of people; and shall we, who are thus favoured and endowed; shall we, who are abundantly supplied with iron and steel, powder and lead; shall we, who have a fleet superior to the maritime force of all the world, and who are able to bring two millions of fighting men into the field; shall we yield up this dear and happy land, together with all the liberties and honours, to preserve which our fathers so often dyed the land and the sea with their blood; shall we,

[1] *Political Register*, 25th February 1804.

thus, at once dishonour their graves, and stamp disgrace and infamy on the brows of our children; and shall we, too, make this base and dastardly surrender to an enemy, whom, within these twelve years, our countrymen have defeated in every quarter of the world? No; we are not so miserably fallen; we cannot, in so short a space of time have become so detestably degenerate: we have the strength and the will to repel the hostility, to chastise the insolence of the foe. Mighty, indeed, must be our efforts, but mighty also is the meed. Singly engaged against the tyrants of the earth, Britain now attracts the eyes and the hearts of mankind; groaning nations look to her for deliverance; justice, liberty, and religion are inscribed on her banners; her success will be hailed with the shouts of the universe, while tears of admiration and gratitude will bedew the heads of her sons, who fall in the glorious contest.'

Although the renewal of war had removed Cobbett's original cause of quarrel with the ministry, he had imbibed so hearty a contempt for its members, and above all for Addington, that he continued to assail it with little intermission. Two or three months before the war was renewed he wrote:—

'The millennium of politics seems to be fast approaching: there is scarcely any distinction of parties left; for, though, we do, indeed, hear talk of the new and the old oppositions,[1] there is in reality no opposition of party, and, if we except a few individuals, a perfect indifference appears to prevail as to the consequences of the present system of public measures. The same men who were alive two years ago are still alive, but their minds seem to have been changed; the rule of the Addingtons and Hawkesburies, which is more like a burlesque of government, than anything that ever appeared before in the world, has rendered public life so ludicrous and disgusting that it really requires more than common fortitude to enable a man of character to interfere, even for the sake of preventing the destruction of his country. The absence of opposition which is

[1] The followers of Grenville and Fox.

to be ascribed to this disgust, to this loathing inspired by the scene altogether, the Addingtons have the modesty to attribute to an universal acquiescence in the *wisdom* of their measures. Happy people! To them all is sun-shine. They live and laugh under a load of contempt which would sink any other of God's creatures to the grave. And well they may laugh, for they are advancing on *à grand pas*, towards a monopoly of everything that is profitable, as well as of everything, which, before their time, used to be accounted honourable.'[1]

Strongly impressed with the iniquities of the ministry, Cobbett's attention was drawn particularly to the affairs of Ireland as the scene of those jobs and peculations, which were too gross to be perpetrated elsewhere. In the last three months of 1803 a series of articles on Irish affairs, signed ' Juverna,' appeared in the *Political Register*. The epistles were not written by Cobbett himself, but by Robert Johnson, a judge of the Irish Common Pleas, a man with an intimate knowledge of Irish official life, with a keen pen, and a strong feeling of indignation against the Government. He openly assailed the Lord Lieutenant, Lord Hardwicke, the Chancellor, Lord Redesdale, and other high officers of State, as at once incapable and malignant. Government resolved upon action, and being unable to ascertain the name of the author, they proceeded against Cobbett, on 24th May 1804, for publishing the articles. The libels were not particularly virulent. If Cobbett himself had been the author they would probably have been much more un-measured. Moreover, the articles dealt with the public actions of public persons, and at the present day would be considered as fair political criticism. But at that time Government insisted that freedom of criticism was

[1] *Political Register*, 19th February 1803.

only permissible within Parliament. The long strain of war, and the nervous apprehensions engendered by the French Revolution, had rendered ministers at once timid and vindictive. They were determined at any cost to prevent the spread of hostile opinions by means of the press. The case was tried before Lord Ellenborough, who summed up strongly against the defendant, and Cobbett was convicted. He saved himself, however, by sacrificing his contributor. He gave the Attorney-General the manuscript of some of the articles, which was in Johnson's handwriting, and appeared as a crown witness at Johnson's trial in November 1805. In consequence he was never called to receive sentence on this conviction.[1]

It would naturally seem discreditable to Cobbett that he should consent to betray his contributor in order to avoid punishment. It is, however, singular that his conduct on this occasion was never made a subject of reproach by his enemies either at the time or at any subsequent period. It seems possible, therefore, that he acted with the consent of Johnson, who may not have cared to shelter himself behind his publisher, and who did not, in fact, incur any severe consequences. But this is merely conjecture; the whole matter is obscure and no authoritative explanation seems attainable. In spite of his docile behaviour it is uncertain whether Cobbett entirely escaped. The Solicitor-General for Ireland, William Conyngham Plunket, brought a separate civil action for damages, two days later, in consequence of a passage in the same series of articles. He had been

---

[1] Howell's *State Trials*, 1821, xxix. 1-54; *Diary of Lord Colchester*, 1861, i. 518; *Political Register*, 2nd June 1804.

denounced as a renegade from his earlier opinions, and
had been accused in no measured terms of proceeding
with undue severity while conducting the prosecution of
Robert Emmet, the United Irishman, from whose family
he had received benefits, on the charge of high treason
in 1803. After twenty minutes' deliberation the jury
awarded Plunket £500 damages.[1] Whether these
damages were actually exacted is uncertain, but it is
not unlikely that Cobbett obtained their remission in
consequence of his bargain with the Attorney-General.[2]

[1] Howell's *State Trials*, xxix. 53-80; *Political Register*, 9th June 1802.
[2] Lord Dalling and Bulwer definitely asserts that Cobbett escaped payment. See *Historical Characters*, ed. 1876, p. 325.

CHAPTER IV

THE CHANGE IN COBBETT'S POLITICAL OPINIONS

THE year 1804 is usually regarded as the period at which
Cobbett definitely abandoned the high Tory opinions of
his earlier life in favour of those strong Radical sentiments which guided his later career. The change was,
however, more gradual than is generally supposed, and
was, in a measure, the result of the great alterations in
English political parties, which began at the end of Pitt's
first ministry.

When Cobbett came to England in 1800 he found all
other political questions overshadowed by the absorbing
interest of the French war. He himself regarded other
issues as entirely subordinate. He engaged enthusiastically in support of the great war minister Pitt, whose
only opponents in Parliament were the section of the
Whig party which had adhered to Fox in resisting the
rupture with France. Pitt's resignation in February 1801
was quickly followed by the negotiations which terminated
in the Treaty of Amiens. Cobbett, true to his hatred of
France, persevered in his advocacy of war, and devoted
himself to opposing Addington's administration. But, in
the meantime, differences began to appear between Pitt
and several of the former members of his government,
among whom may be mentioned Lord Grenville, his
former Foreign Secretary, and William Windham, his

former Secretary at War, and Cobbett's especial patron. The majority of Pitt's cabinet persisted in making an uncompromising resistance to the conclusion of the peace of Amiens, while Pitt himself, alarmed by the serious symptoms of exhaustion displayed by the country, supported Addington in his overtures. The conclusion of the Treaty of Amiens in March 1802 only intensified the discord, while Buonaparte's acts of aggression on the Continent constantly strengthened the party that clamoured for a renewal of the war.

Towards the close of Addington's administration Cobbett considered that there were three classes of public men neither in, nor acting with, the ministry : first, Pitt and his friends, among whom were Lord Melville and Lord Camden; secondly, the New Opposition, consisting of Carlisle, Grenville, Windham, and their supporters ; and thirdly, Fox and his powerful party, the Old Opposition, weakened to some extent by the loss of George Tierney and Benjamin Hobhouse, who had joined Addington's ministry. Pitt and his friends, by giving some measure of support to Addington's administration, completely alienated Cobbett's regard.

'Had Mr. Pitt, when he retired from his majesty's service, left his place to be supplied without any interference of his own ; had he regularly continued his attendance in parliament, speaking and voting merely as a member of that body, supporting those measures that were good, and opposing those that were bad ; had he left the war to be continued, or the peace to be made, by the ministers themselves ; and, had he, when the peace of Amiens came to be discussed, given it that mark of reprobation, which it has been found to merit ; had this been his line of conduct, his return to power would, at this day, have been the undivided wish of the nation, who would have looked

to him as an immovable rock of defence. But he, unhappily
for his country and for his own fame, chose a course entirely
different. The new cabinet was moulded up by his assistance,
and with every appearance of wishing to retain his power after
he had yielded his place, not unaccompanied with some marks
of having retired himself for the purpose of getting rid of his
colleagues, and with a view to returning to exercise absolute
sway amongst others of his own creation. The moment,
too, that he ceased to be minister, he seemed to have
forgotten that he was a member of parliament, and as if it were
beneath him to be anything less than the ruler of the nation, he
imitated the example of secession which had been given him by
his rival orator.[1] In the meantime, however, by whispers and
nods, his followers were instructed to support the ministers, lest
they should sink under their opponents, lest a breach should be
made, and lest the cabinet should fall into the hands of others
whom he hated, or, which was nearly the same thing, over
whom he could not hope to have an absolute control.'[2]

But while the war party, the strength of which lay in
the New Opposition, failed to gain assistance from Pitt,
they received a new and remarkable addition from
another quarter. Charles James Fox, in opposition to
the sentiments of the great bulk of the Whig party, had
distinguished himself in the early stages of the war by
his fearless advocacy of peace. He had sympathised
with the spread of republican sentiment in France and had
warned the English Government of the folly and danger
of attempting to regulate the internal affairs of another
nation. The establishment by Buonaparte of a des-
potism in France had alienated much of his sympathy.
His personal interviews with Buonaparte in Paris after
the conclusion of peace did not enhance his admiration
of the first consul. While he did not doubt his sincere

[1] Fox rarely appeared in Parliament between 1797 and 1802.
[2] *Political Register*, 4th June 1803.

intention to maintain the peace, he considered him 'as a young man who was a good deal intoxicated with his success.'[1] Fresh causes of discontent quickly arose. In September 1801 Buonaparte reorganised the Batavian republic, and towards the close of 1802 he interposed with French troops in the internal affairs of Switzerland. Fox thus saw his two political principles, respect for the sovereignty of the people and for the independence of foreign states, violated by Buonaparte. The effect upon him was such that on 9th March 1803 he felt himself obliged to support a warlike address in the House of Commons. On 24th May, while condemning the resumption of the war because he considered it had been undertaken for the retention of Malta and generally on behalf of British interests, he ridiculed Buonaparte's demand for a restraint of the press and for the expulsion of refugees, and condemned the conduct of France in Switzerland and Holland. After the resumption of the war he made common cause with Grenville in attacking Addington's ministry.

As Fox became more warlike Cobbett's tone towards him became more friendly. In February 1804 an article in the *Register* asserted that it would be unjust 'to deny him the rare qualification of an enlightened, indeed consummate, statesman,' and gently deplored that his philanthropy should have biased him in favour of an unrighteous peace.[2]

At the close of Addington's ministry Cobbett was a staunch supporter of the New Opposition, was amicably

---

[1] Trotter's *Memoirs of the Latter Years of Fox*, 1811, p. 316.

[2] *Political Register*, 4th February 1804. For a further explanation of Cobbett's feelings towards Fox, see his second letter to Pitt in *Political Register*, 6th October 1804.

inclined towards the Old Opposition, and was altogether out of sympathy with Pitt.

'A year ago,' he said in May, 1804, 'it was perceived that the reign of the Doctor [Addington], the scandalous triumph of imbecility, only existed by the division of these parties. The nation felt this, and all men who loved their country were anxious to see a reconciliation take place, and a co-operation so far, at least, as was necessary, to obtain for the country an administration, embracing such a weight of talents and character as might excite confidence at home and respect abroad. It was time, too, to put an end to the effect of party animosities which had lived for ten years, and especially as the cause of these animosities had totally ceased to exist. Participating in this the general feeling of the country, the Old and New Oppositions seemed to make some approaches towards each other during the latter part of the last session of Parliament. This inclination gathered strength before Parliament met again ; and to the satisfaction of every one except the ministers and their creatures, the language of Mr. Fox and Mr. Windham soon indicated, than any further attempts to prolong the differences between them would fail of success. Mr. Pitt and his close adherents still kept aloof, till that gentleman himself began to perceive, that those, by whom he had been constantly supported, and whose support was worth having, were daily joining in those opposition divisions, from which he thought proper to keep away. Thus situated he determined to co-operate with the Old and New Oppositions so far, at least, as was necessary to leave the ministers in a minority ; but without any positive engagement as to the composition of a new ministry leaving himself at full liberty to act, as to that matter, according to the dictates of his own mind. Between the leaders of the Old and New Oppositions there might be, and it is probable there was, an understanding somewhat more friendly, but certainly no specific agreement. No pledge, or even proposal, as to the acceptance of office, or the division of power, had been made by either party. Amongst *all* the parties, however, the object of turning out the tinman ministry was clearly understood to be

G

that of bringing into the power the united talents, character, weight, and influence of the leading men of both Houses, without any distinction as to party, and certainly without any idea of acting upon a principle of proscription.'[1]

This passage shows that Cobbett had thrown in his lot with the parties of Grenville and Fox—the New and Old Oppositions—and that he was disposed to regard the actions of Pitt with unfriendly suspicion. Addington resigned on 30th April 1804, and Pitt was called upon by the king to form a ministry. Pitt requested permission to treat with Grenville and Fox. The king angrily refused, but on 7th May, after a long interview with George III., he obtained permission to include Grenville. When, however, on the next day he communicated with Grenville, Windham, and others of the New Opposition, he found that none of them would consent to take office without Fox. Pitt, therefore, was compelled to draw half of his cabinet from the late Government, and found himself opposed by three parties headed respectively in the Commons by Addington, Windham, and Fox. Addington was reconciled with the Government before the close of the year, and in January 1805 entered the Cabinet as President of the Council, with the title of Viscount Sidmouth, but Windham and Fox remained in opposition until Pitt's death. From these circumstances Cobbett, in spite of the renewal of the war and the change of ministry, found himself still in opposition to the Government. His covert mistrust of Pitt in opposition was changed for a spirit of open hostility to Pitt in office; and he blamed him especially for forming a war administration, from which most of

[1] *Political Register*, 12th May 1804.

the leaders of the war party were excluded. In June he wrote:

'Very deep and general discontent at the conduct of Mr. Pitt, in patching up the present ministry, prevails through the country, and is heard amongst all ranks, and all descriptions of persons.

. . . 'Some faint attempts have been made to conjure up the ghost of Jacobinism and again to make Mr. Pitt the anti-Jacobin hero. If this could be accomplished, then, indeed, were he safe. But, alas! the materials are wanting: Buonaparte has completely extinguished the principle; and, it would be utterly impossible to make any one man in England, except he be an anti-Jacobin by trade, listen, for a single moment, to any harangue upon the subject. The "pilot that weathered the storm" is, therefore, in a situation entirely new: he can expect no support from the persuasion, which prevailed during the last war, that the duration of his power was identified with the existence of the monarchy. Many persons, very anxious for the welfare of that monarchy, entertain an exactly opposite opinion. He has no resource left. He has nothing new to offer. He has no hope to present to the country. All his showy schemes for the extension of trade, the augmentation of riches, and the discharge of debt, have been tried, and have proved to be bubbles. Men have had time to reflect; they have traced him through his measures and the consequences of his measures. Those, who are the least capable of inquiry, compare the state of the country, when he took possession of it twenty years ago, with its present state: they know well, without any reasoning upon the subject, they *feel*, that he has had the absolute command of the nation from that day to this; and they fail not to draw a conclusion by no means advantageous to him, but not, for that reason, the less rational or just.'[1]

In the last four months of 1804, Cobbett published a series of letters to Pitt similar in character to the series addressed to Hawkesbury in 1801. In the introductory

[1] *Political Register*, 16th June 1804.

epistle he justified his abandonment of Pitt by accusing
that statesmen of changing his policy.

'At the preliminaries of peace a new question in politics arose.
I remained upon the old ground; you departed from it. The
Treasury writers have accused me of "deserting Mr. Pitt, whom I
had so highly extolled, and of going over to Mr. Fox, whom I
had so severely censured." And thus I am, by way of allusion,
charged with a crime almost as heinous as any that a man can
commit. But, to desert, a man must first be enlisted, and, if I
might be said to be enlisted, it was in the cause of which I regarded you as the champion; and not in your personal service.
It is very true, that, while in America, and immediately after
my return to England, I did highly extol you; but, Sir, it must
be evident to every one, that this my conduct arose from my regarding you as the great asserter of the cause of my country and
of monarchy. You were always defended and applauded by me
as the person, who was at the head, who was the rallying point of
all those, who were opposed to the principles and the natural
consequences of the French revolution. . . . Your conduct relative to the peace, contrasted with your declared principles and
avowed object as to the war, are all I require to prove, that in
ceasing to be your eulogist and in becoming your assailant, my
conduct has exhibited a perfect consistency. In supporting you,
Sir, what was the object I had in view? Some of your liberal
partisans will probably say, a good round sum of money. But, be
that as it may, what was the object which I professed to have in
view? for here, if anywhere, must be found the marks of desertion.
What, then, was this object? It was, Sir, that which you professed to me, as well as to every man in England and in Europe,
upon several occasions during the war, and particularly in your
speech made in the House of Commons on the 7th June, 1799.
In that speech you declared, that we were in circumstances
which forbade us to stop short of "an adequate, full, and
rational security," that the war might be carried on for any
length of time, "without the creation of new debt"; and that it
would not be difficult "to provide taxes for eight years." . . .
"We shall not," said you, "be satisfied with false security.

War, with all its evils, is better than a peace, in which there is
nothing to be seen but injustice, dwelling with savage delight
on the humbled prostrate condition of some timid suppliant
people." . . . "The time to come to a discussion of a peace,
can only be the time when you can look with confidence to an
honourable issue ; to such a peace as shall at once restore to
Europe her settled and balanced constitution of general polity,
and to every negotiating power in particular, that weight in the
scale of general empire, which has ever been found the best
guarantee and pledge of local independence and general security.
Such are my sentiments. I am not afraid to avow them. I
commit them to the thinking among mankind ; and, if they have
not been poisoned by the stream of French sophistry, and prejudiced by her falsehoods, I am sure they will approve of the
determination I have avowed, and for those grave and mature
reasons on which I found it." I, Sir, had not been poisoned by
the stream of French sophistry; I did approve of the determination that you avowed ; I not only approved of it, I applauded it,
I exulted at it, as my American friends will remember to their
present mortification. But, Sir, because I highly extolled you
for this noble determination, and for the inexhaustible pecuniary
means that you had provided for carrying it into effect, was I to
continue to extol you when you broke a determination so
solemnly avowed, and that, too, under the pretext of husbanding
those pecuniary means. Because I highly extolled the Mr. Pitt of
June, 1799, was I bound to extol the Mr. Pitt of November, 1801,
when he called upon the country for its lasting gratitude towards
those men who had negotiated the preliminaries of peace ? It is
a well-known and undisputed fact, that you yourself, Sir, directed
those negotiations ; that it was at your suggestion they were
undertaken ; that in every stage you were consulted, and that no
stipulation was made without your consent and approbation.
But, if there were any doubt upon this point, there can be none
as to your open conduct in regard to the measure, in which you
did not merely *acquiesce*, which you did not merely approve of
and support, but which you declared to be such as to "afford
matter of *exultation* to the country, and to entitle the ministers
to its warmest approbation and *most grateful thanks*." And, Sir,

did consistency call upon me to support you after such an eulogium in which all your principles had been abandoned, and all your promises falsified? Will any one say, that the peace of Amiens "restored to Europe her settled and balanced constitution of general policy?" Will any one pretend that the peace of Amiens "gave us indemnity for the past and security for the future." To ask the question seems like a sort of mockery. Will it be said, that you were unable to carry on the war? Then Mr. Fox was right; for it was a peace of necessity. But if this was the case, then comes your other difficulty; for, I was deceived by your statements of 1799, to say nothing about the more elaborate statements of your secretary Mr. Rose, whose official pamphlet came forth to aid the deception. I believed you when you so confidently and solemnly declared, that "the war might be carried on for any length of time without the creation of new debt," and that "it would not be difficult to provide taxes for eight years"; and, though I saw you, in two years afterwards, make a peace, in which not only all your avowed objects of the war were abandoned, but by which the ancient honours of the country were surrendered; though I saw the balance of Europe remain completely overset, though the enemy seized state upon state even during the negotiations; and though I clearly saw and explicitly foretold that England would be exposed to that constant and imminent danger, of which every man is now feelingly sensible; in spite of all this, was I still to adhere to you, still to extol you, on pain of being stigmatised as a political deserter! Will any one, even in the purlieus of Downing Street and Whitehall, attempt to maintain a position so repugnant to reason? Because you, either from choice or from necessity, impelled either by your interest, your ambition, or the consequences of your errors, changed your course in politics, throwing aside all the principles which had induced me to follow you, was I bound to change too? Is the mere *name* of Pitt (for there was little else left), sufficient to compensate for the absence of everything that we desire to find in a minister, and is it entitled to political allegiance from all those who have once expressed their attachment to the principles, with which it has been, but no longer is, connected? Is there any one who will pretend, that you are not only so great as to have a right to abandon your principles, without exposing yourself to censure, but to render it a duty in others to abandon theirs for the sake of yielding you support? Is there any one who will venture to urge a pretension so offensive, so insulting to the feelings of the world? And, if not; if it be not insisted, that every man who once supports a principle of yours, becomes by that act solely your bondsman for life, then, I think, if *desertion* be a proper word to employ, it will be allowed that I did not desert you, but that you deserted me.'[1]

The 'Letters' to Pitt were six in number, and appeared between September and December 1804. They were chiefly occupied with two topics—the iniquity of the Peace of Amiens and the ruinous consequences of Pitt's system of finance. They are inferior in ability to the 'Letters to Addington.' This was partly due to the inconsistency of Cobbett's position. While still strenuously advocating the necessity of war, he was continually asserting that the economic condition of the country was very unsatisfactory. In order, however, to evade the remonstrances of those who endeavoured to make the exhaustion of England an argument for the conclusion of peace, he insisted on ascribing it entirely to Pitt's financial measures, and to the corruption and peculations of his official supporters. So paradoxical a view was hardly fitted to form the basis of a popular appeal, and although he is often extremely forcible when urging either the exhaustion of the country or the imperative necessity of continuing the war, he is hardly so convincing when he endeavours to suggest a policy fitted to meet all the requirements of the position.

In March 1805 Cobbett obtained a fresh means of

[1] *Political Register*, 29th September 1804.

attacking Government. In that month the Commission which had been appointed in 1802 to inquire into frauds and irregularities in the several naval departments issued their Tenth Report, which dealt with the office of Treasurer of the Navy. During Pitt's first administration this post had been held in conjunction with higher offices by Henry Dundas, who in 1802 became Viscount Melville and from 1804 held the office of First Lord of the Admiralty. The report showed that during Melville's tenure of office large sums of public money had been applied to other uses than those of the navy, and that his paymaster, Alexander Trotter, had been permitted through carelessness or connivance to draw other sums from the Bank of England and employ them for his private emolument. These revelations caused great indignation, and in spite of Pitt's ardent espousal of the cause of his colleague, of whose probity he was convinced, a motion censuring Melville's conduct was carried in the House of Commons on 8th April by the casting vote of the Speaker. Pitt was greatly afflicted by this occurrence, and indeed his distress in regard to Melville is believed to have shortened his life. After Pitt's death Melville was impeached of high crimes and misdemeanours, and after a trial lasting fifteen days was acquitted on all charges on 12th June 1806. Cobbett entertained no doubt of Melville's guilt. On the appearance of the Tenth Report he declared that 'now there was some fine work cut out for the heaven-born minister.' When Pitt defended Melville's conduct Cobbett pointed out that the defence was insufficient.

'Never,' he declared, 'did a man sink so low in the estimation of the public as William Pitt; when, in his place in the House of Commons, he boldly and unblushingly declared, that the public had not suffered any *actual loss* by the conduct of Melville and Trotter, although it had been distinctly proved, that owing to their malversations, the country had sustained a loss of many millions . . . Yet, because Lord Melville was not what was called a defaulter, because he, at going out of office, paid over to his successor the *mere balance* that he had in his hands, because this was the case, Mr. Pitt contended, that there had arisen from the misapplication of the public money no actual loss to the public. The fallacy of this position is so glaring, that little needs be said in answer to it, for the reader has only to consider himself having large concerns, the disbursements of which are managed by a steward, who instead of calling upon his master for money no sooner than it is wanted, takes care to call for a sum always beforehand, and constantly to keep out at interest for his own emolument, a sum that would otherwise be kept out at interest for the emolument of his master.'[1]

The lax manner in which the funds of the navy office had been dealt with led Cobbett to undertake a general examination into the disposal of the State revenues. He was especially concerned with the way in which sinecure posts and pensions were distributed to the friends and relatives of those in power. As early as 1802 Cobbett had assailed Addington for bestowing the clerkship of the Pells, worth three thousand a year, on his eldest son Henry, a child of twelve.[2] But he now assailed the system on a much greater scale, preparing a series of pension-lists which appeared in the *Political Register*. He asserted that Pitt, since his return to office, had, in the course of ten months, bestowed pensions on obscure individuals to the extent of £38,000 a year. These payments were made from a great variety of

[1] *Political Register*, 4th May 1805.
[2] He died before his father in 1823.

sources, with the intention, Cobbett alleged, of confusing and baffling any one who endeavoured to investigate the accounts. These assaults upon a system for which little could be said were calculated to awaken against Cobbett a vast amount of resentment. In fact, he could not have chosen a course more likely to arouse general enmity. His attacks were sensibly felt by almost every place-holder in England, for few could fail to be conscious that either they or their relatives had benefited by the system. His attacks on individuals, moreover, were direct and outspoken, and sometimes, perhaps, were intensified by the memory of private injuries. Lord Auckland, for instance, as Post-Master General, had formerly slighted Cobbett's complaints. In regard to his wife, who is styled Lady Eleanor Auckland, though her brother, not her father, was first Earl of Minto,[1] Cobbett remarks with an intensity of feeling which gets the better of his grammar :

'Last upon the list comes Lady Eleanor Auckland, with her £500 a year, and which £500 a year I, for my part, do most heartily grudge her. Her husband receives [as a pension] £2300 a year from the public; and observe, that he stands his chance of official emoluments besides, being in place always as often as he can, and when out of place, returning to his pension. Her children, some of them at least, are provided for at the public expense, reversions of sinecures are secured for them. And now comes Lady Eleanor Auckland, with her claim for £500 a year, in addition to what is already enjoyed by her family ! Am I told, that Lord Auckland is poor, and having a large family, has not wherewith to support an appearance suitable to his rank, without some aid from the minister ? My answer is, that we did not compel Lord Auckland to assume that expensive rank : the assumption was his own choice, for his own and his family's gratification, and, not, in any degree, for the advantage, or

---

[1] Even her brother was only a baron in 1803.

the gratification of the King or the people.   It is one thing to apply the public money to the *supporting* of the aristocracy of the kingdom, and another thing to apply it in the *creating* of a new aristocracy.   The former, every man, who wishes to preserve the monarchy will approve of, when the support is unconnected with corrupt influence; but, the latter every man who does not wish to see the monarchy destroyed, must earnestly reprobate.'[1]

A series of such comments on the great class of pension-holders was likely to make Cobbett very heartily disliked.

The death of Pitt on 23rd January 1806 completed the reconstitution of English political parties.   For the moment it also appeared as if Cobbett would at last find himself in accord with the party in power.   In reality, however, a few weeks witnessed his final separation from his old allies and his identification with the new radical party of reform, of which Sir Francis Burdett, Henry Hunt, and John Cartwright were among the leaders.

On the death of Pitt the king sent for Lord Hawkesbury, the Home Secretary, and requested him to carry on the Government.   On Hawkesbury declining the task, George III. invited Lord Grenville to form an administration, which he consented to do on condition that Fox should be admitted to the cabinet.   The ministry of All the Talents was then formed, comprising the principal members of the three parties which had recently acted together in opposition.   The New Opposition was represented in the cabinet by the Prime Minister, Lord Grenville; by Earl Spencer, the Home Secretary; Windham, the Secretary for War; and Earl Fitzwilliam, the President of the Council.   The Old Opposition

[1] *Political Register*, 27th July 1805.

supplied Fox, the Foreign Secretary; Grey, the First
Lord of the Admiralty; Lord Erskine, the Lord Chancellor; and Lord Henry Petty, the Chancellor of the
Exchequer. Sidmouth's party was represented by the
Privy Seal, Lord Sidmouth himself, and the Lord Chief-
Justice, Lord Ellenborough, who, contrary to custom, was
included in the cabinet. In Cobbett's eyes this ministry
had at least one serious defect in the inclusion of Lord
Sidmouth. Notwithstanding this blot it was impossible
for him to view without approval the elevation to power
of those whose conduct in opposition he had so consistently lauded, and at first he unhesitatingly declared
his approbation. But, while he welcomed the new
administration, he demanded from it so extensive a
policy of reform that it soon became evident that no
efforts the ministry were likely to make would be
sufficient to satisfy him. In fact, the necessity of continuing the war with France was the only point of policy
on which he was in full accord with the new Government,
and precisely on this question they needed no support,
owing to the unanimity of public sentiment. But on
questions of home administration, which had now
attained paramount importance in his eyes, Cobbett's
views were such as could hardly be welcomed by any
administration likely to come into office. During Pitt's
second ministry he had centred his attention on finance
and internal government, and the early enthusiasm for
reform, which had driven him to give up his prospects of
promotion and retire from the army, had returned with
redoubled force. He demanded wide-reaching changes
in the army, the exchequer, the Church, and the poor
laws. While utterly out of sympathy with the Radicals

in their belief that English society might be regenerated by an extension of the suffrage, he was in accord with them in condemning the evils of the existing system of administration. He had begun to attack as abuses, institutions which any administration, capable of commanding support in Parliament, was certain to sustain as essential to the wellbeing of the country. In consequence, he was completely disappointed with the conduct of Government. About three months after the formation of the cabinet he said bitterly that the ministers 'took to the Pitt inheritance without any complaint; and the people have a right to demand of them a complete responsibility for all the mischief that shall happen.'[1]

Whether Cobbett was disappointed in regard to any hopes of personal benefit from the new ministry cannot be known with certainty. His strenuous support might well have entitled him to look for some reward. But he himself vehemently denies any such expectation. He states that immediately after he received intelligence that the administration was being formed, he went to Windham, 'and, in the most distinct and decided manner expressed to him my resolution, never to accept of any place of emolument under the Government as long as I lived.'[2] There is no independent testimony to bear out his account of his relations with the Whigs. On the other hand, it has never been established in any instance throughout his life that he attempted to obtain a price in return for political services. His changes of opinion were frequent, but none of them has been traced to any base traffic for gain: usually, in fact, they were detrimental to his

[1] *Political Register*, 12th April 1806.   [2] *Ibid.*, 8th November 1806.

interests. In the present instance, his rupture with the Whigs seems explicable without imputing it to disappointed greed or ambition. Until he was enlightened by the accession of the Whigs to office, he believed that the corruption of the administration was due to Pitt's long tenure of power. When he was disabused, he hastened to denounce his former allies.

Certainly the break was complete. On the acquittal of Lord Melville, who had been impeached for his conduct as Treasurer of the navy, he wrote:

'Really when I contemplate what has passed during the last six months, I cannot refrain from expressing my satisfaction at the triumph of Lord Melville, whom from the bottom of my heart, I believe to be a better and honester man than any one of the Whigs—the professing, the noisy, the clamorous, the disgusting Whigs; I cannot refrain from expressing my hearty satisfaction at seeing these latter baffled by him, who was at any rate, always *frank* in his actions as well as in his words, and who never *sneaked* his way along through the dirt.' [1]

For Fox and Windham alone did he retain any vestige of regard. Some months later he wrote that he considered that the death of Fox completed the degradation of his party:

'There was something in his name, that preserved his party from that utter contempt, into which, as it were at a signal given, they have now fallen. The Grenvilles know well, that the reputation of the Whigs is gone; they know well that all the *good* and sensible men in the country, who were formerly proud to be thought Whigs, have long been disgusted at the base abandonment of principle which their leaders have discovered; and they knew also that merely the name of Mr. Fox, and the high reputation of his talents, were all they had to dread in the way of rivalship for power.' [2]

[1] *Political Register*, 2nd August 1806.   [2] *Ibid.*, 18th October 1806.

Cobbett's personal regard for Windham was much greater than it had ever been for Fox. Windham had been his patron from the time of his arrival in England. Yet he asserts that, from about ten days after the formation of the ministry, he 'had no communication whatever, verbal or written, directly or indirectly, with Mr. Windham,'[1] and this statement is borne out by an entry in Windham's Diary, dated 28th February 1806: 'Came away in carriage with Fox; got out at end of Downing Street, and went to office, thence to Cobbett. Probably the last interview we shall have.'[2] The cause of this sudden cessation of intercourse is a little obscure. Cobbett wishes it to be understood that he voluntarily brought it about to avoid any appearance of dependence on the Government, but this explanation seems hardly adequate. In any case it was soon followed by the termination of their political friendship. Almost the last occasion on which they were agreed was in opposing the public funeral accorded to Pitt. While Windham in Parliament contended that Pitt's life had not been beneficial to his country, Cobbett in the *Political Register* maintained that Pitt had never given proof of any talents except as a debater.

In March Cobbett entered on a prolonged attack on the military department in which, although he abstained for the most part from assailing him directly, Windham, as Secretary for War, was immediately concerned. The occasion was the first report of a commission appointed during Pitt's last administration to inquire into military abuses. Grave cases were discovered of misappropriation

[1] *Political Register*, 8th November 1806.
[2] *Windham's Diary*, ed. Mrs. Baring, 1866, p. 460.

of public funds by officials of the department, but Government, much to Cobbett's disgust, showed no inclination to pursue the matter thoroughly. In fact, they could not do so without raising the whole wide question of administrative corruption, and, so firmly established was the system, that it was probably beyond the power of any ministry, before the passage of the Reform Bill, to sweep it away. Considerations of expediency had no weight with Cobbett, and he severely blamed Windham for protecting corrupt public servants. In the course of his inquiries he came across the case of John Pritchard, a barrack-master in the Isle of Wight, who had been persecuted for exposing the peculations of local contractors, and had finally been dismissed from his post, while Windham was Secretary at War in Pitt's administration, on the pretext of some trifling infringement of the regulations. In 1806 Pritchard appealed to Windham for redress. Windham returned an answer which Cobbett described as 'a letter in which I can discover but little of that frankness, which upon every other occasion I should have expected to meet with in Mr. Windham, and still less of that *indulgence*, that *excessive indulgence*, which, *in other cases*, he has been so anxious to exercise, and has actually exercised.'[1] Although Cobbett subsequently, on several occasions, spoke of Windham with kindness and respect,[2] such an attack showed clearly that their political friendship was at an end. Soon afterwards, in November and December, Cobbett elaborated his reasons for discontent with the ministry in a series of three letters to Windham, which, besides touching more particularly upon the conduct of Sheridan in the Westminster

---

[1] *Political Register*, 26th July 1806.   [2] See *Ibid.*, 8th November 1806.

election, embraced almost the whole scope of home and foreign affairs. In the third letter he dwelt earnestly on the ever-increasing burden of taxation and the distress of the country, and, after commenting severely on the places and pensions enjoyed by members of Parliament and official hangers-on, urged that as a first step for the alleviation of taxation these places and pensions ought to be curtailed in unsparing fashion. In these letters he addressed Windham in a tone of great moderation, very different from that which he had formerly employed towards Hawkesbury and Addington in his famous letters on the peace. Regard for Windham was the last link that bound him to the Government, and even after that link had been broken neither Windham nor Cobbett openly assailed the other. But at Windham's death, in 1810, Cobbett was significantly silent, and under the date 19th February 1809, we find the following entry in Windham's Diary, written probably after perusing Cobbett's attack on the Duke of York in the *Political Register* of the previous day :—'Nearly the whole time from breakfast till Mr. Legge's coming down employed in reading Cobbett. More thoroughly wicked and mischievous than almost any that has appeared yet.'[1]

Although the year 1806 did not witness the complete development of Cobbett's later radical opinions, it was the period when he finally abandoned the attempt to associate himself with either great English political party. From this time he began to regard the causes of the political and social evils which he denounced as deep-seated, and ceased to consider them the result of the evil dispositions

---

[1] *Diary*, ed. Mrs. Baring, p. 488. For points of difference with Windham, see also *Creevy Papers*, 1903, ii. 55.

of individual statesmen. In consequence the character of
his writings changed, and he began to address himself to
a larger audience than the handful of men who controlled
English politics. It will therefore be unnecessary in
future to trace in so much detail the politics of the day,
for after his quarrel with the Whigs, Cobbett ceased to
be concerned so intimately in the fortunes of cabinets.

During the eventful years that followed the foundation
of the *Political Register*, Cobbett had not been entirely
absorbed in politics. He had found time to begin two
literary undertakings of the greatest historical importance : he had commenced the publication of his *Parliamentary Debates* and of his *Parliamentary History*. It is
tolerably certain that the actual labour of compilation
and even the more responsible task of supervision were
delegated to others, but to Cobbett must be awarded the
credit of originally conceiving the project in either case.

The *Parliamentary Debates* was an independent development of part of the general design of the *Political
Register*. From the first publication of that periodical,
in January 1802, Cobbett furnished his readers with an
account of proceedings in Parliament. The comparatively brief summary given in the first two volumes was
reproduced on a larger scale in the supplement to the
second volume, and from that time till the close of 1803
the *Parliamentary Debates* were published as part of the
half-yearly volumes of the *Register*. Early in 1804,
however, it was determined from motives of convenience
to publish the *Debates* separately. Accordingly, *Cobbett's
Parliamentary Debates* was brought out in separate
numbers during the session and afterwards bound in
volumes. The first volume appeared on 7th June, under

the editorship of Cobbett's assistant, John Wright. From
their commencement the *Debates* was a literary, though
not a financial success. The proceedings were reported
at greater length and with more precision than in any
previous attempt at reproducing Parliamentary deliberations.

The great success which attended this work encouraged
Cobbett to supplement it by an account of the proceedings of past Parliaments. *Cobbett's Parliamentary History of England* began to appear in October 1806 and
was completed in thirty-six volumes in April 1820. The
entire series was edited by John Wright, and formed a
work of considerable historical value. There already
existed for the earlier part of the history a work of a
similar character. It was published in twenty-four
volumes between 1751 and 1761, was edited anonymously
'by several hands,' and was entitled *The Parliamentary
or Constitutional History of England from the earliest
Times*. It was brought down to the dissolution of the
Convention Parliament which restored Charles II. This
compilation was used by Wright as a ground-work for
his earlier volumes. He did not, however, content himself with copying. He omitted the accounts of battles,
sieges, and domestic occurrences, with which the *Parliamentary and Constitutional History* abounded. The compilers of the earlier work had also inserted long pamphlets
just as they were printed and sold, and these also
Wright relentlessly cut out. He carefully collated the
Journals of the Lords and Commons and such contemporary or almost contemporary authorities as Sir Simonds
D'Ewes' *Journals of all the Parliaments during the Reign
of Queen Elizabeth*, John Rushworth's *Historical Collec-*

tions, John Nalson's *Impartial Collection*, and Whitelocke's *Memorials*. All these authorities, however, were also employed by the anonymous compilers, in spite of Cobbett's citation of them in his prefaces, as though they had been consulted for the first time. From the Restoration onwards the chief guides to the student in Cobbett's time were *The History and Proceedings of the House of Lords*, published by Ebenezer Timberland, and *The History and Proceedings of the House of Commons*, published by Richard Chandler, both of which covered the period from the Stuart Restoration to 1743. These works were, however, very inferior to the *Parliamentary History of England*. They were compiled without consultation of the Journals of the Houses, and without any indication of the sources whence their materials were drawn. In fact, as Cobbett severely remarks in the preface to the fourth volume of his own history, these materials would seem 'to have been moulded into the form of volumes for the mere purpose of filling up a chasm in a bookcase.' On the other hand, independent records and narratives of parliamentary proceedings were more numerous than for the earlier period. Wright availed himself diligently of his authorities. In consequence, the later portion of the *Parliamentary History* has greater claims to be regarded as an original compilation. From 1743 to November 1774 there was a great lack of records, owing to the jealousy with which Parliament guarded the privacy of its debates, and, though Wright sought with great industry to supply deficiencies, the *Parliamentary History* for that period is shorter and more imperfect than for the preceding years. At a much later date, between 1841 and 1843, Wright supplied this deficiency between the

years 1768 and 1771 by deciphering and transcribing the
manuscript of 'Sir Henry Cavendish's Debates of the
House of Commons during the Thirteenth Parliament
of Great Britain, commonly called the Unreported Parliament.' This manuscript is preserved in forty-eight
volumes in the Egerton Collection in the British Museum.[1]
When Wright, however, had published this report as far
as 27th March 1771, his labours were ended by death,
and the rest of the manuscript still remains unpublished.

From November 1774 Wright had the assistance of
the *Parliamentary Register*, a monthly periodical, founded
by John Almon in 1775, which was continued until 1813.
With the assistance of this compilation he was able to
make the latter part of *Cobbett's Parliamentary History*
tolerably complete. These publications continued to
appear regularly with Cobbett's name on the title-page
until 1811, when they passed out of his hands under
circumstances hereafter to be related.[2] From that time
he ceased to have any concern in them, although in
October 1820 he made an attempt to resume the publication of the Parliamentary debates, and announced the
first volume of a new series of *Cobbett's Parliamentary
Debates*, comprising the deliberations in the first part of
the current session. But either the venture met with no
success, or the labour of preparing it was too arduous,
for the publication was abandoned after the issue of the
first number.

[1] Egerton MSS. Nos. 215-62.   [2] See pp. 167-173.

CHAPTER V

COBBETT'S LIFE AT BOTLEY AND THE DEVELOPMENT
OF HIS RADICAL OPINIONS

IN the year 1804 Cobbett ceased to reside habitually in
London. His own love of the country and his solicitude
for the health of his children may account for his change
of residence. After paying a prolonged visit in the
summer and autumn of 1804 to Southampton and other
places in Hampshire, he bought a farm called Fairthorn
in July 1805, in the parish of Botley, a little village on
the River Hamble, five miles from Southampton and
less than four from Bishop's Waltham. Within a year
or two he purchased two or three small neighbouring
farms, and in May 1808 he acquired eighty-seven acres
consisting chiefly of woodland, which he expected to
increase very much in value during the next twenty
years. Botley was a quiet spot. There was 'no trade,
except that carried on by two or three persons who bring
coals from the Southampton water, and who send down
timber.' Among the inhabitants were two doctors and
one parson. 'All the rest are farmers, farmers' men,
millers, millers' men, millwrights, publicans, who sell beer
to the farmers' men and the farmers; copse-cutters, tree-
strippers, bark-shavers, farmers' wheelwrights, farmers'
blacksmiths, shopkeepers, a schoolmistress, and in short,
nothing but persons belonging to agriculture, to which

118

COBBETT DENYING HIS KING.

indeed, the two doctors and the parson belong as much as the rest.'

Cobbett entered heartily into the country life of the district. His house and garden bordered on the creek of the little river Hamble, in which he amused himself by fishing, sending presents of the fish of the stream—jack, trout, and salmon-peel—to Windham and other friends in town. He also promoted single-stick play by holding a grand match in October 1805 and again in October 1806 which brought together the most skilful players of Hampshire and Wiltshire.[1]

His house also became a constant meeting-place for the more advanced political reformers. Among those who visited him were Lord Cochrane, Lord Folkestone, and Dr. Samuel Parr. Of the first, Miss Mitford, who was also a visitor in company with her father and mother, says:

'Lord Cochrane was there, then in the very height of his warlike fame, and as unlike the common notion of a warrior as could be. A gentle, quiet, mild young man, was this burner of French fleets and cutter-out of Spanish vessels, as one should see in a summer day. He lay about under the trees reading Selden on the *Dominion of the Seas*, and letting the children (and children always know with whom they may take liberties) play all sorts of tricks with him at their pleasure.'[2]

Of Cobbett she says:

'He had at that time a large house at Botley, with a lawn and gardens sweeping down to the Bursledon River, which divided his (Mr. Cobbett's) territories from the beautiful grounds of the old friend, where we had been originally staying, the great squire

---

[1] See Add. MS. 22906, ff. 90, 187.
[2] Miss Mitford, *Recollections of a Literary Life*, 1859, p. 199.

of the place. His own house—large, high, massive, red, and square, and perched on a considerable eminence—always struck me as being not unlike its proprietor. . . . I never saw hospitality more genuine, more simple, or more thoroughly successful in the great end of hospitality, the putting of everybody completely at ease. There was not the slightest attempt at finery, or display, or gentility. They called it a farm-house, and everything was in accordance with the largest idea of a great English yeoman of the old time. Everything was excellent, everything abundant—all served with the greatest nicety by trim waiting-damsels : and everything went on with such quiet regularity, that of the large circle of guests not one could find himself in the way. I need not say a word more in praise of the good wife . . . to whom this admirable order was mainly due. She was a sweet motherly woman, realising our notion of one of Scott's most charming characters, *Ailie Dinmont*, in her simplicity, her kindness, and her devotion to her husband and her children.

'At this time William Cobbett was at the height of his political reputation; but of politics we heard little, and should, I think, have heard nothing, but for an occasional red-hot patriot, who would introduce the subject, which our host would fain put aside and got rid of as soon as possible. There was something of *Dandie Dinmont* about him, with his unfailing good humour and good spirits—his heartiness, his love of field sports, and his liking for a foray. He was a tall, stout man, fair, and sunburnt, with a bright smile, and an air compounded of the soldier and the farmer, to which his habit of wearing an eternal red waistcoat contributed not a little. He was I think the most athletic and vigorous person that I have ever known. Nothing could tire him. At home in the morning he would begin by mowing his own lawn, beating his gardener, Robinson, the best mower, except himself, in the parish, at that fatiguing work.

'For early rising indeed he had an absolute passion, and some of the poetry that we trace in his writings, whenever he speaks of scenery or of rural objects, broke out in his method of training his children into his own matutinal habits. The boy who was first down stairs was called the Lark for the day, and had

amongst other indulgences, the pretty privilege of making his
mother's nosegay and that of any lady visitors. Nor was this
the only trace of poetical feeling that he displayed. Whenever
he described a place, were it only to say where such a covey
lay, or such a hare was found sitting, you could see it, so graphic
—so vivid—so true was the picture. He showed the same
taste in the purchase of his beautiful farm at Botley, Fairthorn ;
even in the pretty name. To be sure, he did not give the name,
but I always thought that it unconsciously influenced his choice
in the purchase. The beauty of the situation certainly did.
The fields lay along the Bursledon River, and might have been
shown to a foreigner as a specimen of the richest and loveliest
English scenery.' [1]

  With equal vividness and even greater power, Cobbett
himself described his home at Botley and spoke of his
manner of bringing up his children, who were, perhaps,
his principal reason for relinquishing his life in town.
After explaining how he aimed at inducing them to love
learning and books instead of compelling them to study
by severity, he says :

  ' But, to do the things I did, you must love *home* yourself ; to
rear up children in this manner, you must *live with them*, you
must make them, too, *feel* by your conduct, that you *prefer* this
to any other mode of passing your time. All men cannot lead
this sort of life, but many may ; and all much more than many
do. My occupation, to be sure, was chiefly carried on *at home* ;
but, I had always enough to do I never spent an idle week, or
even day, in my whole life. Yet I found time to talk with them,
to walk, or ride, about *with them* ; and when forced to go from
home always took one or more with me. You must be good-
tempered too with them ; they must like *your* company better
than any other person's ; they must not wish you away, not fear
your coming back, not look upon your departure as a *holiday*. . . .
  When I went from home, all followed me to the outer gate,

---

[1] Miss Mitford, *Recollections of a Literary Life*, 1859, pp. 199-201.

and looked after me, till the carriage, or horse, was out of sight. At the time appointed for my return, all were prepared to meet me; and if it were late at night, they sat up as long as they were able to keep their eyes open. This love of parents, and this constant pleasure *at home* made them not even think of seeking pleasure abroad ; and they, thus, were kept from vicious playmates and early corruption.

'This is the age, too, to teach children to be *trustworthy*, and to be *merciful* and *humane*. We lived *in a garden* of about two acres, partly kitchen-garden with walls, partly shrubbery and trees, and partly grass. There were the *peaches*, as tempting as any that ever grew, and yet as safe from fingers as if no child were ever in the garden. It was not necessary to forbid. The blackbirds, the thrushes, the white-throats, and even that very shy bird the goldfinch had their nests and bred up their young ones in great abundance, all about this little spot, constantly the play-place of six children ; and one of the latter had its nest and brought up its young ones in a *raspberry-bush*, within two yards of a walk, and at the time that we were gathering the ripe raspberries. We give *dogs*, and justly, great credit for sagacity and memory; but the following two most curious instances, which I should not venture to state, if there were not so many witnesses to the facts, in my neighbours at Botley, as well as in my own family, will show, that *birds* are not, in this respect, inferior to the canine race. All country people know that the *skylark* is a very shy bird, that its abode is the open fields : that it settles on the ground only ; that it seeks safety in the wideness of space ; that it avoids enclosures, and is never seen in gardens. A part of our ground was a grass-plot of about *forty rods*, or a quarter of an acre, which, one year, was left to be mowed for hay. A pair of larks, coming out of the fields into the midst of a pretty populous village, chose to make their nest in the middle of this little spot and at not more than about *thirty-five yards* from one of the doors of the house, in which there were about twelve persons living, and six of these children, who had constant access to all parts of the ground. There we saw the cock rising up and singing, then taking his turn upon the eggs ; and by and by we observed him cease to sing, and saw them both *constantly engaged in bringing food to the young ones*. No unintelligible hint to fathers and mothers of the human race, who have, before marriage, taken delight in *music*. But the time came for *mowing the grass !* I waited a good many days for the brood to get away, but at last I determined on the day ; and if the larks were there still, to leave a patch of grass standing round them. In order not to keep them in dread longer than necessary, I brought three able mowers, who would cut the whole in about an hour; and as the plat was nearly circular set them to mow *round*, beginning at the outside. And now for sagacity indeed ! The moment the men began to whet their scythes, the two old larks began to flutter over the nest, and to make a great clamour. When the men began to mow, they flew round and round, stooping so low, when near the men as almost to touch their bodies, making a great chattering at the same time ; but before the men had got round with the second swath, they flew to the nest, and away they went, young ones and all, across the river, at the foot of the ground, and settled in the long grass in my neighbour's orchard.

'The other instance relates to a house-marten. It is well known that these birds build their nests under the eaves of inhabited houses, and sometimes under those of door-porches, but we had one that built its nest *in the house*, and upon the top of a common door-case, the door of which opened into a room out of the main passage into the house. Perceiving the marten had begun to build its nest here, we kept the front door open in the day time, but were obliged to fasten it at night. It went on, had eggs, young ones, and the young ones flew. I used to open the door in the morning early, and then the birds carried on their affairs till night. The next *year* the marten came again, and had *another brood in the same place*. It found its *old nest* ; and having repaired it, and put it in order, went on again in the former way ; and it would, I dare say, have continued to come to the end of its life, if we had remained there so long, notwithstanding there were six healthy children in the house, making just as much noise as they pleased.' [1]

[1] *Advice to Young Men*, pp. 275-78.

Then passing on to speak more directly of how he induced his children to study, and of how he protected them from the dangers of social dissipation, of romances, and of playhouses, he says:

'We wanted no stimulants of this sort to *keep up our spirits*; our various pleasing pursuits were quite sufficient for that; and the *book-learning* came among the rest of the pleasures, to which it was, in some sort, necessary. I remember that, one year, I raised a prodigious crop of fine *melons*, under hand-glasses; and I learned how to do it from a gardening *book*; or, at least, that book was necessary to remind me of the details. Having passed part of an evening in talking to the boys about getting this crop, "Come," said I, "now, let us *read the book.*" Then the book came forth, and to work we went, following very strictly the precepts of the book. I read the thing but once, but the eldest boy read it, perhaps, twenty times over; and explained all about the matter to the others. Why here was a *motive!* Then he had to tell the garden labourer *what to do* to the melons. Now, I will engage, that more was really *learned* by this single *lesson*, than would have been learned by spending, at this son's age, a year at school; and he *happy* and *delighted* all the while. When any dispute arose amongst them about hunting or shooting, or any other of their pursuits, they, by degrees, found out the way of settling it by reference to some book; and when any difficulty occurred, as to the meaning, they referred to me, who, if at home, *always instantly attended to them*, in these matters.

'They began writing by taking words out of *printed books*: finding out which letter was which, by asking me, or asking those who knew the letters one from another; and by imitating bits of my writing, it is surprising how soon they began to write a hand like mine, very small, very faint-stroked, and nearly plain as print. The first use that any of them made of the pen, was to *write to me*, though in the same house with them. They began doing this in mere *scratches*, before they knew how to make any one letter; and as I was always folding up letters and directing them, so were they; and they were *sure* to receive a *prompt answer*, with most *encouraging* compliments. All the meddlings and teasings of friends, and what was more serious, the pressing prayers of their anxious mother, about sending them to *school*, I withstood without the slightest effect on my resolution. As to friends, preferring my own judgment to theirs, I did not care much ; but an expression of anxiety, implying a doubt of the soundness of my own judgment, coming, perhaps, twenty times a day from her whose care they were as well as mine, was not a matter to smile at, and very great trouble it did give me. My answer at last was, as to the boys, I want them to be *like me* ; and as to the girls, "in whose hands can they be so safe as in *yours*? Therefore my resolution is taken : *go to school they shall not.*"

'Nothing is much more annoying than the *intermeddling of friends*, in a case like this. The wife appeals *to them*, and "*good breeding*," that is to say *nonsense*, is sure to put them on *her side*. Then, they, particularly the *women*, when describing the *surprising progress* made by their *own sons* at school, used, if one of mine were present, to turn to him, and ask, to what school *he went*, and what *he* was *learning*? I leave any one to judge of *his* opinion of her ; and whether *he* would like her the better for that ! "Bless me, so tall, and *not learned* anything *yet*!" "Oh yes, he has," I used to say, "he has learned to ride, and hunt, and shoot, and fish, and look after cattle and sheep, and to work in the garden, and to feed his dogs, and to go from village to village in the dark." This was the way I used to manage with troublesome customers of this sort. And how glad the children used to be, when they got clear of such criticising people ! And how grateful they felt to me for the *protection* which they saw that I gave them against that state of restraint, of which other people's boys complained ! Go whither they might, they found no place so pleasant as home, and no soul that came near them affording them so many means of gratification as they received from me.'[1]

While enjoying rural life and superintending his children's upbringing, Cobbett began also to take a more active share in local political contests. During

[1] *Advice to Young Men*, pp. 280-82.

the ministries of Pitt and Addington he had consoled himself with the reflection that there was a powerful party in the House of Commons as zealous for reform as himself, and only kept out of office by the personal predilections of the king. The first few months of Grenville's ministry completely disillusioned him, and he realised that it was hopeless to look for reform from within Parliament and that therefore it must be sought from without by appealing from the House of Commons to the body of electors. An opportunity for beginning his new form of attack soon offered itself. In the early summer of 1806 Augustus Cavendish Bradshaw, one of the members for Honiton, accepted the office of teller of the Irish exchequer, which forced him to vacate his seat. As this was one of those places which Cobbett considered to be paid far too highly, he resolved that Bradshaw should not be re-elected without opposition, and, failing to find a candidate to oppose him, determined himself to contest the seat, issuing his first letter to the electors on 23rd May. He also posted up a bill, having at the top the quotation from the Book of Job, 'Fire shall consume the tabernacles of bribery,' and announced his intention of refusing to pay for votes. As Honiton was a typical small borough where the burgesses were accustomed to sell their votes to the highest bidder, this announcement did not excite much enthusiasm. 'Most of the corrupt villains,' he says, 'laughed in my face, but some of the women actually cried out against me in the streets, as a man that had come to rob them of their blessing.'[1] On 8th June Lord Cochrane appeared at Honiton. He had just returned from a cruise on the French and Spanish

[1] *Political Register*, 22nd November 1823.

coasts in command of the *Pallas*, in which he had made numerous prizes, disorganised the system of signalling along the French coast, and fought a desperate action off the Isle of Oléron with a French forty-gun frigate and three brigs, which were only saved from capture by the arrival of two more of the enemy's frigates. On seeing Cobbett's appeal for a candidate he at once posted to Honiton, and Cobbett, who did not wish to stand himself if he could find any one else to do so, at once withdrew in his favour. For the moment Bradshaw's popularity was in danger, for Lord Cochrane was known to have made an immense amount of prize money in his late cruise. Bradshaw, who had paid six guineas a head to his supporters at his previous election, had anticipated buying his votes on this occasion at the reduced rate of two guineas. The electors, whom Bradshaw himself had styled at another time 'the most corrupt set of rascals in the world' took advantage of Cochrane's appearance to force their late member to raise his offer to five pounds a head. They then eagerly turned to Cochrane to ascertain by how much he would outbid his rival. To use the words of an independent elector to that gallant seaman during his canvass, 'You need not ask me, my lord, who I votes for, I always votes for Mister Most.' To the great disappointment of the majority, Lord Cochrane refused to bribe at all, and in consequence polled very few votes. The sequel is best told in his own words :

'To be beaten, even at an election, is one thing; to turn a beating to account is another. Having had decisive proof as to the nature of Honiton politics, I made up my mind that the next time there was a vacancy in the borough, the seat should be mine without bribery. Accordingly immediately after my defeat I sent the bellman round the town, having first primed him with an appropriate speech, intimating that all who had voted for me might repair to my agent, J. Townsend, Esq., and *receive ten pounds ten*.

'The novelty of a defeated candidate paying double the current price expended by the successful one—or indeed paying anything—made a great sensation. Even my agent assured me that he could have secured my return for less money, for that the popular voice being in my favour, a trifling judicious expenditure would have turned the scale.

'I told Mr. Townsend that such payment would have been bribery, which would not accord with my character as a reformer of abuses—a declaration which seemed highly to amuse him. Notwithstanding the explanation that the ten guineas was paid as a reward for having withstood the influence of bribery, the impression produced on the electoral mind by such unlooked-for liberality was simply this—that if I gave ten guineas for being beaten, my opponent had not paid half enough for being elected; a conclusion which, by a similar process of reasoning, was magnified into the conviction that each of his voters had been cheated out of five pounds ten.'[1]

In October 1806 there was a general election and Lord Cochrane was returned without difficulty, no mention being made beforehand of payment for his votes. After the election, however, he was approached and peremptorily declined to make any payment whatever, pointing out that his former payment was a recognition

---

[1] Lord Cochrane's *Autobiography of a Seaman*, 1861, pp. 112-13. This work was compiled in Lord Cochrane's old age and was put into shape by his secretary, G. B. Earp. In it these incidents are placed in 1805 and in the *Dictionary of National Biography*, vol. xi. p. 166, the date has been fixed in March 1805—the time of Bradshaw's original return for Honiton —regardless of the fact that it has been stated just before that Cochrane was cruising off the Azores from February to April 1805. There can be no doubt that June 1806 was the actual date, for Cobbett published contemporary accounts of the proceedings at the election in the *Political Register* for 14th and 28th June 1806.

of the disinterested conduct of his supporters, but that any payment under the present circumstances would be a violation of his avowed principles.[1] Needless to say after the next dissolution he did not seek re-election.

The next election in which Cobbett took a prominent share was that at Westminster following the general dissolution in October. He supported James Paull, a fiery little Scot, who had been engaged in business in India—according to his opponents he had been a tailor—and who, on his return to England in 1804, had vehemently attacked Lord Wellesley's administration. The Whigs supported him until the ministry of 'all the Talents' was formed, when the composition of the coalition rendered further assistance impossible. The official Whig candidate was Sheridan, who had been appointed Treasurer to the Navy in February, and who, in Cobbett's opinion, since his appointment had connived at abuses which he had formerly denounced. Sir Samuel Hood was the Tory candidate, and he and Sheridan uniting against Paull succeeded in keeping him out by a moderate majority. During the election Tom Sheridan, who was working zealously on behalf of his father, reflected unnecessarily on Paull's low birth. Cobbett replied:—

' Whence sprang the Sheridans? From a play-actor; from a person of that profession (if it can be called a profession) the followers of which are, in our wise laws, considered and denominated vagabonds. . . . The prohibition of the exercise of this calling is . . . the rule; the toleration of it merely the exception; and most wise is the law, for, if there be any calling lower than all other callings; if there be any one beyond all

---

[1] Cochrane's *Autobiography*, pp. 126-27. He again misdates the election, but is corrected in the *Dictionary of National Biography*.

I

comparison the most degrading, is it not that, wherein the operator, for the purpose of obtaining food and raiment, exhibits his person, displays his limbs, and strains his voice, for the *amusement* of the spectators, to whose occasional and often capricious hissings and peltings it is a part of his profession to submit with a smile and a bow !'[1]

This contest first brought Cobbett into close relations with one of the most conspicuous Radicals of the time —Sir Francis Burdett. Burdett had resided in Paris during the early days of the Revolution, had listened to the debates in the National Assembly, and had imbibed from the members some of their political ideas. Three years after his return to England in 1793, he entered Parliament and distinguished himself by his attacks on the ministry, whom he accused of arbitrary encroachments upon popular rights and assailed for their suspension of the Habeas Corpus Act and their restrictions on the expression of public opinion. In 1802 Burdett was returned for the County of Middlesex after a stubborn contest with George Boulton Mainwaring, the chairman of the Quarter Sessions, who had distinguished himself by opposing inquiries which Burdett had made into the treatment of suspected persons detained under the Habeas Corpus Acts. At the time of the election Cobbett had written violently against Burdett, whom he branded as the friend of the convicted traitor O'Connor, and of the acquitted traitor Horne Tooke.

'To reason with such a man,' he declared, 'would be absurd; he must be treated with silent contempt, or be combatted with weapons very different from a pen.' 'We detest and loathe Sir

---

[1] *Political Register*, 22nd November 1806.

Francis Burdett,' he went on to say, ' we would trample upon him for his false, base, and insolent insinuations respecting his and our Sovereign.'[1]

On Burdett's return for Middlesex in 1802 his opponent Mainwaring petitioned, and, in July 1804, after a protracted inquiry, a new election was ordered. On this occasion Cobbett's attitude was entirely changed. He criticised Mainwaring's conduct and language, extolled Burdett's private character, and while declining to approve his political opinions, urged that it was illiberal under changed conditions to assail him on account of his conduct at a past time.[2]

This attitude of tolerance was soon changed for one of friendship, and by the time of his active intervention in the Westminster election, Cobbett and Burdett had become intimate. Their friendship unfortunately was not more lasting than their former enmity.

Early in 1807 Grenville's ministry, which had been weakened by the death of Fox, was driven from office. In March Lord Howick (afterwards Earl Grey) introduced a bill into the House of Commons to admit Roman Catholics and dissenters into the army and navy. The king took alarm and insisted on the withdrawal of the bill. The cabinet yielded, but informed the king that they reserved themselves the right openly to avow their opinions in Parliament on the subject of the Catholic claims, and to offer him such advice about Ireland 'as the course of circumstances shall appear to require.'[3]   In consequence the king, two days later,

---

[1] *Political Register*, 7th August 1802.
[2] *Ibid.*, 1st September, 8th September 1804.
[3] *Memoir and Correspondence of Viscount Castlereagh*, 1849, iv. 388.

demanded from them a positive assurance that they would never press on him in the future any concessions to the Roman Catholics, and on their declining to give such an assurance, the Duke of Portland was asked to form a ministry. This he succeeded in doing, and thus the Tory party returned to power. The two chief members of the administration were Canning, the Foreign Secretary, and Castlereagh, the Secretary for War. Cobbett saw the downfall of the Whig administration without regret, though he had little sympathy with their successors. He had advanced so far along the path of political reform that the terms Whig and Tory were alike abhorrent to him.

The change of ministry was followed on 29th April by a dissolution of Parliament. Cobbett again supported Paull's candidature at Westminster, and spoke of him with high eulogy. Unfortunately a violent quarrel between Paull and Sir Francis Burdett terminated in a duel, in which both were wounded, Paull so seriously that his life was despaired of. Under these circumstances Cobbett, who strongly objected to duelling, and who at a previous time had severely criticised Paull's propensity for the practice, transferred his assistance to Burdett.[1] For the other seat he supported Lord Cochrane, and to his satisfaction Cochrane and Burdett were returned at the head of the poll, easily defeating Sheridan, while the other candidates, Elliott and Paull, withdrew before the end of the voting.

Cobbett's close association during the Westminster contests with men of such advanced opinions had a marked influence on his political views. Since his

[1] See *Political Register*, 3rd January, 9th May 1807.

alienation from the Whigs he had constantly assailed English politicians with reproaches of incompetence and corruption. He had, however, chiefly confined himself to attacks on practical abuses and on the actual conduct of affairs. But now he began to realise that his quarrel was as much with the system of government as with the men in office, and he adopted several of the leading radical proposals for reform. In particular he began to urge the necessity of revision in parliamentary representation. Parliament seemed to him to be under the control of a ring of stock-jobbers, loan-mongers, placemen, and pensioners, distinct from the ancient landed aristocracy, which he continued to respect, but rapidly supplanting it in power and wealth. This body he designated the 'Thing.' It was kept together by a common interest in corruption, and while its power remained there was no prospect of reform or retrenchment in the public expenditure. The 'Thing' included the class of great manufacturers, whose prosperity was marked by the rapid growth of large towns. Cobbett, inspired by his love of rural scenes, viewed this growth with intense dislike. London, the greatest of all the industrial centres, he constantly designated the 'wen,' regarding it as a visible sign of the distemper of the body politic. In order to overthrow the authority of the 'Thing' Cobbett began to insist upon the benefit of frequent elections, and the importance of removing all place-men as well as pensioners from the Houses of Parliament. In May 1807 in a letter to Spencer Perceval, after quoting utterances by Pitt in 1782, and by Lord Howick in 1806, in favour of the reform of the electorate, he went on to say:

'If those descriptions were true, and if no improvement in the state of the representation has taken place since those descriptions were given, I put it to your justice, whether men ought to be reviled, and punished as traitors, or seditious libellers, because they are discontented under such a state of things: because they wish for, and seek, an improvement in the representation; because, in short, adhering to the principles of that constitution, for the sake of which they are called upon to shed their blood, they desire that a dissolution of the parliament should, to use the words of the Speech, be a recurrence *to the " sense of the people*?" And I put it to your reason, whether the upholding of such a state of things, and whether such revilings and punishings, be the likely means of calling forth the zeal of the people, if need shall be, in defence of the government?'[1]

His denunciations of the House of Commons itself became extremely vehement. Having no longer any faith in the good intentions of either political party, he assailed both with invective. Portland's ministry he designated as 'ousted Treasury clerks' and as the 'no popery faction,' while all who were opposed to them were massed under the general name of 'the rump of whiggism' and treated with even greater contumely. His opinion of the state of Parliament was not more despondent than that which he entertained of the general condition of the nation. He depicted the people as too much oppressed by taxation and dispirited by poverty, to be able any longer to take an interest in public affairs, except so far as they immediately affected their economic condition.

'There was a time, when a cry about Jacobinism, or danger to the church, would have had great weight. But those cries have seen their day pass, every man's attention being now turned *to the*

----

[1] *Political Register*, 16th May 1807.

abuses in the expenditure of the public money. . . . This, I repeat it, is the sole point upon which men's attention is now earnestly fixed. Of the affairs of the Continent ; of conquests in South America, and of means of defence at home, they have not leisure to think. The reading of tax papers, and the providing for the incessant demands of the tax-gatherer, take up all their time. Their present grievous burdens is the only subject upon which they can be expected to think ; and whilst they feel these burdens, they know that enormous peculations remain un-punished ; they see no hope of preventing them for the future ; and they feel as men must feel under such circumstances. The last three years have brought to light most important truths relating to the public expenditure and to the representation in parliament. These truths must, and will, have their effect in due time ; but until then, it is perfectly useless to endeavour to fix the general attention upon any other object.' [1]

Impressed by the serious condition of the nation Cobbett began to declare that a great political change was inevitable. He was roused to indignation by seeing parliamentary seats openly advertised for sale, and addressed a letter to the electors of Westminster, headed by copies of several such advertisements, of which one may serve as a specimen :

' A BOROUGH.—A Gentleman of fortune and respectability will hear of one, by immediately applying to Mr. Prince, Bookseller, Old North-street, Red Lion-square.'—*Morning Post*, 1st May 1807.

After calling attention to these transactions, and shew-ing the absurdity of calling a general parliamentary election an appeal to the people, he exclaimed :

' From one corner of the kingdom to the other corruption extends his baleful, his serpent-hatching wings. Can this last ?

[1] *Political Register*, 2nd May 1807.

Ought it to last? Of what avail is it that the miscreants engaged in this infamous traffic call us jacobins and levellers? Will any one of them say, that this ought to be? Has any one of them the ingenuity to find out any thing, even in imagination, worse than this? Politicians may endeavour to alarm us with cries of revolution, and divines may preach to us about hell; but if the one can find any thing more disgraceful, or the other any thing more damnable, than what is described in these advertisements, I beseech them speedily to exhibit it to our view. *Fifty-seven* of these advertisements have I read in the London daily papers, and I defy any man living to produce me, in the history of the whole world, anything so completely descriptive of national degradation. . . . Again I call upon our accusers, upon those, who, for hire, denominate us jacobins and levellers, and who cry aloud for the preservation of the constitution, to say, whether the constitution sanctions these things. If it does, what an infamous imposture it is! and, if it does not, it is we, and not our revilers, who are endeavouring to support the constitution of England. Aye, it is we who would restore and support the constitution; the real constitution; that constitution which so strictly forbids the buying or the selling of a single vote, much more a seat in parliament; that constitution which inhibits peers from any sort of interference in elections, and that supposes it impossible that any peer should, in any way, send a member to the Commons' house; that constitution, in short, which forbids, in the strongest terms, and under severe penalties, every one of the abuses, of which we complain; and yet have the hireling revilers the audacity to reproach us with *a wish to overturn the constitution!* In such a state the country cannot long remain. No country has ever long remained in such a state. Those who have an evident interest in perpetuating abuses of all sorts, may endeavour to terrify the people with the consequences of what is called a revolution; and from a revolution, in the usual sense of the word, as applied to politics, God preserve us! but a *change*, and a great change too, must come, and come it will, in one way or another, and that at no distant day.'[1]

[1] *Political Register*, 9th May 1807.

Cobbett's language and sentiments had begun to take that Radical colour which was characteristic of his later years. In the *Political Register* for 21st March 1807 he defended the toast 'our Sovereign, the Majesty of the People,' given at one of Sir Francis Burdett's dinners, and only declined to give the sentiment his full approbation because it was not 'of plain and unequivocal meaning.' In the same number he derided a correspondent who had spoken of 'our beloved king, in whose defence every true Englishman would shed the last drop of his blood,' asking him whether it did not seem uncalled-for, if not impertinent, for a grey-coated individual to put himself forward in that way, when the king had about two hundred thousand gentlemen in red and blue coats, including sixteen thousand Hanoverians, who had nothing else to do but to support him, his officers, and his kingdom. At Burdett's dinner the king's health had been omitted, and Cobbett, who had formerly been distinguished for the ardour with which he had expressed his devotion to the king's person, defended this omission on the ground that it was a matter of taste, and that the company had scorned to be guilty of hypocrisy, and proceeded to say that since the introduction of so many Hanoverian soldiers, and the exemption of the king's funded property from income-tax, although he retained his loyalty unshaken, he did not choose to come forward with voluntary expressions of his admiration of the king's conduct.

Finally, in regard to foreign affairs, Cobbett about this time abandoned his former attitude of uncompromising hostility to France, and instead of the fiery patriotic ardour which characterised former utterances adopted a tone of ironic banter, which was extremely galling to his opponents. Writing of the Continental War in July 1807, just after the news had arrived that the French had taken Dantzig, he says:

'The *shaking-fit* seems to have returned to many persons. They really seem to have thought, that the Boulogne fleet would never be heard of again! And now they are filled with dread. For my part, I feel *less* apprehension than formerly. Not that I should like a set of upstart, unprincipled villains, who would swear truth out of the world, to hold the rod over me, to pillage me in virtue of one of their accursed decrees, to send their civil hirelings to rob me, while their foreign armed ruffians stood by to keep me in awe;[1] no, God forbid that I should like this, that I should ever bring my mind patiently to contemplate submission so degrading; but I have from long thinking upon the subject, brought myself to a conviction that the French never will succeed in bringing us into this state. The *why* and the *wherefore* I might have some little difficulty in detailing; but the conviction I entertain, and under it I am easy; and, what is more, I am fully persuaded, that, however some persons may tremble, this conviction is felt by ninety-nine out of every hundred men in the nation. I do not *reason* much upon the matter. I have done asking how the French can get here or to Ireland, and how we are able to repel them. I know the enemy to be powerful by land, and that he may soon become powerful by sea; I see the force of all Europe collected against us, and I have considered in detail the probable acts of such a conqueror; but, when I consider who (*sic*) we have for Commanders, and particularly for Commander-in-Chief; when I consider the strength of our armies; when I consider the extent of our immense resources, and the manner of distributing those resources; when I consider, in short, the whole of the force and state of the nation, the whole of the scene that lies before me, I stop not to reason, but involuntarily exclaim, Buonaparte, I set thy utmost ingenuity, power, and malice at defiance!

---

[1] All this is double-edged.

I fear one thing, indeed, and that is that our gallant friends, *the Hanoverians*, will not be able to get at the French. This was a dirty trick in the Danes, who are said to have shut (out of pure envy, I dare say) the Sound against our expedition![1] I was always afraid of something of this sort. I said, that the Hanoverians would arrive too soon or too late ; and now, curse light upon the Danes, they are stopping them! The *Courier* recommends war against the Danes, and so do I. I would sell the shirt off my back to support war against the Danes. What right had they to stop our expedition? Now it will come back again, Lord Cathcart and all, without having got even a glimpse of the French.'[2]

This effusion, in which Cobbett parodied the style of the *Morning Post*, provoked Francis Jeffrey to inquire ' whether any man, capable of serious counsel or of proper feeling, could possibly conceive such a crisis of such a country as a suitable subject for derision, or for such asinine attempts at irony and humour as are exhibited in this passage.'[3]

It is often a difficult problem to determine when devotion to party should give place to larger feelings of patriotism, and, like many men of strong opinions, Cobbett was hardly sufficiently conscious of the difficulty. There can be little doubt, however, that by sneering at the army and attacking the king he alienated many who lent a ready ear while he assailed the ministry, or even when he proceeded to inveigh against the condition of

[1] The expedition referred to was the expedition under Admiral Gambier and Lord Cathcart, which early in September 1807 bombarded Copenhagen and took possession of the Danish fleet to prevent its being used by Napoleon. At the time Cobbett wrote its destination was unknown, and it was supposed that it was proceeding to the Baltic to assist the Prussians.

[2] *Political Register*, 18th July 1807.

[3] *Edinburgh Review*, 1807, x. 405.

Parliament.   But it would be misleading to represent
Cobbett as indifferent, much less hostile, to the success
of the English arms.   At heart he was a patriot, though
his low opinion of the abilities of the Government made
him savage in his onslaughts on their measures.   Yet he
welcomed the tidings of victory.   A striking instance of
this may be given.   In the passage just quoted he gibed
at the expedition under Gambier and Cathcart while he
believed it bound on a hopeless errand in Prussia.   But
on learning of its true destination and success he candidly
avowed his mistake.

'When the expedition was going out, I, like the French,
laughed at it; but I, like the French, thought it was bound to
the Prussian territories, and had in view "the deliverance of
Europe" after the old Pitt fashion.   The enterprise was really
well conceived and well executed.   It is, I hope, a mere
beginning of what we ought long ago to have finished.'

In questions of patriotism it is dangerous to adopt an
ambiguous position.   Cobbett inevitably was misunderstood.   He was regarded as an incendiary and a traitor
by those in authority, and in either character was considered worthy of punishment.   But for a time he went
on unharmed.   So absorbed was he in current affairs that
outside the *Political Register* his literary life was almost
entirely barren.   His only enterprise of note between 1805
and 1815 was the commencement of *Cobbett's Complete
Collection of State Trials*, and in the actual preparation
of this work he had no share.   It was under the nominal
editorship of his assistant, John Wright, who delegated
the task of compilation to a professional lawyer, Thomas
Bayley Howell, a barrister of Lincoln's Inn.   Cobbett
had no personal liking for this man.

'He always seemed to me to be a little *screely* fellow. Sharp and clever, but feeble of body and not very strong of mind.'[1]

Howell had been an undergraduate of Christ Church, Oxford, and was distasteful to Cobbett on that account.

'I know,' he wrote to Wright, 'what your *college* gentlemen are. They always have, and will have the *insolence* to think themselves *our betters*; and our superior talents, and power, and weight, only excite their envy.'[2]

At the commencement of the negotiations concerning the State Trials, Howell wished to have a partner's share in the profits of the undertaking, but to this Cobbett would not consent.[3] He wrote to Howell proposing other terms, but failed to receive a prompt reply. He at once concluded that he was delaying in order to obtain a better bargain, and becoming very angry at the slight, determined to break off negotiations.

'Depend upon it,' he wrote to Wright, 'he thought I offered him too little. Depend on it, though I'll engage such an offer was never before made in the world. *Go* to him no more. *Send* to him no more. . . . Get an amanuensis, and leave me to give him his *congé*. What £2,400 certain not enough for the editing of such a collection! Damn his college insolence. What apology can he possibly make?'[4]

Wright, however, understood better than Cobbett the difficulties of the undertaking, and represented that Howell would be a very valuable coadjutor from his knowledge of the sources of information, while it would be dangerous to break with him and leave him to offer

---

[1] Cobbett to Wright, 9th December 1808. Add MS. 22907, f. 90.
[2] *Ibid.*, 7th December 1808. Add. MS. 22907, f. 88.
[3] *Ibid.*, 28th October, 12th Nov. 1808. Add. MS. 22907, ff. 64, 76.
[4] *Ibid.*, 7th December 1808. Add. MS. 22907, f. 88.

himself to a rival publisher. He convinced Cobbett that it was better to make at least a temporary arrangement.

'You have done very right about Mr. Howell. I am afraid he will not suit us, but if we get along for a Part or two, we shall be the better able to do without him, and he the less able to play us any trick.'[1]

Wright also persuaded Cobbett that Howell was not seeking for better terms, but he removed that suspicion only to find a darker substituted; '*Where* the devil can he be? I am afraid he is an opium-eater.'[2] However, shortly after, Cobbett received a note from Howell informing him 'all's well,' and though still puzzled by such casual treatment on the part of a scribbler, he suffered his resentment to subside. The first eleven volumes were issued under Howell's supervision between 1809 and 1811, and the work continued under his editorship until his death in 1815. In 1811 the control passed from Cobbett's hands, under circumstances to be related later,[3] and his name was replaced on the title-page by that of Howell. Twenty-two more volumes enabled Howell and his son to bring the collection to an end in 1826, but with these Cobbett had nothing to do.

[1] Cobbett to Wright, 9th Dec. 1808.　Add MS. 22907, f. 90.
[2] *Ibid.*　　　　　　　　　　　　[3] See pp. 167-173.

CHAPTER VI

COBBETT IN PRISON

WHEN the Tory ministry came into office in March 1807, Cobbett, realising that they were likely to take stronger measures than their Whig predecessors against hostile newspaper critics, was for some time extremely cautious in the conduct of his journal. Writing to his assistant John Wright, he says:

'I am resolved that with this letter I will begin a new *manner* of expressing myself. I see the fangs of the law open to grasp me, and I feel the necessity of leaving no hold for them, and even no ground for silly cavillers, upon the score of "coarseness or violence."' [1]

For a time these cautious counsels prevailed, but in 1808 he was roused into renewed vehemence by the commencement of the Peninsular War. He assailed the conduct of the campaign by the Government in a very damaging manner, and on the conclusion of the Convention of Cintra, made a violent attack on Sir Arthur Wellesley, insinuating, perhaps with some truth, that he owed his command rather to his political connections than to his military abilities.[2] A new administrative scandal increased the vehemence of his attacks. In January 1809, Colonel Wardle, a member of the House

---

[1] Cobbett to Wright, 10th May 1807, Add. MS. 22906, f. 282.

[2] See Cobbett to Folkestone, 9th October 1808, in *Creevy Papers*, 1903, i, 89-90.

of Commons, brought the most serious charges against the Duke of York, who held the office of Commander-in-Chief. The Duke was accused of permitting his mistress, Mrs. Clarke, to traffic in commissions, and although no charge of personal corruption was established against him, he was forced to resign his office. This grave scandal gave Cobbett an admirable opportunity for assailing the established order, and he availed himself of it fully. His *Register* was very widely read, and Government felt the force of its assaults. During 1808 and the early months of 1809 he daily became bolder, losing much of his old dread of legal coercion. On 4th February 1809, he replied to the complaint of Charles Yorke and Canning, that a series of libels had been published against the Duke of York, by citing and quoting the writings of Pope and Swift, Akenside and Churchill, as proofs that it was no new licence to inveigh against corruption, and he concluded a defence of public criticism of rulers by exclaiming:

'Upon one thing I am resolved, be the consequences to myself what they may, and that is, to continue to exercise the freedom of writing and of speaking, as my forefathers were wont to exercise it, as long as I have my senses, and the power of doing either one or the other.'

Yet all the while the *Register* was being keenly watched by every member of the Cabinet in the hope that an opportunity for punishment might arrive. On 7th May 1809, Charles Abbot, at that time Speaker of the House of Commons, records in his diary, that, while he was going home from church with Spencer Perceval, the Chancellor of the Exchequer, the conversation turned on Cobbett. Perceval said that:

' he thought Cobbett had at last committed himself in his paper upon the House of Commons' vote, for rejecting Lord Folke-stone's motion for a committee to inquire into the sale of all places in the State, etc.'

When Abbot was shown the paper, however, he did not think the attack more violent than others made daily in the opposition papers, nor did he consider that it would be of any use to proceed against Cobbett on account of it.[1] In fact to any one accustomed to modern freedom of criticism there is nothing very remarkable in the article. It is a clever commentary on Canning's speech in opposition to Folkestone's motion, and contains many general allegations of corruption, but no direct personal accusations. Perhaps the most pungent passage is one in which, addressing Canning, Cobbett says :

' No sir, there is no one but a fool or a rogue, who is so unjust as to accuse any of you " of having *nothing* in view but the emoluments of *office* "; for, seeming to bear in mind the maxim of St. Paul, that it is being worse than a heathen to neglect one's own kindred, most of the public men of our day, with filial and paternal and conjugal tenderness, take care to make pretty decent provision for their mothers and fathers, sisters and brothers, wives, children, and other relations ; there being from the maxim of the apostle only this trifling deviation, that he seems to have meant such provision to have proceeded from a man's own private means, while the provision we have been speaking of proceeds from the means of the public, and those means, too, of which members of the House of Commons are, by the constitution, considered as the stewards.'

Political intolerance had reached a high pitch in England when a Cabinet minister could contemplate a prosecution on the ground of such a paragraph as this.

[1] *Diary and Correspondence of Lord Colchester*, 1861, ii. 183.

K

A few weeks later Cobbett irretrievably compromised himself. On 24th June, the *Courier*, an evening newspaper, which had atoned for an earlier career of opposition by becoming a ministerial journal, published the following paragraph:

'The mutiny among the local militia which broke out at Ely, was fortunately suppressed on Wednesday by the arrival of four squadrons of the German Legion Cavalry from Bury, under the command of General Auckland. Five of the ring-leaders were tried by a court-martial, and sentenced to receive five hundred lashes each, part of which punishment they received on Wednesday, and a part was remitted. A stoppage for their knapsacks was the ground of complaint that excited this mutinous spirit, which occasioned the men to surround their officers, and demand what they deemed their arrears. The first division of the German Legion halted yesterday at Newmarket on their return to Bury.'

This incident raised Cobbett to extreme indignation. It angered him at once as a patriot, an old soldier, and an opponent of the Government. In the next number of the *Register* he selected the paragraph from the *Courier* as a motto and launched into a vehement comment:

'Local Militia and German Legion.—See the Motto, English Reader! See the motto, and then do pray recollect all that has been said about the way in which Buonaparte raises his soldiers. Well done, Lord Castlereagh! This is just what it was thought your plan would produce.[1] Well said, Mr. Huskisson. It really was not without reason that you dwelt with so much earnestness upon the great utility of the *foreign* troops, whom Mr. Wardle seemed to think of no utility at all.[2] Poor gentleman! he little

---

[1] Lord Castlereagh, the Secretary for War and the Colonies, had introduced a system which was retained till the end of the war, by which the regular army was to be fed by volunteering from the militia as well as by recruiting.

[2] See *Parliamentary Debates*, 1809, xiv. 1081-2, 1110-1.

imagined how a great genius might find useful employment for
such troops. He little imagined that they might be made the
means of compelling Englishmen to submit to that sort of
discipline, which is so conclusive to the producing in them a disposition to defend the country at the risk of their lives.   Let
Mr. Wardle look at my motto, and then say whether the German
soldiers are of *no use*.   *Five hundred lashes* each !   Aye, that is
right !   Flog them ; flog them ; flog them !   They deserve it, and
a great deal more.   They deserve a flogging at every meal time.
"Lash them daily, lash them duly."   What shall the rascals
dare to *mutiny*, and that, too, when the German Legion is so
near at hand !   Lash them, lash them, lash them !   They *deserve*
it.   O, yes ; they merit a double-tailed cat.   Base dogs !   What,
mutiny for the sake of *the price of a knapsack* !   Lash them !
Flog them !   Base rascals !   Mutiny for the price of a goat's
skin ; and, then, upon the appearance of the *German soldiers*,
they take a flogging as quietly as so many trunks of trees !—I do
not know what sort of a place ELY is ; but I really would like to
know how the inhabitants looked one another in the face, while
this scene was exhibiting in their town.   I should like to have
been able to see their faces, and to hear their observations to
each other, at the time.   This occurrence at home will, one
would hope, teach *the loyal* a little caution in speaking of the
means which Napoleon employs (or, rather, which they say he
employs), in order to get together and to discipline his conscripts.
There is scarcely any one of these loyal persons who has not, at
various times, cited the *hand-cuffings*, and other means *of force*,
said to be used in drawing out the young men of France ; there
is scarcely one of the loyal who has not cited these means as a
proof, a complete proof, that the people of France *hate Napoleon
and his government*, assist *with reluctance in his wars*, and would
fain see another revolution.   I hope, I say, that the loyal will,
hereafter, be more cautious in drawing such conclusions, now
that they see that our "gallant defenders" not only require
physical restraint in certain cases, but even a little blood drawn
from their backs, and that, too, with the aid and assistance of
German troops.   Yes ; I hope that the loyal will be a little more
upon their guard in drawing conclusions against Napoleon's

popularity. At any rate, every time they do, in future, burst out in execrations against the French for suffering themselves to be "chained together and forced at the point of the bayonet to do military duty," I shall just republish the passage which I have taken for a motto to the present sheet.'[1]

This attack was so violent, so damaging, and, in the eyes of the ministers, so mischievous, that they resolved to take action. Cobbett did not hear of their intention until three weeks later. On learning his danger, he wrote to Wright, his London assistant :

'I have a most serious business to impart to you, and that is, that I hear, from Mr. White,[2] that the hell-fire miscreants are about to prosecute me for the article about the *flogging of the local militia*. . . . It is quite useless to *fret* and *stew* about this. —I must meet it.—They may, probably, confine me for two years, but, that does not kill a man, and may, besides, produce even good effects, in more ways than one.'[3]

Wright took a more serious view of the situation than Cobbett, and, without his authority, attempted to approach the Government through John Reeves, the king's printer, whose friendship Cobbett had preserved in spite of his political change. On hearing of this, Cobbett wrote indignantly to Wright :

'I am fully prepared for the *worst*, and therefore, am no longer under any *anxiety*. I would rather be *gibbetted* than owe my life to the intercession, such as you speak of, and such as I am afraid you *half solicited*. I told you to keep very *quiet*. Ask no questions; only be sure to tell me precisely what you hear.—I am not afraid of them. Times are coming on when we shall all

---

[1] *Political Register*, 1st July 1809.
[2] Holt White, Cobbett's solicitor.
[3] Cobbett to Wright, 22nd July 1809, Add. MS. 22907, f. 177. The words in italics are underlined in the original.

have enough to do; but, in the meanwhile, I shall not worry myself to death with apprehension.'[1]

Three months later he said :

'I hold the thing in contempt; . . . I am no more afraid of the rascals than I would be of so many mice.—And, really, if we have an *honest* jury, it will be a famous thing altogether.'[2]

A little later he wrote :

'I have read the trial of Tooke all through.[3] . . . Really, I do not wonder at Sir F.'s[4] attachment to him. Never did man show such courage and so much public virtue! What villains he had to deal with! His life is a history of the damned hypocritical tyrannies of this jubilee reign.'[5]

In February 1810 the Government failed in an attempt to convict James Perry, the editor of the Whig *Morning Chronicle*, of seditious libel for asserting, in reference to the talk of a regency, that—

'Of all monarchs since the Revolution, the successor of George III. will have the finest opportunity of becoming nobly popular.'

Perry had only transcribed the paragraph from the *Examiner*, the organ of John and Leigh Hunt ; but his trial came on before theirs, and the jury found him not guilty.[6] Although Cobbett had often abused Perry soundly since his breach with the Whigs, he naturally

---

[1] Cobbett to Wright, 18th August 1809, Add. MS. 22907, f. 189.
[2] *Ibid.*, 19th November 1809, Add. MS. 22907, f. 216.
[3] Probably his trial for libel in 1777, when he was convicted, but possibly his trial for high treason in 1794, when he was acquitted. See Howell, *State Trials*, xx. 651-802 ; xxv. 1-748.
[4] Sir Francis Burdett.
[5] Cobbett to Wright, 8th January 1810, Add. MS. 22907, f. 234.
[6] *State Trials*, xxxi. 335-368.

testified the liveliest joy at his acquittal, and spoke enthusiastically of his service to the nation.[1]

Early in 1810 the House of Commons sent John Gale Jones, a democratic surgeon, to Newgate for announcing to the public the result of a debate on the Walcheren Expedition by means of a placard. A long letter, signed by Sir Francis Burdett,[2] was published in the *Political Register*, denying the right of the House to imprison any but its own members. This Perceval considered a breach of privilege, and he formed a resolve to commit Burdett to the Tower, and to order Cobbett's attendance at the Bar of the House.[3] But though Burdett was arrested in his house by an armed force a fortnight later, and remained in the Tower until the prorogation of Parliament towards the close of June, no action was taken against Cobbett. As Burdett's letter had been printed in the *Register*, that periodical was read to the House, and Cobbett remarked with grim satisfaction :

'So, then, the honourable House have, at last, resolved to have *The Register* read to them. That is one sign of amendment, and if they do but follow it up by a similar motion every week, it cannot fail to do them a great deal of good, if anything in the world can do them good.'[4]

In spite of this ordinary feeling of confidence, however, at times he looked forward to the ordeal with misgiving. He knew the merciless spirit of the ministry, and shrank from finding himself placed in their power by an adverse

---

[1] Cobbett to Wright, 25th March 1810, Add. MS. 22907, f. 253.
[2] Cobbett claimed that he composed it.
[3] Lord Colchester's *Diary*, ii. 240.
[4] Cobbett to Wright, 28th March 1810, Add. MS. 22907, f. 257.

verdict. The very uncertainty of his position shook him. Early in 1810 he remarked :

'I really do not know which I ought to ask for; a trial or a *nolle prosequi*. My character and fame call for the former; but, then, my health and my dearly beloved family call for the latter, or for anything that shall preclude the chance of a villainous sentence. However, I am, really, rather indifferent about the matter.'[1]

In May he learned that a prosecution was decided on, and on 15th June the case came on in the Court of King's Bench before Lord Ellenborough, the Lord Chief-Justice, a judge already noted for his severity towards political offenders. The prosecution was conducted by Sir Vicary Gibbs, who had made himself famous by his defence of Horne Tooke on the charge of high treason in 1794, but who now, as Attorney-General, prosecuted opinions which he had formerly defended. Cobbett had early resolved to conduct his own defence.

'Nothing upon earth, illness excepted, shall make me forego this resolution. I am also resolved to defend ; that is to justify ; and, to render the affair a great public question.'[2]

A few months before, Perry, conducting his own case, had obtained an acquittal, and at an earlier date, in 1777, Horne Tooke had defended himself against a somewhat similar charge of libel, and, though unsuccessful, had earned an immense reputation. But Tooke was a man of extraordinary forensic ability, and had actually studied for some terms at the Inner Temple before his father compelled him to take orders. Cobbett recognised Tooke's legal qualifications, but failed to comprehend

[1] Cobbett to Wright, 30th January 1810, Add. MS. 22907, f. 244.
[2] *Ibid.*, 19th November 1809, Add. MS. 22907, f. 215.

their importance. He thought he could turn a trial in an English court of law into a debate on general principles.

'Mine,' he said, 'must be a defence of a different sort [from Horne Tooke's]: less of law knowledge and more of a plain story and an appeal to the good sense and justice of my hearers.'[1]

He had no conception how seriously ignorance of methods of procedure might embarrass his defence. Besides, at this period of his life at any rate, his power as a speaker was very inferior to his ability as a writer. The fearless dogmatism and unqualified strength of assertion which characterised the controversial products of his pen, were not so marked when he addressed an audience by word of mouth. On this occasion his speech was disappointing. Once or twice there were flashes of eloquence, as when in defence of his censure of the court-martial he said :

'What! is every man who puts on a red coat, to be from that moment deserted by all the world; and is no tongue, no pen, ever to stir in his defence?'

But these gleams of fire died away into faltering hesitation. He continually qualified his arguments by damaging admissions of possible error. He complained that his cause had been prejudiced by the slanders of his opponents. Early in his defence his ignorance of legal rules brought him into difficulty. He had intended to show that much stronger things had been said concerning the cruel treatment of English soldiers by leading statesmen of the Whig party, than any contained in his

[1] Cobbett to Wright, 8th January 1810, Add. MS. 22907, f. 234.

own article. But unfortunately the collection he had
prepared of the utterances of Lord Grenville, Samuel
Whitbread, and other well-known politicians was entirely
composed of extracts from speeches delivered in Parliament, and when he began to read them he was at once
checked by Lord Ellenborough, who told him that he
could not allow speeches stated to have been spoken in
Parliament to be read to the jury, though he did not
object to extracts from other sources being brought
forward.   This completely upset Cobbett's argument.
He had relied on showing that there was nothing unusually severe in his comments, that in numerous cases
harsher censures had been passed, and that therefore it
was extravagant to represent his remarks as dangerous
to the community.   But he had forgotten that utterances
by a Member of Parliament in his place in the House
were specially privileged, and, as he was unprovided with
other instances of severe criticism, he could not establish
his contention.   Several times he endeavoured to introduce his extracts, but on each occasion he was sternly
checked by the judge. These rebuffs completely dis-
comfited him, and, after citing some instances of bad
behaviour on the part of the German Legion, he sat
down. No parts of his defence were more injudicious
than his deprecating references to his article, his admission that it 'was somewhat angry and hasty,' that
it was hyperbolical and 'perhaps clumsily and badly
written,' and his plea in excuse that 'it was certainly
written in a great hurry.'   It ought to have been clear
to so clever a man that his best chance was to enlist
the sympathies of the jury on behalf of the militiamen,
and on his own behalf as their champion, and that if he

himself admitted that his criticism was hasty and exaggerated, he would find it very difficult to persuade them that it was not also libellous. It is never quite fair to judge of the value of speech from the effect produced by a reproduction of it in print. But Francis Place, the Radical breeches-maker, who assisted Cobbett to prepare his defence and listened to its delivery, also speaks most disparagingly of its effect.

'Cobbett,' he says, 'made a long defence, a bad defence, and his delivery of it and his demeanour were even worse than his matter. He was not at all master of himself, and in some parts where he meant to produce a great effect he produced laughter. So ludicrous was he in one part the jury, the judge, and the audience all laughed at him. I was thoroughly ashamed of him, and ashamed of myself for being seen with him.'[1]

Cobbett called no witnesses and after his lame defence the Attorney-General had an easy task. His reply is chiefly noteworthy for his crushing rejoinder to Cobbett's complaint that he had been traduced by his political opponents and that in consequence of the misstatements made about him in the press, the jury could hardly have come into court unbiased:

'Mr. Cobbett—the most calumniated—the most libelled man in the whole world. I am not a constant reader of Mr. Cobbett's works, much of them is doubtless unknown to me, but I have certainly seen enough of them to be able to pronounce him not the most calumniated man in the world.'

Lord Ellenborough in charging the jury gave a strong opinion against the defendant:

[1] Wallas's *Life of Place*, 1898, p. 117. Place afterwards sided very strongly with Burdett in his quarrel with Cobbett, so that his description of Cobbett's failure may be heightened.

' In cases like the present, the law requires me to state my opinion to the jury, and where I have held a different opinion to that which I have of the present case, I have not withheld it from the jury. I do pronounce this to be a most infamous and seditious libel.'

The jury found the defendant guilty in five minutes, without leaving the box, and Cobbett having departed for Botley before the verdict, was immediately followed by a tipstaff of the court, who brought him back to London on 20th June to give bail for his appearance in court to receive judgment.[1]

Almost immediately after the verdict Cobbett resolved to try the plan by which he had succeeded in averting sentence in 1804 and to seek terms from Government: in return for an assurance that he would not be called upon to receive judgment, he was prepared to discontinue the *Political Register*. In a letter to Wright[2] he mentions that a suggestion had been made to him, but does not describe its character. It was probably a proposal that he should seek those good offices from John Reeves, which he had rejected before the trial.[3] At any rate within a week the negotiation had commenced. Cobbett prepared a Farewell Article for insertion in the *Register* and forwarded a copy to Reeves together with a statement of his former services and his claims on Government for indulgence.[4] In this article he gives as his reason for putting

---

[1] For a full report of the trial, see *The Times*, 16th June 1810.

[2] See Mr. E. Smith's *Life of Cobbett*, ii. 119. Mr. Smith quotes almost the entire letter, but does not give the date, and I cannot find the original among Wright's collection at the British Museum.

[3] See Reeves's evidence in the *Book of Wonders*, Part the Second, 1821, p. 42.

[4] Cobbett to Wright, 25th and 26th June 1810; Add. MS. 22907, ff. 279, 281.

an end to the *Register* that the country itself had condemned him through its representatives, the jury. He could not be reproached for deserting the cause of the press, for while several newspapers had attacked him, not one had uttered a word in his defence. He then proceeds to pledge himself never to publish anything anonymously, and states that he 'never will again, upon any account, indite, publish, write, or contribute towards any newspaper or other publication' so long as he lives.[1]

Cobbett believed that his submission would be accepted. On Wednesday the 27th June he sent the Farewell Article to Wright, saying:

'I enclose to you the remainder, and the last that I shall write for the *Register*. It is all dull enough, but I do not know what I could say more short of downright begging.'[2]

Wright himself did not believe that the ministers would be merciful, and he was keenly alive to other perils of the position. The overtures were getting known to the dismay of Cobbett's friends and the open joy of his foes. Convinced that Cobbett was being beguiled, he resolved on a bold step. Late on Wednesday afternoon he waited on Reeves and told him that unless he obtained a positive assurance that Cobbett would not be called on for judgment, he would not discontinue the *Register*, whatever directions he might receive from Cobbett. He then wrote to Cobbett warning him of his danger and telling him what he had said to Reeves. As it was too late for the post he made up a mail coach parcel and

---

[1] This article, though suppressed after it had been set up in type, was carefully preserved by Wright and published at a later date in his preface to the *Report of the Action, Wright* v. *Clement*, 1819.

[2] Add. MS. 22907, f. 282.

despatched it that night. On Thursday Cobbett received Wright's note and also a letter from Reeves which convinced him that the ministers were playing with him. After saying that his letter and enclosure had been handed to Mr. Yorke,[1] who would see what could be done on the subject with Mr. Perceval.[2] Reeves hinted that the Government might find themselves obliged to direct the Attorney-General to ask for judgment, but that even in that case Cobbett's submission would have great weight with the court in mitigation of the punishment inflicted.[3] Perceval in fact was resolved not to forego vengeance, but he was willing to obtain the additional satisfaction of submission. Cobbett was too shrewd to be beguiled by so open a snare. He wrote instantly to Wright :

‘ I will not sacrifice fortune without securing freedom in return. It would be both baseness and folly. . . . Now therefore unless, *before* you get this, you know for a CERTAINTY, that I am not to be called upon, *suppress the article sent you*, stuff in something to fill up *one sheet*, and put the little *notice* I now send you at the head of that sheet. Leave me to manage the rest. In conversation with *any* one say you do *not know* what I intend to do ; that it will depend upon circumstances and the like.’ [4]

In truth it was high time that Cobbett broke off the negotiation. Members of Government treated his offers with scorn. According to Wright the Attorney-General remarked ‘ that —— —— Cobbett has offered to give up his *Register* provided we do not call him up for judgment.’

---

[1] The first Lord of the Admiralty.
[2] Then Prime Minister. He succeeded the Duke of Portland who died in November 1809.
[3] Reeves to Cobbett. Add. MS. 22907, f. 291.
[4] Add. MS. 22907, f. 283.

Another member of administration is reported to have said, 'Why, here's Cobbett squeaking; he'll give up the *Register*, if you won't send him to Newgate,' and suggested that possibly he might go a little further and write for Government. The reply to this was 'Damn him, he has changed too often already—he would not be worth a louse for us!'[1] On the other hand the venerable Major Cartwright, who had a sincere admiration for Cobbett's effort in the cause of freedom,[2] came to Wright in great dismay on hearing the rumour.

Cartwright was reassured, but the failure of the negotiation left Cobbett nothing to do but to await the utmost that the ministry could inflict. He felt the strain acutely. On 2nd July[3] he wrote fretfully to Wright, who had urged him to celebrate the rupture of negotiations by writing 'something powerful' in the *Register*.

'If you had my affairs to arrange and six children about you, you would not, I imagine, think much about writing "something powerful this week." I must do as well as I can till this suspense is over, and then I shall do much better.'[4]

The suspense was soon ended. On 5th July he was called up for judgment, and on 9th July he was sentenced. Such an interest was taken in the trial that from an early hour Westminster Hall was crowded and the court could only be approached with difficulty. The throng was so dense when the judges entered that the court could not be cleared, and Lord Ellenborough was obliged to

---

[1] *The Times*, 11th July 1812.
[2] See Miss Cartwright's *Life and Correspondence of Major Cartwright*, 1826, i. 327-28.
[3] This is the most probable date. The letter is only dated 'Monday, noon.'
[4] Add. MS. 22907, f. 294.

allow strangers to remain.   Cobbett was condemned to
imprisonment for two years, to pay a fine of a thousand
pounds to the king, and at the end of the two years to
give bail himself in three thousand pounds, with two
sureties in one thousand each, for his keeping the peace
for seven years.   He himself seemed little affected by
the sentence : his deportment during its delivery was
unembarrassed and he left the court with a smile on his
face.[1]   His printer, Thomas Curson Hansard, and his
publishers, John Budd and Richard Bagshaw were also
prosecuted for the libel and sentenced, Hansard, to three
months' imprisonment, and Budd and Bagshaw to two
months respectively.   Hansard had only printed the
Register from the beginning of 1809, so that he early
paid the penalty for being connected with Cobbett.

Cobbett's sentence excited very various opinions.
James Swann, a papermaker, who supplied Cobbett's
publications, said that the sentence was generally condemned, even Cobbett's most violent opponents admitting
that it was too severe.   On the other hand Cobbett himself, in a vigorous passage, described both verdict and
sentence as being received by his enemies with exultation :

'The Borough-mongers had me shut up in Newgate. . . . They
thought, that this horrible punishment, which was inflicted only
because they dreaded my pen, but, professedly because I had
expressed my indignation at the flogging of English Local
Militia Men, in the heart of England, under the force of
Hanoverian bayonets and sabres ; they thought, that this savage
sentence would break my heart, or, at least, *silence me for ever*.
It was, indeed, a bloody stab.   They thought they had got rid
of me.   Just after the verdict of guilty was found, Perceval met

---

[1] *The Times*, 6th and 10th July 1810.

his brother-in-law Redesdale at the portal of Westminster Hall. They *shook hands and gave each other joy!* Chucklehead but crafty Curtis [1] met Tierney in the Hall. "Ah, a, ah! We have got him at last," said Curtis. "Poor Cobbett! Let him be *bold now!*" The old place-hunter answered: "Damn him! I hope they'll *squeeze* him!" They did squeeze indeed; but their claws, hard as they were, did not squeeze hard enough.' [2]

At a later time Cobbett depicted in unfading colours the grief which the sentence occasioned his children and his own feelings of hatred towards his oppressors.

'The blow was, to be sure, a terrible one, and, oh God! how was it felt by these poor children! It was in the month of July, when the horrible sentence was passed upon me. My wife having left her children in the care of her good and affectionate sister, was in London, waiting to know the doom of her husband. When the news arrived at Botley, the three boys,—one eleven, the other nine, and the other seven years old, were hoeing cabbages in that garden, which had been the source of so much delight. When the account of the savage sentence was brought to them, the youngest could not for some time be made to understand what a *jail* was, and when he did, he all in a tremor exclaimed, "Now, I am sure, William, that Papa is not in a place *like that!*" The other in order to disguise his tears, and smother his sobs, fell to work with the hoe, and *chopped about like a blind person.* This account, when it reached me, affected me more, filled me with deeper resentment, than any other circumstance. And oh, how I despise the wretches who talk of my *vindictiveness*; of my *exultation* at the confusion of those who inflicted those sufferings! How I despise the base creatures, the crawling slaves, the callous and cowardly hypocrites, who affect to be "*shocked*" (tender souls!) at my expressions of *joy*, at the death of Gibbs, Ellenborough, Perceval, Liverpool, Canning, and the rest of the tribe, that I have

[1] Sir William Curtis, Lord Mayor of London in 1795-96, and an army contractor.
[2] *Political Register*, 22nd August 1818.

COBBETT CONFOUNDED.

already seen out;[1] and at the fatal workings of *that system*, for endeavouring to check which, I was thus punished! What! I am to forgive, am I, injuries like this, and that, too, without any *atonement*? Oh no! I have not so read the Holy Scriptures; I have not from them learned that I am not to rejoice at the fall of unjust foes; and it makes a part of my happiness, to be able *to tell millions of men* that I do thus rejoice, and that I have the means of calling on so many just and merciful men to rejoice with me.'[2]

Cobbett was removed to Newgate immediately after sentence. Of his place of confinement he wrote:

'I was well aware, that a prison, though I had never seen the inside of one in my life, must differ very materially from a dwelling-house. I was aware of many of the disagreeable circumstances attendant on such a state; but I had no idea of the *reality*. That part of the prison, to which I was committed, consisted of a yard and divers rooms. The rooms were numerous, the yard about 35 feet by 25 feet. Each room contained, or was intended to contain two, three, or more, beds. Each bedroom was locked up at about nine o'clock at night, and kept locked till about seven o'clock in the morning. The doorway leading from the passage of the rooms to the yard, was also locked. The windows were barred with iron. The walls that surrounded the yard were the sides of houses; and of course there could be little sun or air. But the *companions*! What companions had I? Men guilty of the most odious and detestable crimes. Swindling, Fraud, Embezzlement, and even of those crimes which are too horrid to name, but which have been committed by so many within the last two or three years. With wretches like these I was destined by my sentence to dwell for two years; I, who had never *seen* the inside of a jail in my life time, and who, amidst all the temptations of youth, had been eight years in a regular regiment without ever being, in a single instance, confined for a single moment! One fact will enable the reader to judge of the society I was sentenced to

---

[1] Written in 1829.   [2] *Advice to Young Men*, 1837, pp. 283-84.

L

keep for two years. There was a man taken out and *sent to Botany Bay* two days after I entered the prison. He was taken out of the same part of the prison, and, perhaps, out of the very room, in which I was to have slept for two years, if I lived so long. Here was I, then, sentenced to live for *two years* amongst *felons* and men guilty of *unnatural crimes*, and to pay a thousand pounds *to the King*; aye, *to the King*, at the end of that time! I have three sons; and, if any one of them ever forgets *this*, may he that instant be . . . not stricken dead; but, worse than that, bereft of his senses. May he become both *rotten* and *mad*. May he, after having been a gabbling, slavering half-idiot all the prime of his life, become, in his last days, loathsome to the sight, and stinking in the nostril! I am, however, not at all afraid, that any child of mine will merit this curse; for, they have all been shown the horrid place where their father was sentenced to be imprisoned, and, I am satisfied that nothing more will be necessary. From the place and the society here described I was ransomed by my purse; but while I say this, I must beg to be understood, as hinting no complaint against the keeper, who gave up the best part of his own house to me, from whom I and my family and friends always received the most civil and kind treatment, and whom I believe to be a very honest and humane man.'[1]

Cobbett's first anxiety after his incarceration was in regard to the future of his family, liable to be left penniless owing to his financial difficulties.

'On the third day after I entered the accursed jail, I wrote [to a friend] requesting him, in case of my death, to send for, and take care of my wife and children. From him I, *as quickly as possible*, received an answer, containing amongst others these words: "Give thyself no trouble about Nancy and the children. If thee should die, which I hope thee will not for many years to come, thy dear family shall find a home under my roof, and shall be to me and to all of us *as our own kindred*." . . . And who was this man? It was James Paul, a Quaker farmer, of Lower

[1] *Political Register*, 18th July 1812.

Dublin township in the State of Pennsylvania; a native American, from a Yorkshire father and mother; a man, on whom I had never conferred a favour to the amount of the value of a pin; but under whose hospitable roof I and my wife had spent many and many a happy day, always treated as a son and daughter of the family, though both of us *English*, and in no way related to this family.

'Having written this letter to Mr. Paul, I was quite tranquil on the score of provision for wife and children. I wanted not to wait for *an answer*: all that was necessary was, to make *sure of his getting my letter*, and of that I took care. So that, the truth is, the greatest load of all was off from my mind at the end of three days. I wanted *no answer* to my letter; I was *sure* that my family would be provided for: I was *sure* that the tigers would never be able to make them beg their bread, nor to cram them into a workhouse; and it is curious, but not more so than true, that I took delight in reflecting on the innocent and happy life that my children would lead in case of my perishing in the hellish jail. . . . Such was the friendship of James Paul. No wonder that I named a son after him, and no wonder that that son should, when he signs, never fail to stick the *Paul* into his name; a name that will be honoured by my children's children, as synonymous with all that is frank, sincere, benevolent, kind, and generous.'[1]

Other manifestations of kindness helped to console him. He was fortunate enough to be in the custody of the sheriff, Matthew Wood, himself an ardent reformer, who did all he could for his comfort and permitted visitors free access to him. Among these who came frequently was Francis Maseres, cursitor baron of the Exchequer, who invariably appeared in his wig and gown, in order, as he said, to show his abhorrence of the sentence. He had also many other sympathisers.

'During my imprisonment the conduct of my friends was such as was naturally to be expected from men who regarded

[1] *Political Register*, 10th April 1830.

me as suffering in the public cause. The attentions of all sorts ; the acts of real, solid service, were as numerous and as great, perhaps, as any man ever received in a like space of time. But the circumstance of this sort, which gave me the most pleasure, was, that during the two years, I was visited by persons whom I had never seen before, from *one hundred and ninety-seven cities and towns of England, Scotland, and Ireland,* the greatest part of whom came to me as the deputies of some society, club, or circle of people in their respective places of residence. I had the infinite satisfaction to learn from the gentlemen who thus visited me, that my writings had induced those who had read them to think. This fact, indeed, of being visited by persons from almost every considerable town in the kingdom, speaks a language that cannot be misunderstood.'[1]

Cobbett's life in prison was one of activity. He had numerous interests to occupy his time. In the first place he had to superintend the management of his farm at Botley. He has described how, while attending to the farm, he also furthered the education of his children.

'I had a *farm* in hand. It was necessary that I should be constantly informed of what was doing. I gave *all the orders,* whether as to purchases, sales, ploughing, sowing, breeding, in short, with regard to everything, and the things were in endless number and variety, and always full of interest. My eldest son and daughter could now write well and fast. One or the other of these was always at Botley, and I had with me, having hired the best part of the keeper's house, one or two besides, either their brother or sister. We had a hamper with a lock and two keys, which came up once a week, or oftener, bringing me fruit and all sorts of country fare. . . . This hamper, which was always at both ends of the line looked for with the most lively interest, became our *school.* It brought me *a journal* of *labours, proceedings,* and *occurrences,* written on paper of shape and size uniform, and so contrived, as to margins, as to admit of binding. The journal used, when my eldest son was the writer, to be

[1] *Political Register,* 18th July 1812.

interspersed with drawings of our dogs, colts, or anything that he wanted me to have a correct idea of. The hamper brought me plants, bulbs, and the like, that I might *see* the size of them, and almost every one sent his or her *most beautiful flowers*, the earliest violets, and primroses, and cowslips, and bluebells, the earliest twigs of trees, and in short everything that they thought calculated to delight me. The moment the hamper arrived, I, casting aside everything else, set to work to answer *every question*, to give new directions, and to add anything likely to give pleasure at Botley. *Every hamper* brought one "*letter*," as they called it, if not more, from every child, and to *every* letter I wrote *an answer*, sealed up and sent to the party, being sure that that was the way to produce other and better letters, for though they could not read what I wrote, and though their own consisted at first of mere *scratches*, and afterwards, for a while, of a few words written down for them to imitate, I always thanked them for their "*pretty letter*," and never expressed any wish to see them *write better*, but took care to write in a very neat and plain hand *myself*, and to do up my letter in a very neat manner.

'Thus, while the ferocious tigers thought I was doomed to incessant mortification, and to rage that must extinguish my mental powers, I found in my children, and in their spotless and courageous, affectionate mother, delights to which the callous hearts of these tigers were strangers. "Heaven first taught letters for some wretch's aid." How often did this line of Pope occur to me, when I opened the little "*spuddling* letters" from Botley. This correspondence occupied a good part of my time, I had all the children with me turn and turn about; and in order to give the boys exercise, and to give the two eldest an opportunity of beginning to learn French, I used, for a part of the two years to send them for a few hours a day to an Abbé, who lived in Castle Street, Holborn. All this was a great relaxation to my mind, and when I had to return to my literary labours, I returned *fresh* and cheerful, full of vigour, and *full of hope* of finally seeing my unjust and merciless foes at my feet; and that, too, without caring a straw on whom their fall might bring calamity, so that my own family were safe, because, say what any one might, the *community taken as a whole*, had *suffered this thing to be done unto us.*

'The paying of the work people, the keeping of the accounts, the referring to books, the writing and reading of letters, this everlasting mixture of amusement with book learning, made me, almost to my own surprise, find at the end of two years that I had a parcel of *scholars* growing up about me, and long before the end of the time I had *dictated many Registers* to my two eldest children. Then there was *copying* out of books, which taught *spelling correctly*. The calculations about the forming of affairs forced arithmetic upon us; the *use*, the *necessity* of the thing, led to the study. By and by we had to look into the *laws* to know what to do about the *highways*, about the *game*; about the *poor*, and all rural and *parochial* affairs. I was, indeed, by the fangs of government, defeated in my fondly-cherished project of making my sons farmers on their own land, and keeping them from all temptations to seek vicious and enervating enjoyments; but those fangs, merciless as they had been, had not been able to prevent me from laying in for their lives a store of useful information, habits of industry, care, and sobriety, and a taste for innocent, healthful, and manly pleasures; the fangs had made me and them pennyless, but had not been able to take from us our health, or our mental possessions, and these were ready for application as circumstances might ordain.'[1]

But while Cobbett thus kept up his spirits by tending his farm and educating his children, his attention was frequently distracted by more harassing cares. Owing to his law expenses, which, with his heavy fine, amounted to six thousand pounds, he found himself on the verge of financial ruin. His affairs, for some time past, had been in a disordered state. His land at Botley was mortgaged, and he had other outstanding liabilities.

'Every one will easily imagine,' he said, in a heightened picture of his first days in prison, 'that every debt that I owed,

[1] *Advice to Young Men*, 1837, pp. 284-88.

of every description, came pouring in for payment. . . . Almost every one stood aloof except my creditors (never the last to visit you in such a season), who pressed on amain, so that I really forgot that I was in a prison, so great and so numerous were the torments arising from my pecuniary concerns, which, if I had been at large, would have given me no trouble and no care at all. I was looked upon as a man *given over by the doctors*; and every one to whom I owed a shilling, brought me sighs of sorrow, indeed; but, along with these, brought me his *bill*.'

In fact, in spite of Cobbett's offhand manner of speaking of his finances, he was seriously involved. While at Botley, he had been content to live a country life, leaving to his assistant, Wright, the entire management of his literary affairs. He had kept no accounts and made no investigations. All transactions with printers, publishers, paper-makers, and other tradesmen, were left entirely in Wright's hands. Wright, however, as Cobbett should have known, was by no means a competent man of business. He had at a former time made shipwreck of his own affairs.

The history of Cobbett's dealings with Wright forms a dark and doubtful chapter, beset at every step with contradictory statements. John Wright was the son of a clerk in a manufacturing house at Norwich. In early life he came to London, and afterwards set up as a bookseller in Piccadilly, opposite Old Bond Street, where his shop became the general morning resort of the friends of Pitt's ministry, as Debrett's was of the opposition. He became Cobbett's London agent, and lodged him in his house on his arrival in England in 1800. Two years later he failed in his business, and found himself in Cobbett's debt, and early in 1803 Cobbett had him confined in the Fleet. On the circumstances of this imprisonment a direct conflict of evidence exists. Cobbett asserts that the committal was made with Wright's knowledge and consent; while Wright maintains that he was enticed to Peel's coffee-house, arrested there, and thrown into prison.[1] He was shortly after released, and entered Cobbett's service. Cobbett draws a vivid picture of his destitute condition at this time.

'The fact is he was totally friendless; he had not a soul to give him or lend him a penny; relations, parents, every one had turned their backs on him. He was but at one little remove from beggary. From this state I raised him; I, in all human probability, preserved him from the ranks of the army or from utter destruction. I voluntarily put him in the way of living reputably and even of gaining a competence for old age. . . . He has been lodged, fed, and nursed, in my house, weeks and months, without the cost of a farthing; when he had not a soul to give or lend him a meal; when he was houseless, bedless, breakfastless, and almost shirtless, compassion and not interest, dictated to me and to Mrs. Cobbett to feed and lodge him; and, to such misery was he reduced, that we paid for his very washing.'[2]

Without rhetoric, the facts are that Wright entered Cobbett's service in 1803, and lived for a time as a member of his household, and afterwards in a room in Panton Square. He acted as assistant-editor of the *Political Register*, read all Cobbett's manuscript contributions in order to eliminate indiscreet utterances, and to correct the grammar and phraseology,[3] and superintended all the details of sending the periodical to press. Also, as has been stated already,[4] he acted as editor of the *Parlia-*

---

[1] For Cobbett's statement, see Add. MS. 31126, f. 103.
[2] Add. MS. 31126, ff. 111, 112.
[3] See Add. MS. 22906, f. 29.   [4] See pp. 114-17.

mentary Debates and the *Parliamentary History*, and
supervised the issue of the *State Trials*. In addition he
performed innumerable domestic services. He looked
after his house when Cobbett was away from town, and
Cobbett's letters to him teem with commissions for himself and his family. He was constantly employed in
Cobbett's money matters. The following letter may
serve as an instance of Cobbett's manner of writing to
him :

'I have received fifteen pounds from you this day by post ;
but, no newspaper of any sort has come to hand this day ! This
is the devil. This is just what would drive me mad. Pray
see into the cause instantly. Send a packet by mail-coach on
Wednesday night by all means.' [1]

Here is another, which illustrates Cobbett's financial
methods :

'Damn Le Maire. Pray settle the matter somehow or other,
and may I suffer death, when I am so caught again. See the
damned lawyer and settle somehow.'

This is endorsed ; 'Paid by Mr. Budd's acceptance
£53 10s.' [2]

In return for these services Wright was entitled to two-
thirds of the profits of *Cobbett's Parliamentary Debates*
and to half the profits on the *Parliamentary History* and
the *State Trials*. These terms at first sight appear
liberal, but as a matter of fact none of these publications realised any profit while they were in Cobbett's
hands, so that actually Wright was entitled to no re-

---

[1] Cobbett to Wright, 23rd December 1805, Add. MS. 22906, f. 116.
[2] *Ibid.*, 9th November 1807, Add. MS. 31126, f. 22.

muneration for his labours upon them. For his other work he received nothing. To this fact Hansard bore emphatic witness at a later date in the libel action, Wright *v.* Clement. In reply to the question, ' How was Mr. Wright remunerated ? ' he said :

' I happen to know that he was not remunerated at all ; even his incidental expenses were denied, unless, for instance, he produced the back of every twopenny post letter.'

To the further interrogation :

' Then he never had remuneration, or anything allowed him, unless he could produce a voucher ? ' he answered, ' No ; not one farthing.'[1]

Under these circumstances, although Cobbett may have been perfectly sincere in his statement that he befriended him through ' compassion and not interest,' it is plain that he obtained a valuable servant on very moderate terms. The worth of Wright's services was, however, literary rather than financial. He kept no systematic accounts, and Cobbett justly complained that he failed to inform him of the inadequacy of the returns from the *Debates,* the *History,* and the *Trials.* Consequently Cobbett had an exaggerated view of the pecuniary value of these publications. When his heavy law expenses had to be met he contemplated relieving himself by disposing of the copyright. Before this was done it was necessary that his accounts with Wright should be settled. Then or earlier it was discovered that the actual sale of these periodicals had not equalled the preliminary expenses.

[1] *Report of the Action Clement* v. *Wright, taken in Shorthand by Mr. George Farquharson,* 1819, p. 30.

It is obvious, therefore, that Wright, in order to live, for he had no other means, must have anticipated some part of his share of the profits. He himself acknowledged that there was a balance against him of about £500, but Cobbett demanded of him a full account of all his pecuniary transactions, accompanied by vouchers, receipts, and other testimony. This demand filled Wright with dismay. He was conscious that to satisfy it was beyond his power, and he represented that the complicated nature of the accounts rendered it impossible. In 1808 Cobbett himself had written to him, when refusing Howell's request to be allowed a partners' share in the profits of the *State Trials*, saying,

'Only think of having another person invested with a right, a *legal* right, to make us account, *us* whose accounts the devil himself would never unravel. I would not take such a weight upon myself for all the profits of all the books in the universe. No, no; you and I were never made to have our accounts examined by anybody but ourselves.'[1]

But now he was inexorable and Wright finally produced what documents he could. His only memoranda for most of the sums he had transmitted to Cobbett were Cobbett's informal acknowledgments in the course of his correspondence. When he had made as adequate a statement as was in his power, Cobbett claimed that there was a deficit of £12,000, due to some extent to liability as partner for a portion of the expenses of printing and publishing the *History*, the *Debates*, and the *Trials*. After a good deal of wrangling the matter was referred for legal arbitration to William Cooke of

---

[1] Cobbett to Wright, 28th October 1808, Add. MS. 22907, f. 64.

Lincoln's Inn, still remembered for his book on bankrupt laws, who decided in Cobbett's favour for £6500. There were some very sharp passages between Cobbett and Wright during the proceedings. Cobbett constantly charged Wright with debiting him with sums which he had not received. It is impossible to determine the exact truth in regard to the matter, for only Cobbett's account of the transactions survives and that in a very incomplete state,[1] in the shape of the rough drafts of several memorials prepared by him for submission to various officials. They are filled with the bitterest accusations against Wright, and assert that he was again and again convicted of peculation. But when some time later these accusations were made the subject of a libel action, Cobbett virtually admitted their falsity by abandoning the plea of justification, which he had at first entered. On the other hand, as has been already shown, Wright must have been to some extent in Cobbett's debt, but it is unlikely that he owed so large a sum as £6500, even when his liabilities as a partner for preliminary expenses were included. His careless book-keeping must have rendered it impossible for him to account for many sums that passed through his hands and for all of these he would be liable. He was unable to satisfy the arbitrator's award and was forced to mortgage his share in the *Parliamentary History* and *Debates* and in the *Collection of State Trials*. Cobbett, also being pressed for money, was compelled to sell his interest in those works, and finally, after a great deal of wrangling, the entire property passed into Hansard's hands, who removed Cobbett's name from the title-page of the *Parlia-*

[1] In Add. MS. 31126.

mentary Debates, substituting his own, and continued Wright in his post of editor. Hansard also removed Cobbett's name from the *Collection of State Trials*, replacing it by Howell's. Thus by parting with the greater part of his literary property and by availing himself of the liberality of friends, among whom Colonel Bosville and Sir Francis Burdett may be particularly mentioned, Cobbett was enabled, though seriously impoverished, to preserve his farm at Botley and to realise a sufficient sum for his immediate needs.

The time which was not absorbed by the importunities of his creditors, the care of his family, and the attentions of his friends, was devoted by Cobbett chiefly to the conduct of the *Register*, which his quarrel with Wright threw, early in 1811, entirely into his hands. His articles on political and social subjects were numerous, but, with one exception, were hardly of permanent interest. That exception was the important series of letters on the financial state of the nation entitled 'Paper against Gold,' which appeared in the *Political Register* in 1810 and 1811. For some time past the high price of bullion had attracted attention. This rise, together with the fall of the exchange, became especially marked in 1809, and in September Ricardo commenced to write a series of letters in the *Morning Chronicle* under the title, 'The High Price of Bullion, a Proof of the Depreciation of Bank Notes,' in which he showed that English paper money had considerably depreciated from its face value since the passage of the Bank Restriction Act in 1797, which rendered it inconvertible. This doctrine ran counter to the more generally received theory according to which the value of paper money had remained normal, while that of gold and silver had considerably appreciated owing to the increased demand for them in consequence of the war. The Bullion Committee, which was appointed a few months later, in making its report in September 1810, adopted most of the principles laid down by Ricardo, and recommended a resumption of cash payments as a suitable remedy for the inconveniences consequent on the depreciation. In the following session, Francis Horner, who had been chiefly concerned in obtaining the appointment of the committee, moved a series of sixteen resolutions embodying their opinions. He was, however, strenuously resisted by Government, which regarded the proposal for the resumption of cash payments as fraught with peril, and his resolutions were rejected. A few days later a set of counter-resolutions introduced by Vansittart, who shortly after became Chancellor of the Exchequer, were proposed and carried. These resolutions, which had been drawn up at Perceval's request, affirmed that an immediate resumption of cash payments was undesirable, that the restriction had no connection with the unfavourable state of the exchanges, and that the promissory notes of the Bank of England were held in public estimation to be equivalent to the legal coin of the realm. This last conclusion occasioned considerable ridicule as it was perfectly well known that bank notes were worth only about eighty per cent. of their face value in specie. But, notwithstanding Canning's declaration that no assembly of reasonable men could be persuaded to give their concurrence, all the resolutions were passed. As a necessary corollary a bill was passed in July making bank notes legal tender, avowedly because gold was so appreciated that for currency purposes it was unprocurable. The notoriety attained by this discussion and the fact that the Government was maintaining a bad cause induced Cobbett to enter the field.

He has left an interesting account of his final decision :

'The next day after Gibbs, Ellenborough, and their associates, had got me safe into Newgate, an American friend of mine, who had the clearest and soundest head of almost any man I ever knew in my life, and for whom I had and still have a very great personal regard, came to see me in a very miserable hole, though better than that to which I had been sentenced, and from which I finally ransomed myself at the expense, for *lodging alone* of *twelve hundred pounds*. Being seated, one of us on each side of a little bit of a table, he said, looking up into my face, with his arms folded upon the edge of the table, "Well ! they have *got you*, at last. And *now what will you do*?" After a moment or two I answered "What do you think I ought to do?" He then gave me his opinion, and entered pretty much into a sort of plan of proceeding. I heard him out and then, I spoke to him, in much about these words : "No, Dickins, that will never do. This nation is drunk, it is mad as a March hare, and mad it will be till this beastly frolic (the war) is over. The only mode of proceeding to get satisfaction requires great patience. The nation must suffer at last, and greatly and dreadfully suffer, and in that suffering it will come to its reason, and to that justice of sentiment which are now wholly banished. I shall make no immediate impression by tracing the paper system to its deadly root. The common people will stare at me, and the rich ruffians will sneer ; but the time must come when all will listen ; and my plan is to *write that now* which I can hold up to the teeth of my insolent enemies and taunt them with in the hour of their distress." "Aye," said he, "but the *worms* may be taunting you before that time,"—"No matter," said I "for though fame, after the worms have been at work, is a foolish thing, recollect that I have *no other line to pursue*. By pursuing this, I secure a *chance* of final success and satisfaction, and by no other can I perceive a possibility of obtaining even that chance." I then described to him the outline of what I intended to do with regard to the paper system ; and after passing a very pleasant afternoon, during which we selected and rejected several titles, we at last fixed upon that of "*Paper against Gold,*" which I began to write and to publish in a few weeks afterwards, and which, at the end of thirteen years, I hold up to the noses of the insolent foes who then exulted over me, and tell them, "This is what you got for my having been sentenced to New-gate ; this was the produce of that deed by which it was hoped and believed that I was pressed down never to rise again." I did not expect that the public would pay attention to what I wrote. I cared nothing about it. I no more looked for any effect from it within ten years than a farmer looks for the wheat harvest in March. But I was sure that the time of harvest would come : I was quite sure of that ; and I enjoyed by antici-pation more pleasure, so far as I know, than I enjoy at this moment.'[1]

In the treatise itself he says that, after seeking for instruction on questions of finance from Adam Smith, George Chalmers, and others without much success, he read in 1803 Paine's *Decline and Fall of the English System of Finance.*

'Here,' he said, 'was no mud to obscure my view ; the stream was clear and strong : I saw the whole matter in its true light, and neither pamphleteers nor speechmakers were, after that, able to raise a momentary puzzle in my mind.'[2]

It would of course be idle to expect from Cobbett any profundity of reasoning on the subject. The value of his

---

[1] *Political Register,* 20th July 1822.
[2] *Paper against Gold,* ed. 1815, p. 442.

contribution lay in its clearness of arrangement, which made it easily intelligible to the majority of his readers. He commanded a large audience and his advocacy of the abolition of paper money was sufficient to make it an article of faith with many advanced reformers. His treatise appeared in the form of letters addressed to the people in and about Salisbury, who were, at the time, suffering greatly from the failure of a bank in that city. Cobbett was not only opposed to an inconvertible paper currency, but to a paper currency of any kind. He vehemently assailed the institution of the national debt, maintaining that, while it was the inevitable result of the nation's appetite for war, it was no less certain to bring about the destruction of its prosperity. While deserving considerable credit for insisting that to decree the resumption of cash payments would not in itself be sufficient to restore the credit of the Bank of England, an assumption made by the Bullion Committee, he was inclined too much to assert that depreciation of the currency was the inevitable result of any increase in the amount of paper in circulation, making no allowance for the growth of commercial transactions in the country. But whatever the theoretical value of Cobbett's economic opinions, he gave them henceforward a prominent place in his utterances. The letters entitled *Paper against Gold* appeared in the *Political Register* between 30th August 1810 and 2nd August 1811. They were twenty-eight in number and were republished in two volumes in 1815, with four additional letters and an appendix. Several subsequent editions appeared, the latest being that of 1828.

Long after the publication of these letters, in fact

M

almost to the close of his life, Cobbett continued to give his views on finance and the currency a prominent place in the *Register*. He deserves credit for pointing out, what was generally ignored, that to permit the holders of stock created during the period of depreciation to reap the full benefit of the resumption of cash payments in the enhanced value of their holdings would be an act of injustice to the general body of taxpayers. He insisted that before the resumption of cash payments the National Debt must be abolished, otherwise the nation would be crushed by exchanging a debt in depreciated paper for one in gold. In accordance with these opinions he confidently asserted, on the passage of Peel's Bill in 1819, that it would be impossible to give it full and immediate effect, and he offered, if he were mistaken, to give Lord Castlereagh leave 'to put me on a gridiron and broil me alive, while Sidmouth stirs the fire, and Canning stands by making a jest of my groans.'[1] He was not altogether mistaken in his predictions. Although the date of Peel's Bill is rightly regarded as marking the return of the country to a sound financial policy, yet it was impossible to give full and immediate effect to the changes which those who supported Peel had in contemplation. It was found necessary from time to time to pass a number of measures to mitigate the violence of the remedy, and in spite of these palliatives the heavy taxation necessitated by the burden of the debt occasioned so much distress, that in all probability the country was only saved from grave economic disaster by the extraordinary development of its industries, and the consequent increase in its wealth. Cobbett stoutly

[1] *Political Register*, 13th Nov. 1819.

"The Gridiron."

Lord Althorp: "Oh! positively you must have a broil."
Cobbett: "Ah mammy, don't ask me."
Sir R. Peel: "You cannot object to so equitable an adjustment."

maintained to the end of his life that his prognostications had been correct. He frequently placed a woodcut of a gridiron at the head of the *Register*, and on 9th April 1826 he held a Feast of the Gridiron at the London Tavern to celebrate the fulfilment of his prophecies up to that time.

CHAPTER V

COBBETT AND PARLIAMENTARY REFORM

ON Cobbett's release from Newgate, on 9th July 1812, he was entertained at dinner at the 'Crown and Anchor' Tavern in the Strand by his political admirers, Sir Francis Burdett taking the chair, and about six hundred persons being present. On the morning of the same day a vehement attack upon his conduct had appeared in *The Times*. The writer sheltered himself under the pseudonym of 'A Fellow Sufferer under unjust Persecution.' After attacking several points in Cobbett's conduct with extreme bitterness he went on to state that 'no sooner was Mr. Cobbett convicted, than he endeavoured to gain the forgiveness of Government, and to prevail upon the Attorney-General to refrain from calling him up for judgment.' The opening paragraphs of the suppressed 'Farewell Address' were then quoted, and the epistle closed with a caution to Sir Francis Burdett against any longer lending his name to 'the support of such dupery.'[1] This letter, reprinted on a handbill, was distributed at the door of the 'Crown and Anchor' before the dinner and placed under the soup-plates of the diners. Although the statements which it contained were fairly accurate, there was something cruel in launching such a charge on the day of the prisoner's liberation, and something exquisitely mean

[1] *The Times*, 9th July 1812.

in making it anonymously. In fact Cobbett's assailant blundered in his method of attack, and the indignation he aroused blinded many to the truth of his assertions. Cobbett, however, was aware of his serious peril, and he met the gravest charge by peremptory denial. He admitted, indeed, that he had contemplated discontinuing the *Register*, but stated that he did so solely 'because I was apprehensive that I could not exercise the same liberty that I had heretofore enjoyed, and because I would not consent to lower the tone I had heretofore held.' He also stated emphatically that if he had made the discontinuance of his *Register* a condition of his punishment being remitted or mitigated, or if he had even acceded to such a proposition, when made to him, then he would have abandoned his principles. But he denied that he had ever made such a proposition—that such a proposition had ever been made to him—that he had ever entertained such an idea—that he had ever thought of it. Next week he referred in the *Register* to the accusations and, after stating them categorically, repeated the denial which he had already given to the charge of negotiating with Government, stating that that charge was 'false,' 'wholly destitute of truth,' and 'invented as much as any fairy tale was ever invented.'[1]

It is impossible, after following the details of the negotiation in Cobbett's letters to Wright and in those of Reeves to Cobbett, to avoid the conclusion that Cobbett at this great crisis entered on a course of prevarication and actual falsehood unworthy of an upright man. Yet, if it is permissible to make conjectures concerning those secret springs of action that must always

---

[1] *Political Register*, 18th July 1812.

remain concealed, it may be surmised that it was anger rather than apprehension that influenced his conduct. The cowardice of the anonymous letter in *The Times*, the malice which launched the accusation to humble him in his hour of triumph roused him to anger, and, obeying his impulse, he gave his accusers the lie direct. It may be urged in partial extenuation that, although it is perfectly clear from Reeves's first letter to Cobbett that his proposals and Farewell Article were placed in Yorke's hands, it is possible Cobbett had forgotten this, perhaps never fully realised it in the absorbing interest of the rest of the contents.[1] Such a failure of memory would also account for his firm conviction that Wright was the author of the letter to *The Times*, and that Wright alone knew enough about the negotiation to have written it, a conviction which afterwards bore disastrous fruit and which it is difficult to account for, if Cobbett remembered that his article had actually been laid before the ministers. At a later date, in January 1817, in reply to a renewed attack in *The Times*,[2] Cobbett in a letter in the *Register*, addressed to his political adversary, George Rose, made a modified statement which further bears out this view.

'Walter says that I made a proposition to government to this effect; that, if the proceedings were dropped; that is to say that if I were *not brought up for judgment*, but suffered to remain unmolested, *I never would publish another Register or any other thing*. Now, . . . suppose this to have been *true*. Had I not a *right* to do this? Was there anything dishonest and base in this? I was under no obligation to continue to write. The

---

[1] Immediately after receiving Reeves's letter Cobbett sent it to Wright, with whom it remained, so that he had no opportunity of looking at it again.

[2] *The Times*, 14th Nov. 1816.

country had done nothing for me. I was in no way bound to sacrifice myself and family if I could avoid it. I was in the state of a soldier surrounded by an irresistible enemy; and has a soldier so situated ever been ashamed to ask his life and to accept of it upon condition of *not serving again during the war*?

'I might let the thing rest here. This answer would be complete, were I to allow the charge of Walter to be *true*; but, the charge is basely false. *No proposition of any sort was ever made by me, or by my authority, to the Government.* The grounds of the charge were as follows. A few days before I was brought up for judgment, I went home to pass the remaining short space of personal freedom with my family. I had just begun farming, and also planting trees, with the hope of seeing them grow up as my children grew. I had a daughter fifteen years of age, whose birthday was just then approaching, and, destined to be one of the happiest and one of the most unhappy days of my life, on that day my dreadful sentence was passed. One son eleven years old, another nine years old, another six years old, another daughter five years old, another three years old, and another child nearly at hand. You and Perceval might have laughed at all this. It was your turn to laugh then; but, the public will easily believe, that, the apprehensions of an absence of years, and the great chance of loss of health, if not of life, in a prison, produced nothing like laughter at Botley! It was at this crisis, no matter by what feelings actuated, I wrote to my attorney, Mr. White, in Essex Street, to make the proposition stated above. But, fits of fear and despair have never been of long duration in my family. The letter was hardly got to the post-office at Southampton before the courage of my wife and eldest daughter returned. Indignation and resentment took place of grief and alarm; and they cheerfully consented to my stopping the Letter. Mr. Peter Finnerty was in my house at the time; a post-chaise was got; and he came up to London during the night *and prevented Mr. White from acting on the letter*. . . . If I am asked how it happened, that *Walter* came in possession of the fact of my having written to Mr. White the letter which was recalled by Mr. Finnerty, I answer, that I cannot tell; but,

that I suspect, that it was communicated to him (with a suppres-
sion of the recalling) by a wretch whom *he knows* to be without
an equal in the annals of infamy, not excepting the renowned
Jonathan Wild, and which wretch I will, when I have time,
drag forth, and hold him up to the horror of mankind.'[1]

With this partial avowal Cobbett closed his utterances
on the subject. His story was still far from the true one,
but it was at least more plausible than his first uncon-
ditional denial. The incident did him much harm with
his former adherents, especially with the more uncompromising reformers. Among others, Leigh Hunt in the
Examiner attacked him violently for his timidity and for
whining about being torn from his home.

On his release from prison Cobbett dared not continue
proprietor of the *Register* in consequence of the heavy
bonds he had been sentenced to give, that he would keep
the peace for seven years. He was in consequence
obliged to transfer the property and a considerable part
of the profits to another[2] until the time for which he was
bound over should have expired. The *Register* was very
famous and had an immense circulation, while his own
renown as a writer never stood higher. James Smith
made him the subject of one of the best parodies in
Rejected Addresses, and he found himself a centre of
literary attentions, not often equally friendly in character. But before long he began to perceive that the
popularity of the *Register* was declining, and in the next
two or three years he lost a number of his subscribers.
The clergy, among whom at one time he had many
supporters, were alienated by his advocacy of the cause
of Daniel Isaac Eaton, a little London bookseller, who

---

[1] *Political Register*, 4th January 1817.   [2] *Ibid.*, 10th April 1830.

had incurred many convictions for retaining blasphemous and seditious books, and who in March 1812 had been sentenced to stand in the pillory for publishing the third part of Paine's *Age of Reason*.[1] Cobbett confirmed their hostility by attacking the system of tithes and by indulging in theological excursions, in which he gave utterance to heterodox views on many subjects. In like manner the smaller landowners resented his advice that they should make the cause of the labourers their own, and he finally disgusted them by opposing the Corn Bill of 1815, which prohibited the importation of corn when the price was lower than eighty shillings a quarter. Nor were his descriptions of the farmers themselves likely to conciliate them.

'When I saw the plain-dressed and industrious farmers of Pennsylvania, it seemed to me, that I was still amongst those of England, the former being, I confess, rather more hospitable and better informed, the natural consequences of their easy circumstances, and of the universal habit to *read* which prevails in America. But, the English farmer has, of late years, become a totally different character. A fox-hunting horse ; polished boots ; a spanking trot to market ; a " Get out of the way or by G—d I'll ride over you" to every poor devil upon the road ; wine at his dinner ; a servant (and sometimes in *livery*) to wait at his table ; a painted lady for a wife ; sons aping the young 'squires and lords ; a house crammed up with sofa's, piano's, and all sorts of fooleries.'

Moreover, the stirring events on the Continent, the triumphs of British arms, and the rapture of victory, drew the attention of people generally from domestic affairs. Distress was still acutely felt, but there was a general expectation that prosperity would follow the

[1] See *Political Register*, 13th June 1812.

permanent establishment of peace, and this led to a disinclination to seek for remedies of other kinds. Cobbett, on the other hand, had devoted his periodical largely to financial disquisitions, to attacks on paper money, and to warnings of the danger of increasing the National Debt. These subjects, never intrinsically popular, might well seem flat and stale to a nation intoxicated with victory. In 1815 he found himself with few friends or adherents, his existence hardly recognised by the political press.

But, when it became evident that peace would not bring in its train economic prosperity, the spirit of discontent returned sevenfold, and people began to again pay attention to Cobbett, who had steadily maintained throughout the delirium of triumph, that the causes of national distress were too deep-rooted to be affected by the cessation of the war.

'Before the year 1816 had expired,' said Cobbett at a later time, after speaking of the national rejoicing that had followed the Peace, 'my affairs began to take a different turn. The "*reckoning*" had not been paid; "*dear old Blucher*," as the nasty tax-eating women called him, was gone away to "*dear* Brunswick," and had left us all the *score* to pay. "*Agricultural distress*" began to make the nation listen to the call for *parliamentary reform*; and the latter part of 1816, saw the kingdom agitated from one end to the other.'[1]

There were in fact serious industrial disturbances, accompanied by the extensive destruction of machinery, which had marked the Luddite movement of 1812. But there were signs of intellectual earnestness about the new movement which had been lacking in the former

[1] *Political Register*, 10th April 1830.

riotous upheaval.   Cobbett had been ostracised by the
more advanced reformers, because they suspected him
of insincerity.   But as the reform movement gradually
permeated the yet unfranchised classes, it brought him
adherents who had no ears for past scandals and whose
loyalty could be shaken by no stories of bygone hesita-
tions.   He set himself to gain the attention of the discontented and distressed multitudes, and to show them
that the true remedy for the ills of the State was to be
found, not in rioting and violence, but in parliamentary
reform.   He began to travel about the country, speaking
whenever he found an opportunity, addressing crowds
in the market-places or talking with humble labourers
on the road or at the doors of their cottages.   He visited
meetings of freeholders called by the county gentry to
consider remedies for the prevalent distress, and, though
he did not always succeed in persuading them to adopt
his own expedients, he was able at least to publish his
opinions on the causes of poverty and discontent.

In this new field of political enterprise Cobbett was
aided by the great seaman, Lord Cochrane, who had
for many years resided in Hampshire in his immediate
neighbourhood.   Lord Cochrane had, in the previous
year, been convicted of being concerned in a fraudulent
scheme to influence the price of stocks by means of
false intelligence of the defeat and death of Napoleon.
He had been sentenced to a year's imprisonment, and
to stand in the pillory, and fined £1000.   The trial and
sentence reflect indelible disgrace both on the Government and on the presiding judge, Lord Ellenborough,
who openly favoured the prosecution.   Lord Cochrane's
innocence has recently been questioned, yet he actually

gave the information which led to the apprehension of the real perpetrator of the fraud immediately he had intelligence of it.[1] He was not made to stand in the pillory, for Government feared a riot, but he was dismissed from the navy, and was thus enabled to turn his whole attention to politics.

In consequence of Cobbett's exertions the *Register* began to be read widely among classes which journalism had hitherto failed to reach, especially among the skilled workmen of the towns. The price of the *Register*, a shilling and a halfpenny, was too high to enable them to contribute singly, but it became customary to unite to purchase a copy, which was read aloud to the whole company. Strenuous opposition was offered to these meetings by Cobbett's political opponents, and after considerable hesitation he resolved to meet the case by reducing the price of the *Register* to twopence. In announcing his resolution he wrote:

'Events are pressing upon us so fast that my Register, loaded with more than half its amount in *stamp* and other expenses incidental to the stamp, does not move about *sufficiently swift* to do all the good it might do. I have therefore resolved to make it move *swifter*.' He went on to say that the stamped *Register* was 'read in meetings of people in many towns, and one copy was thus made to convey information to scores of persons'; but that he finds in public-houses 'the landlords have objected to *Meetings for Reading the Register being held at their houses*, for fear they should LOSE THEIR LICENCES. This was what had never struck me. I had heard of the Register having been banished from *Officers' Mess-Rooms*, from the *Mess-Rooms on board of Ship*, from numerous *Reading-Rooms*, which must necessarily be under the controul chiefly of the busy

[1] For a careful statement of the case against Lord Cochrane see Mr. J. B. Atlay's *Trial of Lord Cochrane*, 1897.

Clergy, the Pensioners, the Taxing People, and the like; but satisfied that all these are but as dust in the balance, when we are talking of the *public*, the *energetic people*, I disregarded all these marks of hostility . . . seeing that thousands upon thousands of *real men* were *hearing* in the *Reading-meetings* at Public-houses.   But I had not yet heard of the alarm about the LICENCES! The moment I heard of that . . . I saw at once that my readers or *hearers* (or at least the greater part of them) must either be driven out into the high-roads and waste-lands, or that they must be supplied with reading at a cheap rate.'

Accordingly on 2nd November 1816, while continuing to issue the stamped edition of the *Register* at a shilling and a halfpenny, he also published an unstamped edition at twopence, at the same time reprinting several back numbers in the cheaper form. He avoided the stamp-duty of sixpence a copy on newspapers by omitting all items of news. The cheap form was registered as a pamphlet by paying a duty of three shillings for the whole impression.

At the same time Cobbett adapted his style of writing to his audience. The first cheap number was No. 18, famous for containing the 'Address to the Journeymen and Labourers of England, Wales, Scotland and Ireland.' Its inception was due to a suggestion of Lord Cochrane that Cobbett should write an essay dissuading the populace from acts of violence.

'I said before we parted that this should be done. But as it was impossible for me to prove to the people what was *not* the cause of their misery, without proving to them what *was* the cause . . . without pointing the *remedy*; as the remedy, at last, came to a Reform of Parliament; and, as I still feared that the best time was not come for urging on this great question, I delayed, from time to time, the fulfilment of my promise to my neighbour, who, on his part, never saw me without pressing me hard upon the subject; and on the 2nd of November, I wrote the No. 18, being an Address to the Journeymen and Labourers on the aforementioned subject.'

In the opening part of the Address Cobbett claimed that the whole of the country's wealth and resources were the outcome of the labour of the people :

'FRIENDS AND FELLOW-COUNTRY MEN,—Whatever the Pride of rank, of riches, or of scholarship may have induced some men to believe, or to affect to believe, the real strength and all the resources of a country, ever have sprung and ever must spring, from the *labour* of its people; and hence it is, that this nation, which is so small in numbers and so poor in climate and soil compared with many others, has, for many ages, been the most powerful nation in the world; it is the most industrious, the most laborious, and, therefore, the most powerful. Elegant dresses, superb furniture, stately buildings, fine roads and canals, fleet horses and carriages, numerous and stout ships, warehouses teeming with goods; all these, and many other objects that fall under our view, are so many works of national wealth and resources. But all these spring from *labour*. Without the journeyman and the labourer none of them could exist; without the assistance of their hands, the country would be a wilderness, hardly worth the notice of an invader.

'As it is the labour of those who toil which makes a country abound in resources, so it is the same class of men who must, by their arms, secure its safety, and uphold its fame. Titles and immense sums of money have been bestowed upon numerous naval and military commanders. Without calling the justice of these in question, we may assert that the victories were obtained by *you* and your fathers, and brothers and sons in co-operation with those commanders, who, with *your* aid, have done great and wonderful things; but, who, without that aid, would have been as impotent as children at the breast.

'With this correct idea of your own worth in your minds, with what indignation must you hear yourselves called the Populace, the Rabble, the Mob, the Swinish Multitude; and with what greater indignation, if possible, must hear the projects of these cool and cruel and insolent men who, now that you have been, without any fault of yours, brought into a state of misery, propose to narrow the limits of parish relief, to prevent you from marrying in the days of your youth, or to thrust you out to seek your bread in foreign lands, never more to behold your parents or friends? But, suppress your indignation, until we return to this topic, after we have considered the *cause* of this present misery, and the measures which have produced that cause.' This cause he asserted to be 'the *enormous amount of the taxes*, which the Government compels us to pay for the support of its army, its placemen, its pensioners, etc., and for the payment of the interest on the debt.'

After pointing out that the burden of the debt on the taxpayers had been considerably increased by the introduction of an inconvertible paper currency, he said :

'We next come to consider what have been *the causes of this weight of taxes*.   Here we must go back a little in our history, and you will soon see that this intolerable weight has *all proceeded from the want of Parliamentary Reform.*'

He went on to indicate that Parliament, and, through Parliament, the government of England was in the hands of a small number of persons, who, instead of administering the country for the welfare of its inhabitants, had turned their power to selfish ends, and especially to the emolument of themselves and their friends.   To deprive them of this power it was necessary that the House of Commons should be elected by the bulk of the people, and in this manner be made amenable to the wishes of the nation.   After pointing out the evils of the existing system, especially those arising from the immense influence of fund-holders who supported the maintenance of an inconvertible paper currency, he concluded :

'I have no room, nor have I any desire, to appeal to your passions upon this occasion. I have laid before you, with all the clearness I am master of, the causes of our misery, the measures which have led to those causes, and I have pointed out what appears to me to be the only remedy—namely, a reform of the Commons', or People's, House of Parliament. I exhort you to proceed in a peaceable and lawful manner; but, at the same time, to proceed with zeal and resolution in the attainment of this object. If the *Skulkers* will not join you, if the "decent fire-side gentry" still keep aloof, proceed by yourselves. Any man can draw up a petition, and any man can carry it up to London, with instructions to deliver it into trusty hands, to be presented whenever the House shall meet.' [1]

Having thus pointed out what he believed to be the true remedy for the prevailing distress, Cobbett proceeded to dissuade the labouring classes from the use of violence. On 30th November he published his *Letter to the Luddites*, a defence of machinery which, says Miss Martineau, 'must have been far more effectual than a regiment of dragoons.' [2] In this appeal he urged the workmen to refrain from outrage, and spoke with sorrow of the destruction which they had already accomplished:

'Judge you, my good friends, what pain it must have given me to hear you accused of acts, which I was not only unable to justify, but which, in conscience and in honour, I was bound to condemn! I am not one of those, who have the insolence to presume that men are *ignorant*, because they are *poor*. If I myself have more knowledge and talent than appears to have fallen to the lot of those who have brought us into our present miserable state, it ought to convince me, that there are thousands and thousands, now unknown to the public, possessed of greater talent, my education having been that of the common soldier grafted upon the plough-boy. Therefore, I beg you not to suppose that I address myself to you as one who pretends to any superiority in point of rank, or of natural endowments. I address

[1] *Political Register*, 2nd November 1816.
[2] *History of England during the Thirty Years' Peace*, 1849, i. 49.

you as a friend who feels most sincerely for your sufferings; who is convinced that you are in error as to the cause of these sufferings; who wishes to remove that error; and, I do not recollect any occasion of my whole life when I have had so ardent a desire to produce conviction.

'As to the *particular* ground of quarrel between you and your employers, I do not pretend to understand it very clearly. There must have been faults or follies on their side at some time or other, and there may be still; but, I think, we shall see, in the sequel, that those circumstances which appear to you to have arisen from their *avarice*, have in fact arisen from their want of the *means*, more than from their want of *inclination*, to afford you a competence in exchange for your labour; and, I think this, because it is to their *interest* that you should be happy and contented.

'But, as to the use of *machinery in general*, I am quite sure, that there cannot be any solid objection. However, as this is a question of very great importance, let us *reason it together*. Hear me with patience; and, if you still differ with me in opinion, ascribe my opinion *to error*, for it is quite impossible for me to have any *interest* in differing from you.'

He proceeded to point out that the use of machines discriminated civilised from savage man, and that the total abolition of machinery would make it impossible for almost any one to support life. He then went into some detail to show that in particular trades the introduction of machinery benefited, rather than distressed, the workers, and forcibly urged that the widespread poverty was due, not to the malevolence of employers, but to the disorganisation of industry in consequence of the debased state of the currency, and to the heavy load of taxation with which trade was oppressed.

Such weighty appeals issued in a cheap form attracted enormous interest. The circulation of the *Register* went up to forty or fifty thousand a week.[1]

[1] *Monthly Magazine*, Jan. 1817, p. 544.

N

Cobbett himself has drawn an interesting picture of the excitement caused by his 'Address to the Journeymen and Labourers.'

'The effects of No. 18 were prodigious. It occupied the conversations of three-fourths of all the active men in the kingdom. The whole town was in a *buz*. The labouring classes of the people seemed as if they had never heard a word on politics before. The effect on their minds was like what might be expected to be produced on the eyes of one bred up in the dark, and brought all of a sudden, into broad daylight. . . . Amongst the striking and *instantaneous* effects of this Cheap *Register* was the *unlocking of the jaws* of the London Press with regard to me and my writings. For nearly *five years* I had been unable to extort a word from this press. The hirelings of the *ministry* hated me because I exposed the acts of the ministers; the papers attached to the *Whig* faction hated me because I proved that the faction was as hostile to the people as the ministers themselves; and the papers which took, as to object, the same side with myself, though they could not, if they spoke at all, refrain from approving, *chose to say nothing*, so that the silence was as complete as if it had been the result of a direct and most *solemn convention*. . . . There were besides, what the French call the *Chutchutments* or the *Whisperings*, to contend with, and it is quite surprising how they are managed, and what effects they produce in London, and thence throughout the kingdom. The word starts from Whitehall and away it goes in every direction. A gentleman in Berkshire was pointing out to a *Parson* in that county in the summer of 1816, something to read in "Cobbett," "Cobbett!" said the other, "Does *he* write *now*?" The crafty Priest knew well enough that I did, but it was his business to cause it to be believed, that I was *become of no consequence*.

'Upon the appearance, however, of No. 18 away went all the *Chutchutments*, and all the pretendings of ignorance; and the corrupt part of the press, instead of its apparently *sworn silence*, treated the public with vollies of lies and execrations against me that never had a parallel in the world. It seemed as if the curses of these hirelings had, for years past, been kept *without sound,* like those of Mandeville's sailors, which having been uttered during a terrible *hard frost,* filled the air with their crackings when the *thaw* came. No. 18 seemed to have a similar effect upon the long suppressed falsehoods and execrations of Walter, Stewart, Perry, and others in London ; and the very air was filled with the sound of their abominable abuse. To all this abuse I opposed nothing but the consciousness of my integrity.' [1]

An independent witness, Samuel Bamford, the Lancashire weaver and poet, has borne equally strong testimony to Cobbett's wide influence :

' At this time the writings of William Cobbett suddenly became of great authority ; they were read in nearly every cottage hearth in the manufacturing districts of South Lancashire, in those of Leicester, Derby, and Nottingham ; also in many of the Scottish manufacturing towns. Their influence was speedily visible ; he directed his readers to the true cause of their sufferings — misgovernment ; and to its proper corrective—parliamentary reform. Riots soon became scarce, and from that time they have never obtained their ancient vogue with the labourers of this country. Let us not descend to be unjust. Let us not withhold the homage, which with all the faults of William Cobbett, is still due to his great name. Instead of riots and destruction of property, Hampden clubs were now established in many of our large towns, and the villages and districts around them ; Cobbett's books were printed in a cheap form ; the labourers read them, and thenceforward became deliberate and systematic in their proceedings.' [2]

Although Cobbett was using all his influence to deter the artisans and labourers from outrage and plunder, he was considered by Tories and by many of the Whigs to be directing their energies in a more dangerous direction. In his scheme of parliamentary reform he included

[1] *Political Register,* 2nd August 1817.
[2] Bamford's *Passages in the Life of a Radical,* Manchester, 1859, pp. 6-7.

a large extension of the franchise, and thus he proposed to raise the great masses of labourers and mechanics into active politicians. To the great majority of the existing parties it appeared that Cobbett proposed to make 'the most impatient and uncontrollable materials of our social system the most preponderating.'[1] The ever-increasing demand for reform sounded in their ears like the knell of England's greatness, and Cobbett's open scorn of their sincere efforts to palliate the distress by means of charity roused them to anger.

Their view of Cobbett's work was set forth by a writer in the *Quarterly Review*, who concurred with Bamford in his estimate of the influence of the *Register*, though he held a different opinion of its value. He asserted that the extent of mischief done by 'this ferocious journal' was not to be calculated.

'Its ignorant readers receive it with entire faith: it serves them for law and for gospel—for their creed and their Ten Commandments. They talk by it, and swear by it; they are ready to live by it; and it will be well if some of these credulous and unhappy men are not deluded to die by it; they would not be the first victims of the incendiary press.'

After recounting how Cobbett had denounced the efforts of the charitable to relieve the distressed, and had told the people of Birmingham that they were 'coaxed and threatened, with a basin of carrion soup in one hand and a halter in the other,' he inquired:

'Why is it that this convicted incendiary, and others of the same stamp, are permitted week after week to sow the seeds of rebellion, insulting the Government, and defying the laws of the country? . . . We have laws to prevent the exposure of un-

[1] Miss Martineau, *History*, i. 49.

wholesome meat in our markets, and the mixture of deleterious drugs in beer. We have laws also against poisoning the minds of the people, by exciting discontent and disaffection;—why are not these laws rendered effectual, and enforced as well as the former?'[1]

The reviewer was mistaken in thinking that the existing laws were sufficient to check Cobbett's teaching. Warned by experience, Cobbett was careful to avoid libel. He dealt only with general subjects, such as the condition of the country and the folly and selfishness of its rulers. He plainly told the people that to employ violence would be to place themselves at the mercy of those rulers. But he called upon them to assemble and petition, and to bend all their energies to obtaining the control of the supreme legislative power. Cobbett, said Francis Place, 'was too ignorant not to see[2] that the common people must ever be imbecile . . . when not encouraged and supported by those who have money and influence.'[3] Place, however, was wrong, if he thought that Cobbett was not aware that the multitude would require leadership: he intended to reserve that office for himself, and not to hand it over to reformers of the class of Burdett and other of Place's friends.

Cobbett's opponents made great efforts to write him down. He was assailed from all quarters and by both the recognised political parties. A journal appeared early in 1817, entitled *Anti-Cobbett*, which was entirely devoted to attacking him. It was written with so much ability that the editorship was usually ascribed to William Gifford. These assaults delighted Cobbett, for they gave

---

[1] *Quarterly Review*, October 1816, p. 275.
[2] Obviously the 'not' should be deleted.   [3] Add. MS. 27809, f. 17.

him the notoriety which was essential to his position. The actions of his allies gave him more disquietude than the writings of his enemies. In December 1816 rioting broke out in London itself, and many of the more extreme agitators, among whom the two Watsons were conspicuous, began to ridicule the practice of petitioning, and to advocate openly an appeal to force. Government took the alarm and passed a number of Acts to cope with the emergency, among them being a bill for the suspension of the Habeas Corpus Act. Cobbett's position then became impossible. He had been denounced in Parliament by Lord Sidmouth as one of those whom the existing law could not restrain. With these new powers the ministry would be able to imprison him at their discretion. He therefore resolved to leave the country and to seek refuge in the United States of America.

'My choice (leaving all considerations of *Personal Safety* out of the question) lies between *silence* and *retreat*. If I remain here, all other means will be *first* used to reduce me to silence; and, if all those means fail, then will come the *dungeon*. Therefore, that I may still be able to write, and to write *with freedom*, too, I shall write, if I live, *from America*.'[1]

His departure was hastened by an overture from Government. He received,

'A proposition *to see Lord Sidmouth and to retire to my estate with a compensation for the loss of the income from my writings*. . . . I do not *assert* that his Lordship authorised such communication; but, I assert, that I had such a proposition made to me by a person, whom I believe and have *good reason* to believe, was authorised by his Lordship to make it.'[2]

[1] *Political Register*, 5th April 1817.   [2] *Ibid.*, 12th July 1817.

A good many years afterwards he referred to the offer in more detail :

'If I had had a mind, even in 1817, to touch the public money, I might have remained in safety, and with *ten thousand pounds in my pocket*; or, at least, such an *offer was made me*, by a gentle man in whose word and authority I firmly believed. The sole condition was, *future silence*. I gave no answer, but, with my two eldest sons, resolved upon flight, it being manifest that *silence* or a *dungeon* must attend my staying ; and observe, a dungeon was *silence*; for the use of pen, ink, and paper was not to be allowed to the victims.'[1]

He hesitated openly to defy Government by rejecting their offer, lest they should use their new powers to deprive him of his liberty.

'I gave *no answer*; and while the answer was expected, I departed. I did not think it *safe* to give an answer. To remain at large in England, and be *silent*, is what I could not have endured. I should have died in a month. And, the probable consequences of *the vengeance* which would, *to a certainty*, have followed my being shut up in a dungeon, and away from my family, were such as I could not have lived in expectation of, without being driven to madness.'[2]

On 22nd March 1817 he left London with his sons, William and John, and proceeded by Lichfield to Liver-pool, where he embarked for New York in the ship *Importer*, on 27th March. At Liverpool he wrote his farewell address to the readers of the *Register*. It was dated 28th March and published on 5th April, as soon as his agents had news that he had actually em-barked. In it Cobbett announced the suspension of the *Register*, but assured his readers that it would reappear within four months. After commenting on the attitude

---

[1] *Political Register*, 10th April 1830.   [2] *Ibid.*, 12th July 1817.

of those in power towards the working-classes he proceeded to defend his own actions:

'I have no desire to write libels. I have written none here. Lord Sidmouth was "*sorry to say*" that I had not written anything that the Law Officers could prosecute with any chance of success. I do not remove for the purpose of writing libels, but for the purpose of being able to write what is *not* libellous. I do not retire from a combat with the Attorney-General, but from a combat with a dungeon, *deprived of pen, ink, and paper.* A combat with the Attorney-General is quite *unequal* enough. That, however, I would have encountered. I know too well what a trial by *Special Jury* is. Yet that, or any sort of *trial*, I would have stayed to face. So that I could have been sure of a *trial*, of whatever sort, I would have run the risk. But against the absolute power of imprisonment, without even a *hearing*, for time unlimited, in any jail in the kingdom, without the use of pen, ink, and paper, and without any communication with any soul but the keepers—against *such a power* it would have been worse than madness to attempt to strive. Indeed, there could be *no striving* in such a case, where I should have been as much at the disposal of the Secretary of State as the shoes which he has upon his feet. No! I will go, where I shall not be as the shoes upon Lord Sidmouth's and Lord Castlereagh's feet, I will go where I can make *sure* of the use of pen, ink, and paper; and these two Lords may be equally sure, that in spite of everything that they can do, unless they openly enact or proclaim a *Censorship* on the Press, or cut off all commercial connection with America, you, my good and faithful countrymen, shall be able to read what I write.'

In accordance with this promise the *Political Register* appeared again on 12th July, and from that date was regularly published in London under the supervision of his sons, while Cobbett contributed articles from America.

The care with which the publication of his farewell address was delayed, until it was known that Cobbett had actually sailed, was not, however, due entirely to an apprehension of hindrance on the part of Government. That he had cause to fear loss of liberty, if he continued his political writings while residing in England, is undoubtedly true. An interesting and striking proof of his danger may be adduced. On 19th March, three days before Cobbett left London, Robert Southey said in a memorandum to Lord Liverpool:

'You have passed laws to prevent men from tampering with the soldiers, but can such laws be effectual? Or are they not altogether nugatory while such manifestoes as those of Cobbett, Hone, and the *Examiner*,[1] etc., are daily and weekly issued, fresh and fresh, and read aloud in every ale-house where the men are quartered, or where they meet together? . . . I did hope that the first measure after the suspension of the Habeas Corpus Act, would have been to place the chief incendiary writers in safe custody.'[2]

But while there is strong probability that it was fear of loss of liberty that actually induced Cobbett to leave the country, the haste with which he fled was due also to the embarrassed condition of his affairs. Had it become known that he was leaving England, his creditors would have taken immediate steps to prevent him. His farm at Botley was mortgaged for sixteen thousand pounds, and he owed besides nearly twenty thousand pounds more.

'I had to move,' he said afterwards, 'merely with a trunk, and as quick as a postchaise would carry me. . . . I left books, papers, and even the great part of my shirts and coats behind.'

'The "celebrated" Cobbett,' said the *Quarterly Review*, 'fled from his creditors. That he should do this is perfectly natural;

---

[1] The Hunts' paper.
[2] Yonge's *Life and Administration of Lord Liverpool*, 1868, ii. 298-99.

the thing to be admired is, that such a man should have creditors to flee from. Had he staid at Liverpool another tide, he would have been brought back, and consigned to Newgate or the King's Bench for the remainder of his life.'[1]

There is considerable exaggeration in this statement, but there is little doubt that Cobbett's creditors would have hindered his departure from England had they been able. In the first *Register* which he sent from America, he inserted the following paragraph:

'I hereby publicly give notice to every person with whom I may have any pecuniary engagements, that, if they proceed to any acts of legal malice ; that if they give any obstruction to the performance of anything that may be to my advantage, and that may tend to alleviate in some small degree, the blow which the Borough-mongers have given me in a pecuniary way ; I hereby solemnly give notice to all such persons, be they who they may, that I will not only never pay them one single farthing, if I should have heaps of money, but that, on the contrary, I shall consider them as *aiders and abetters of the Borough-mongers*, and that whenever the day of justice shall arrive, I will act towards them accordingly.'[2]

Cobbett landed at New York on 5th May 1817, after an absence of nearly seventeen years. The change in his position during the intervening period was very remarkable. In 1800 he had left the United States full of ardour for the party in authority in England, and resolved to uphold it by all means in his power. In 1817 he returned a fugitive, driven from England by the party which he had formerly supported, by means of repressive measures for which his own writings had been a principal

---

[1] *Quarterly Review*, January 1819, p. 135.

[2] *Political Register*, 12th July 1817. See also *Correspondence between Mr. Cobbett, Mr. Tipper, and Sir Francis Burdett*, 1819 ; and *A Defence of Mr. Cobbett*. Both pamphlets are in the British Museum Library, 1103, e. 40 (25 and 26).

occasion. In 1800 he had vehemently declared that injustice and oppression were the natural outcome of democratic rule. In 1817 he was preaching with equal emphasis that the political and economic salvation of England could only be attained by extending the franchise. When he left New York he had departed cursing with his last utterance the corruption and tyranny of American institutions. When he returned a stern and bitter experience had taught him that political liberty can never mean utter licence, and had disposed him to regard the faults of the United States with more tolerant eyes. In one of his contributions to the *Register*, after enumerating some of the physical advantages of New England, he says:

'And then to see a free country for once, and to see every labourer with plenty to eat and drink! Think of *that*! And never to see the hang-dog face of a tax-gatherer. Think of *that*! No Alien Acts here! No long-sworded and whiskered Captains. No Judges escorted from town to town and sitting under the guard of dragoons. No packed juries of tenants. No Crosses. No Bolton Fletchers. No hangings and rippings up. No Castleses and Olivers. No Stewarts and Perries. No Cannings, Liverpools, Castlereaghs, Eldons, Ellenboroughs or Sidmouths. No Bankers. No Squeaking Wynnes. No Wilberforces. Think of *that*. No Wilberforces!'[1]

It would be natural to expect that the advent of so notable a man would have excited considerable stir. But such was not the case. America, like England at a later time, was too much accustomed to political refugees to show much enthusiasm on their behalf. Cobbett had acquired some popularity in the years immediately preceding his arrival, by his strong condemnation of the

---

[1] *Political Register*, 3rd October 1818.

action of the English Government before and during the war with the United States, which broke out in 1812 and continued to December 1814. Several of his articles were reprinted in America as pamphlets, much as in former times his attacks on Priestley and the French Revolution were reprinted by the Tories in London. But these articles by themselves were too slight to give him fame, and Cobbett on his arrival took no steps to make himself more notable. His eyes were continually fixed on the country he had left, and from the time of his arrival he consistently acted as if he regarded his exile as temporary. The day after he landed he left New York and buried himself in a country inn in Long Island. A few weeks later he acquired a small farm at Hyde Park near North Hempstead. His residence in America lasted for more than two years, which were among the most uneventful of his life. During the first of these his history is preserved in unusual detail in a journal which he kept regularly, and afterwards published in London and New York in 1818 and 1819, together with some papers on agricultural and other subjects, under the title of *A Year's Residence in the United States of America.* The work reached three editions, both in England and America. It was intended chiefly as a guide to emigrant farmers, and his own farm was depicted in glowing terms. These eulogies were not altogether sustained by an English radical, Henry Bradshaw Fearon, who made a sentimental pilgrimage to Cobbett's dwelling.

'Upon arriving at Mr. Cobbett's gate, my feelings, in walking along the path which led to the residence of this celebrated man, are difficult to describe. The idea of a person self-banished, leading an isolated life in a foreign land—a path rarely trod, fences in ruins, the gate broken, a house mouldering to decay, added to much awkwardness of feeling on my part, calling upon an entire stranger, produced in my mind feelings of thoughtfulness and melancholy.'[1]

Fearon was rash enough to publish this description, which Cobbett highly resented, as well as the statements that he thought meanly of the 'American people,' and that he felt 'no hesitation in praising himself.' He retorted that, while he took Fearon for a tailor, his son William thought he was a shopkeeper's clerk. In defence of his farm he said :

'The *path*, so far from being *trackless*, was as beaten as a highway. . . . The house is large, and very sound and commodious. The avenues of trees before it, the most beautiful that I ever saw. The orchard, the fine shade and fine grass all about the house, the abundant garden, the beautiful turnip-field ; the whole a subject worthy of admiration ; and not a single drawback. A hearty, unostentatious welcome from me and my sons. A breakfast such, probably, as the fellow will never eat again.'[2]

This little altercation gave keen joy to persons of different political opinions from the disputants, and the *Quarterly Review*, after paternally admonishing Fearon on the danger of associating with men like Cobbett, declared its readiness to accept his account of the state of the farm in preference to Cobbett's own description.[3]

Early in January 1818 Cobbett resolved to go to Pennsylvania in order, as he said, to request the State Legislature to redress the great loss and injury he had sustained at the close of his former residence there, in

[1] *Sketches of America*, 1819, p. 64.
[2] *A Year's Residence in the United States*, 1822, pp. 348-54.
[3] *Quarterly Review*, January 1819, p. 136.

consequence of the tyranny of M'Kean. He arrived in Philadelphia on the evening of the 13th of January, but finding that the legislature was sitting at Harrisburg, he proceeded thither, and remained in the neighbourhood for nearly a month prosecuting his claims. He was full of admiration for that part of America, and contrasted its prosperity with the depressed condition of rural England.

'It is a curious thing to observe the *farm-houses* in this country. They consist, almost without exception, of a considerably large and a very neat house, with sash-windows, and of a *small house*, which seems to have been *tacked on* to the large one; and the proportion they bear to each other, in point of dimensions is as nearly as possible, the proportion of size between a *cow* and *her calf*, the latter a month old. But, as to the *cause*, the process has been the opposite of this instance of the works of nature, for it is *the large house which has grown out of the small one*. The father or grandfather, while he was toiling for his children, lived in the small house, constructed chiefly by himself, and consisting of rude materials. The means accumulated in the small house, enabled the son to rear the large one, and though, when *pride* enters the door, the small house is sometimes demolished, few sons in America have the folly or want of feeling to commit such acts of filial ingratitude, and of real self-abasement. . . . The progress of wealth and ease and enjoyment, evinced by this regular increase of the size of the farmer's dwellings, is a spectacle, at once pleasing, in a very high degree, in itself, and, in the same degree, it speaks the praise of the system of government, under which it has taken place. What a contrast with the farm-houses of England! There the *little* farm-houses are falling into ruins, or are actually become cattle-sheds, or, at best, *cottages*, as they are called, to contain a miserable labourer, who ought to have been a farmer, as his grandfather was. . . . The *farmer* has indeed *a fine house*; but what a life do his labourers lead! The cause of this sad change is to be found in the crushing taxes; and the cause of them, in the Borough usurpation, which has robbed the people of their best right, and, indeed, without which right they can enjoy no other.'[1]

Cobbett did not succeed in the object of his mission, and in consequence he records that he quitted Harrisburg very much displeased. This was his most considerable expedition during his stay, and it was also the only time he approached any American legislative or judicial body. His failure further disinclined him to take any part in American affairs, and he turned with increased energy to English matters.

Soon after his arrival in America he had begun to put into execution a project which had been in his mind for some time, 'for assisting in the acquirement of book-learning all those against whom the Borough-mongers have, in a great degree, closed the door to such learning, and whom they have the insolence to denominate the "Lower Orders."' In order to effect this object, he designed to write and publish at a cheap rate an *English Grammar*, a *History of the Laws and Constitution of England*, a *History of the Church and of Religion in England*, and a *View of the Present State of the Income, Debt, and Expenses of the Kingdom*. Of the three latter only fragments were ever executed, but the *Grammar* was published in London in December 1818, under the title 'A Grammar of the English Language in a series of Letters. Intended for the use of Schools and of young persons in general; but, more especially for the use of soldiers, sailors, apprentices, and ploughboys.' The success of this grammar was very great. Ten thousand copies were sold in a few weeks, and it reached a third edition in less than three months. Besides

[1] *A Year's Residence*, p. 29.

possessing the merits of clearness and simplicity, it was certainly the most readable grammar ever published. It was in the form of letters addressed to his son, James Paul. Two of the original letters (Nos. 22 and 23) are preserved in the British Museum in Cobbett's handwriting.[1] Cobbett took most of the illustrations of the rules he laid down either from domestic incidents or from current politics. Thus in the chapter on the Etymology of Verbs, to illustrate tense, he says: 'The queen [Caroline] *defies* the tyrants; the queen *defied* the tyrants; and the queen *will defy* the tyrants'; as an example of the use of participles, 'a *working* man is more worthy of honour than a titled plunderer who lives in idleness.' As nouns of multitude he instances 'mob, parliament, gang,' and as an example of faulty construction he gives 'The gang of borough-tyrants is cruel, and are also notoriously as ignorant as brutes.' He also added an appendix of specimens of false grammar culled from the writings of Dr. Johnson, Dr. Watts, and other eminent literary men, and from recent state papers drawn up by his political opponents. Many editions have since been published, one of the most recent being that by Thomas Embley Osmun, writing under the pseudonym of Alfred Ayres, which was published in New York in 1884. The work is not without errors. In the Second Letter Cobbett asserts that prosody 'means neither more nor less than what is expressed by the more common word Pronunciation,' and in the following page he confounds etymology with accidence. Such misstatements were retained in editions issued long after his death.

---

[1] Add. MS 22169.

On 20th May 1819 a serious misfortune befell Cobbett. His house was burned to the ground, and with it was destroyed a great part of his farming stock, corn, and hay. He was compelled to seek shelter in a tent 'the walls of which were made of *Morning Chronicles* and *Couriers* pasted upon laths that were a foot asunder.' By seriously crippling him in purse, this calamity probably hastened his return to England. The state of affairs was favourable to his return. The suspension of the Habeas Corpus Act, which he so justly dreaded, had only been temporary, and was not renewed, and the panic in regard to conspiracy had for the moment died down. Moreover, serious dissensions among the Radicals threatened to destroy his hold on the public, and he felt that his presence was urgently needed. But before his departure he resolved on an act of eccentricity, which aroused much controversy.

By this time he had completely altered his opinion of Thomas Paine, whom in earlier life he had described as 'this Ragamuffin Deist.' He sincerely regretted the scurrilous *Life of Paine* which he had published in the *Censor*. Perhaps with a view to undoing some of his past work, he actually composed a new and sympathetic biography, which, however, he did not publish. It remained in manuscript in the possession of Cobbett's daughter, Miss Eleanor Cobbett, until it was printed in 1892 by Mr. D. M. Conway as an Appendix to his *Life of Thomas Paine*.

Paine himself was buried at New Rochelle, not far from New York, in a piece of waste land, having been refused interment in the Quaker burial-ground. To Cobbett, in his later phase of feeling, Paine's burial-place seemed unworthy, and he resolved to remove his bones to England.

'Paine lies in a little hole under the grass and weeds of an obscure farm in America. There, however, he shall not lie unnoticed, much longer. He belongs to England. His fame is the property of England; and if no other people will show that they value that fame, the people of England will.'

He accordingly dug up Paine's coffin and announced his intention of taking it with him. He was refused a passage in the *Amity*, the vessel in which he originally intended to embark, but he sailed in the *Hercules*, and on 20th November 1819 arrived at Liverpool. On the following morning he proceeded to the Custom House, whither his luggage had been brought for the usual inspection, and where a number of spectators had assembled. When the last trunk was opened and sundry deeds and manuscripts removed, a division of woollen appeared, and Cobbett, standing up, said to those around, 'Here are the bones of the late Thomas Paine.' This intelligence excited a sudden and visible sensation, the crowd pressing round to view them. Cobbett improved the occasion by remarking, 'Great indeed must that man have been, whose very bones attract such attention.' The officer took out the coffin-plate and after lifting up several of the bones, replaced the whole and passed them. Cobbett took them with him to London.

His return made a great stir in England. The reformers in many of the northern towns received him with addresses of welcome. At Manchester the authorities were alarmed and brought several pieces of cannon into the town. Hussars were placed on the road to Liverpool to give immediate information of his movements.[1] The borough officials also desired him not to make a public entry into the town. At Bolton, John Heyes, the bellman, was imprisoned for announcing that Paine's bones had been brought by Cobbett to Liverpool.[2] At Coventry Cobbett was turned out of the Craven Arms for addressing the crowd from the window. In his speeches and writings he continually deprecated any resort to violence, and espoused the cause of reform with unusual moderation of language. The exploitation of Paine's bones, however, moved his opponents at once to ridicule and to resentment. Paine was at the height of his renown as an atheist and revolutionary, and this reputation Cobbett himself had formerly done his utmost to enhance. The association of the two names exposed Cobbett to reproach. People will forgive inconsistency in a convert from error, but Cobbett, in the eyes of most of his countrymen, was one who had wilfully fallen from truth. He and his imported bones were welcomed with shouts of derision. Lampoons and caricatures were alike employed as weapons against him. In one of the former the ghost of Tom Paine addressed Cobbett in a night vision :

> ' O rascal, why my name afresh
>   Dost thou lug forth in canting tones,
> The worms content were with my flesh,
>   But thou hast robbed me of my bones.'

He implored him to restore his bones, but Cobbett was obdurate :

> ' Awake, he cried, "Avaunt ye fears !
>   'Tis but a dream my mind dethrones,
> Come, let me bellow in thy ears,
>   I 'll see thee damned, I 'll keep thy bones."'

[1] *Political Register*, 4th December 1819 ; *The Statesman*, 29th November, 1819.

[2] Clegg's *Annals of Bolton*, 1888, p. 74.

Paine's bones also drew a pungent epigram from Lord Byron written in January 1820—

> 'In digging up your bones, Tom Paine,
>   Will Cobbett has done well :
> You visit him on earth again,
>   He'll visit you in hell.'

He sent these lines to Tom Moore with a note in which he said,

'Pray do not let these versicles go forth with my name, except among the initiated, because my friend Hobhouse has foamed into a reformer, and, I greatly fear, will subside into Newgate.'[1]

Finding that the bones aroused ridicule rather than enthusiasm, Cobbett, after a short time ceased to exploit them, but they remained in his possession until his death in 1835. In January 1836 his effects were publicly sold to pay his debts. The auctioneer refused to offer the bones for sale, and the Lord Chancellor, on reference being made to him by the official receiver, declined to recognise them as part of the estate or to make any order in regard to them. They, therefore, remained at the receiver's office until 1844, when they were given to Mr. Tilly of 13 Bedford Square, East, London. Beyond this date their history has not been traced.[2]

On his arrival in London Cobbett was entertained at a public dinner at the 'Crown and Anchor' Tavern, as on his release from prison in 1812, but Sir Francis Burdett, who had taken the chair on that occasion, was

---

[1] See *Byron's Letters and Journals*, ed. Prothero, 1900, iv. p. 395. Byron's apprehensions in regard to Hobhouse were well grounded. When he wrote Hobhouse *was* in Newgate.

[2] See *A Brief History of the Remains of Thomas Paine*, 1847, quoted in *Notes and Queries*, IV. i. 201-3 ; and Conway's *Life of Paine*, ii. 427.

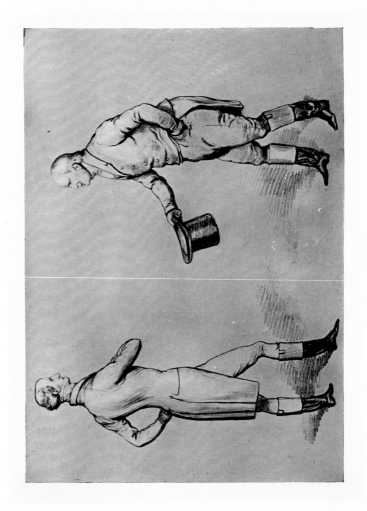

COBBETT AND BURDETT.

"A characteristic interview."

not present. Burdett had not kept pace with Cobbett
in his later progress in reform. He did not desire any
considerable reconstruction of the constitution, but rather
a removal of abuses, which in his opinion were entirely
alien to its spirit. He therefore shrank from the extreme
projects which now began to frame themselves in the minds
of many of the Radical leaders, and which at a later
time were more definitely set forth by the Chartists.
Cobbett, to whom moderation was hardly intelligible,
assailed him violently in the *Register* and asserted that
he had fallen into the hands of a Westminster clique,
who had perverted his mind. The first difference
occurred in May 1816, when Burdett and his friends
chose Lord Brougham as their candidate for Lord
Cochrane's seat. Cobbett disliked Brougham as a Whig,
and an enemy of thorough reform.[1] To these political
differences was added an unhappy wrangle about money.
Sir Francis Burdett in 1812, while Cobbett was in
prison, had advanced him £2000, and in January 1816
£700 more, besides £300 advanced to Wright in 1810,
which Cobbett asserted that he never received. Cobbett
claimed that the £2000 was a gift, while Sir Francis
Burdett more accurately described it as a loan, for
which he held Cobbett's bond. At a later date Cobbett
admitted his indebtedness, but claimed rather incon-
sequently that his persecutions entitled him to exemption from repayment.[2] He never repaid the money, and,
after his death, when Burdett was asked to subscribe to
a memorial to him, he sent the bond to the committee
telling them to take his subscription out of it.

As Sir Francis Burdett was not available, the chair

---

[1] See *Political Register*, 1st June 1816. [2] *Ibid.*, 25th May 1822.

at the banquet was filled by Henry Hunt, a zealous reformer of the advanced school, known as Orator Hunt and as Bristol Hunt, from his connection with that city. The feast passed off successfully, but on its conclusion Cobbett was arrested for debt on leaving the tavern. He was subsequently bailed by Hunt, and by Dolby the publisher of the *Register*; but he found himself extremely embarrassed financially. He made various attempts to collect money, none of which were successful. In spite of the fact that Paine was almost bald when he died he offered for sale gold rings containing a lock of Paine's hair, accompanied by a certificate of genuineness. These were to be had at a guinea each, exclusive of the goldsmith's charge for gold and workmanship. The profits were to be devoted to raising a monument to Paine, but unfortunately there was no demand for the rings. He next proposed a fund of £5000 for furthering the cause of reform, to be raised by twopenny subscriptions, to be entitled 'Cobbett's Fund for Reform,' and to be handed over to him to be dealt with at his discretion.[1] The expedient actually brought in some hundreds, but in the meantime he received another severe financial blow. The passage of the Six Acts at the beginning of 1820, which he always regarded as aimed particularly against himself, and which were undoubtedly intended to deal with a small class of which he was a prominent member, destroyed the sale of his *Register*.

'The dungeon-bill,' he said,[2] 'had *not silenced* me; another dungeon-bill would only have made me go back to America; and that would not have answered the purpose. Therefore the "*envy of surrounding nations*" resorted to *a law* to *prevent cheap*

[1] *Political Register*, 6th January 1820.   [2] *Ibid.*, 10th April 1830.

publications. . . . My *Register* was sold for *twopence*, of which, after expenses and allowances, there was about a penny for me; but a thousand pence make 4*l.* 3*s.* 4*d.*; and that would amount at only 20,000 copies to 84*l.* a week, or 4368*l.* a year. The *admiration* calculated all this. It, therefore, in order to promote *mental improvement* amongst the *"lower orders"* passed a law to compel me to sell the *Register* for *sixpence*; and to *prevent me from gaining money by it*, to put into each *Register two sheets and a quarter of paper*, each sheet being, at the least, twenty-one *inches one way and seventeen inches the other way!* Or, if I did not choose this, to have a stamp and to pay the *"envy"* fourpence (besides the paper-tax) out of every sixpence that I received. . . . The *"admiration"* further enacted, that any pamphlet, *under the price of sixpence*, might be published *occasionally*; but *not periodically*, oftener than *once a month*; but in order to prevent publishing weekly *under different titles*, the *"envy"* enacted, that a *monthly* pamphlet should not be published, except at *the end* of the month! Clever "admiration"! *"Noblest assembly* of freemen in the world!"[1] It does make my blood boil to think, that I am thus made the instrument of taking thousands a year out of the pockets of the best men in the country to give to this thing and its taxeaters.'

This is a fairly accurate description of the effect on the *Political Register* of the 'Act to subject certain Publications to the Duties of Stamps upon Newspapers and to make other Regulations for restraining the Abuses arising from the Publication of Blasphemous and Seditious Libels,' introduced by Lord Castlereagh into the House of Commons on 3rd December 1819, and passed into law early in the following year. It destroyed Cobbett's chie financial resource by making it almost impossible to derive a large profit from a newspaper or periodical

---

[1] Sir James Graham thus designated Parliament in a speech delivered in the House of Commons on 12th February 1830.

publication, and in consequence he found himself in considerable necessity.

While thus struggling with poverty he made an attempt to enter Parliament, standing for Coventry on the death of George III. in January 1820. To provide for his election expenses he employed the proceeds of Cobbett's Fund for Reform, and supplemented them by issuing a circular to seventy gentlemen of fortune requesting them to subscribe ten pounds each. Of the election itself Cobbett has left a very amusing description in a series of letters to his son, James Paul, in the *Political Register*. He met with a triumphal reception on arriving at Coventry. His opponents had assembled their followers to attack him but they were routed by his partisans, who afterwards drew him into the town with acclamations. By means of extensive bribery and treating, however, the mob was afterwards turned against him, and during the course of the election he nearly fell a victim to a savage attack made on him near the polling-booth. After valiantly defending himself for some time he was only rescued by the gallantry of Frank Sergeant, one of his supporters. The crowd then assembled in large numbers, and when he attempted to speak, shouted him down.

'The way I managed the brutes, was well calculated to sting them and their employers to madness. I have, perhaps, as much of *good-humour* on my countenance, naturally, and as little of the gloomy, as any man that ever lived; and I defy the Rich Ruffians of Coventry to say, that the *thousand pounds a day* (for that was about the sum), which they expended on their savages, ever took away that good humour for a moment! My way was to stand and look upon the yelling beasts with a most good-humoured smile; turning my head now and then, leaning it, as it were to take different views of the same person, or the same group. I now and then, substituted something of *curiosity* instead of the general total *unconcern*, that was seated upon my face. Now and then, I would put my mouth close to the ear of some friend that stood by me, and then point to some beast that was foaming with rage, giving him at the same time a laughing look, such as we bestow upon a dog that is chained up and barking at us. Then another time, when half a dozen fresh-drenched brutes were bursting forth close under my nose, I would stretch up my neck, and look, with apparently great curiosity and anxiousness towards a distant part of the crowd, as if to ascertain what was passing there; and this I would do with so much apparent earnestness and continue in that attitude so long, that the beasts really seemed, sometimes, as if they were going mad! I never had so good an opportunity to *philosophise* before. A friend, who saw these man-brutes said, that they shook his faith in *the immortality of the soul*. But, I see no reason at all for any such conclusion. I believe, and have long believed, that there are more *sorts* of men than there are of dogs. The mere circumstance of a creature's walking upon *two legs*, is no proof that he is of the same *sort* or *kind* as I am, or as any other man of mind is. I really looked at and heard these brutes, till they became a subject of amusing speculation; and I could not help concluding that it would be a species of impiety to consider them as partaking in the smallest degree, of the nature of such men as Pope or Paine. . . . The word *fellow-creature* is generally very foolishly used. All *created* things, whether animate or inanimate, are *fellow-creatures*. A Warwickshire savage, or his employer, is, therefor, my *fellow-creature*; but so is a bug, a flea, or a louse, as Swift observes, and as I may hold these latter things wholly beneath me in nature, so I trust I may the former. I am sure I should be very miserable, if I could believe myself to be of the *same* nature.

'This, or something very much like it, was the train of my ideas, while contemplating the horrid groups at the Booth.[1] A

---

[1] Perilous ideas for a democrat. It is doubtful whether Cobbett could ever properly be called one.

parcel of frogs or toads croaking in a pool of dirty water, could as soon have disturbed the muscles of my face as these miserable and degraded things could have done it. When one of these beasts attempted to strike me, however, the feeling became *different*! He reached over the side of the Booth, and caught me by the collar, which was instantly repaid by a blow in his face, for, as Swift says, "if a *flea* or a *louse* bite me, I'll kill it, if I can."[1]

During the election Cobbett was annoyed in many petty ways. The gentry in the neighbourhood of Coventry used all their influence against him. The landlord of the Bull Head Inn, at the village of Marsden, five miles from the borough, was threatened with the loss of his licence unless he instantly and illegally expelled Cobbett, who was staying at his house. On the first day of the voting Cobbett headed the poll, but on the second day he states that his opponents captured the approaches to the booth and his supporters dared not vote for fear of being stabbed or otherwise maltreated. He obtained in all five hundred and seventeen votes and was beaten by a majority of nearly one thousand. His successful opponents were Edward Ellice, a great London merchant, formerly a Radical, but at that time a Whig, who in 1830 became Secretary to the Treasury under Lord Grey, and Peter Moore, a Whig and an Indian Nabob.[2]

The cost of this contest completed the ruin of Cobbett's fortunes. In June he became bankrupt[3] and the farm at Botley was sold to discharge his debts. The creditors were few and acted generously, some, among whom was

[1] *Political Register*, 25th March 1820.

[2] For an account of this election see the *Black Dwarf*, edited by Thomas Jonathan Wooler. Vol. iv.

[3] *The Times*, 19th July 1820.

Sir Francis Burdett, neglecting to present their claims. One of his creditors actually gave him a pound note and a few shillings that he might, for form's sake, have something to surrender to the Commissioners. And he added, when narrating this fact many years afterwards :

'I must do those commissioners the justice to say, that they, seeing a great crowd in Guildhall staring at me, behaved toward me in a manner that showed the best of feelings ; put no questions to me, dismissed me in a minute, and very kindly shook me by the hand when I went away. . . . The old Lord Chancellor,[1] though he had advocated the bills that had ruined me, signed my certificate *out of rule* : "It is *too late*," said the officer, "his Lordship will not sign any more until such a day." I wrote my name upon a bit of paper, and begged him just *to show* it to the Chancellor. When he came out, he smiled with surprise, and said, "His Lordship *will* sign it."'[2]

The bankruptcy, however, was by no means the climax of Cobbett's misfortunes. At that very time he was involved in an affair, which, when it came to an issue, about six months later, seriously injured his reputation as well as his purse. He had not always regarded Orator Hunt with so much favour, as when he was entertained by him at the Anchor Tavern. On 10th April 1808, he had written a note to his assistant Wright, in which he warned him to have nothing to do with Hunt, whom he described as riding 'about the country with a whore, the wife of another man, having deserted his own.' This note contained some other communications in regard to Westminster affairs, and Wright rather injudiciously handed the original to the Westminster Committee immediately after receiving it. In June 1818, when Hunt with Cobbett's support was contesting the re-

[1] Lord Eldon.   [2] *Political Register*, 10th April 1830.

presentation of Westminster with Burdett, this note was remembered, and Wright was asked to allow the Committee to have it again. This he had the meanness to do. Francis Place handed it to Thomas Cleary who read it at the hustings with no intimation in regard to the person to whom it was addressed. The letter was the more damaging because the charge contained in it was strictly true. Cobbett from America promptly disavowed the letter and pronounced it a forgery.[1] The falsehood of this assertion is manifest, for the original is still preserved with the rest of his correspondence with Wright at the British Museum. Hunt, however, accepted and probably believed Cobbett's disavowal and showed that his friendship was unshaken by continuing to co-operate with him.

But although the attempt to sow dissension between Cobbett and Hunt failed in its direct intention, it brought serious consequences in its train. Cobbett was extremely exasperated at Wright's action, and in the *Register* for 6th March 1819, in a letter addressed to Major Cartwright, he assailed his former assistant in unmeasured terms:

'You, my dear Sir, know the history of this Wright; you know all his tricks, all his attempts. The public do not, and I will not now trouble the public with a detail, which, if put in a suitable form, would make a *romance* in the words of *truth*, far surpassing anything that was ever imagined of moral turpitude. I will execute this task one day or other. If the caitiff should put forth anything by way of palliation in the meanwhile, there is Mr. Walker,[2] there is Mr. Margrave, there

---

[1] *Political Register*, 28th November 1818, 6th March 1819; Cleary's defence is contained in *Ibid.*, 19th December 1818. See also a copy of the pamphlet entitled *A Letter to Major Cartwright*, by Thomas Cleary, preserved among the Place Papers. Add. MS. 27809, f. 180.

[2] Peter Walker of Worth, Sussex.

is my attorney, there are the documents, there is Mr. Swann,[1] there is Sir Francis Burdett himself, there is my son John, who, though he was then a child, will never forget the big round drops of sweat, that, in a cold winter's day, rolled down the caitiff's forehead, when he was *detected* in fabricating accounts, and when I took Johnny by the hand (who had begun whimpering for "poor Mr. Wright") and said: "look at that man, my dear! Those drops of sweat are the effect of detected dishonesty! Think of that, my dear child, and you will always be an honest man!"'

These and many other calumnies were brought forward in this remarkable letter, partly in support of the contention that the attack on Hunt was a forgery, but partly also in simple malice against the man, who, as he believed, had betrayed him twice to his enemies.[2] Wright immediately took means for clearing his reputation. Cobbett was at that time out of his reach in America, but he brought an action for libel against the publisher, William Innell Clement, which came on in the court of King's Bench, on 10th December 1819, after Cobbett's return to England. He obtained five hundred pounds damages and promptly commenced a second action against Cobbett himself. Another action was brought by Thomas Cleary, whom he had likewise attacked in the *Register*.[3] Cleary *v.* Cobbett came on a little before noon on 4th December 1820. Brougham, who was for the plaintiff, moved the postponement of the trial till after the hearing of Wright *v.* Cobbett. As Cobbett, who was defending himself, was not present,

[1] James Swann, the Oxfordshire Papermaker, who supplied the *Register*, and was also a personal friend of Cobbett's.

[2] The first time in regard to the negotiations for suppressing the *Register* in 1810.

[3] *Political Register*, 28th November, 5th December, 26th December 1818.

this request was granted by the Lord Chief-Justice. But on the rising of the court Cobbett made his appearance and explained that on his entering the court that morning the door-keeper had seized him by the collar and thrust him out, in spite of his statement that he was defendant. The door-keeper being summoned admitted the truth of this statement, and in consequence the trial was ordered to proceed on the following day. Cobbett admitted the authenticity of the letter, but dwelt with so much effect on the evident malice which had actuated those who published it, that the jury awarded Cleary only the trifling damages of forty shillings.[1] On 11th December the cause of Wright v. Cobbett was brought on. Cobbett had entered a plea of justification and Wright anticipated an opportunity of rebutting the accusations of fraud and dishonesty which Cobbett had made against him so freely. But at the last moment Cobbett withdrew his plea of justification and based his defence on the fact that his son (and not himself) was the present proprietor of the *Register* and that his sons had altered the manuscript of the libels by inserting Wright's name, and in many other material respects. This plea was too evidently an evasion to meet with success. The Lord Chief-Justice summed up strongly against the defendant, and the jury awarded Wright one thousand pounds damages.[2]

The immediate result of the verdict was the appearance of a notice in the *Register* on 20th January 1821, stating formally that it was now published by Mr. John Cobbett,

[1] *Political Register*, 9th December 1820 ; *The Times*, 5th and 6th December 1820.

[2] For a full report of the trial, see the *Book of Wonders*, Part the Second, 1821.

at 1 Clement's Inn. In spite of the fact that the damages and costs of the action were paid by George Rogers of Southampton, who on several occasions had assisted him most generously, Cobbett was reduced to very low circumstances. Yet, notwithstanding his extreme need, his spirit was undaunted. Addressing the electors of Westminster he wrote:

'They have now, they say, *sunk* me in good earnest! Never was a man so often sunk! This is no sinking! This is what the sailors call merely "*shipping a sea*"; that is to say, taking a wave on board, which only gives the vessel a "*heel*," but by no means prevents her from keeping on her course; and, gentlemen, you will see that this, like every other "*sinking*" that I have experienced, will be at last a *mounting* in place of a sinking.'[1]

Ten years later he wrote in regard to this time of tribulation:

'In January 1821 my family, after having for years been scattered about like a covey of partridges that had been sprung and shot at, got *once more together*, in a *hired lodging* at Brompton; and our delight, and our mutual caresses, and our tears of joy, experienced no abatement at our actually finding ourselves with ONLY THREE SHILLINGS IN THE WHOLE WORLD; and at my having to borrow from a friend the money to pay for the paper and print off the then next Saturday's *Register*.'[2]

From Brompton he shortly after removed to Kensington, where he cultivated a plot of land as a seed-farm, and prepared to retrieve his fortunes by his writings.

[1] *Political Register*, 16th December 1820.
[2] *Ibid.*, 10th April 1830.

CHAPTER VIII

THE ten years of Cobbett's life between 1820 and 1830 form the period of his greatest literary activity. In them the greater part of his most famous works were written. He did not retire from politics, for they never ceased to form the absorbing interest of his life, but his political activity was more spasmodic, interspersed with periods of comparative retirement and repose. After his lawsuit with Wright he found himself in straitened circumstances, and very much discredited in the eyes of the world generally. Many of the extreme reformers had never quite approved of his flight to America. Wooler, the editor of the *Black Dwarf*, for instance, taunted him with cowardice, while the more moderate reformers were alienated by his abuse of Sir Francis Burdett. For a space Cobbett almost abandoned the topic of parliamentary reform, and threw all his energy into an impassioned advocacy of the cause of Queen Caroline, trusting to time to restore his ascendency over the minds of his followers. Among other important services which he rendered her he composed the famous 'Letter from the Queen to the King.' According to his son, John Morgan, he wrote it on the night of 6th August 1820. The next morning it was copied by his daughter Anne, and before night it was in the Queen's hands.

Caroline was delighted with it. She signed the paper and sent it off to Windsor just as it was, fearing that if she delayed her legal advisers might counsel her not to let it go. It was returned unopened, but it was published in *The Times* a week later, and was copied by every journal in the kingdom. The authorship was a matter of debate: while the *New Times* conjectured that 'a more classical pen may have here and there polished off the vulgarity of the author of the *Twopenny Register*,' the *Courier* attributed it to Dr. Parr or Dr. Reynolds. The epistle was chiefly occupied with a remonstrance against the injustice of dissolving Caroline's marriage by Act of Parliament, and concluded with a melodramatic protest against the treatment which she had received:

'You have cast upon me every slur to which the female character is liable. Instead of loving, honouring, and cherishing me, agreeably to your solemn vow, you have pursued me with hatred and scorn, and with all the means of destruction. You wrested from me my child, and with her my only comfort and consolation. You sent me sorrowing through the world, and even in my sorrows pursued me with unrelenting persecution. Having left me nothing but my innocence, you would now, by a mockery of justice, deprive me even of the reputation of possessing that. The poisoned bowl and the poniard are means more manly than perjured witnesses and partial tribunals; and they are less cruel, inasmuch as life is less valuable than honour. If my life would have satisfied your Majesty, you should have had it on the sole condition of giving me a place in the same tomb with my child; but, since you send me dishonoured to the grave, I will resist the attempt with all the means which it shall please God to give me.' [1]

When not occupied with the case of Queen Caroline,

[1] For the text of the letter with an account of the circumstances under which it was written, see *Selections from Cobbett's Political Works*, vi. 32-8.

Cobbett carried on a vigorous warfare against his political opponents. He was fond of putting his attacks on his adversaries in a dramatic form. He brought his enemies on the stage and made them condemn themselves out of their own mouths. Of course such an artifice can never be quite convincing, but as handled by Cobbett it was often very effective. Here is a specimen in which the characters are an upright judge, and Mr. Canning, who had supported Castlereagh's coercive measures:

'Judge—What complaint have you to make, Mr. Canning, against these men, whom I see there, behind you, looking so thin and pale, clothed in rags, and having padlocks on their mouths and thumb-screws on their hands?

'Mr. Canning—Oh! don't you know them? I thought all the world knew them! They are the Radicals.

'Judge—The Radicals, Sir! What does that name mean?

'Mr. Canning—Mean! (what a fool the man must be—*aside*). Mean! Why it means everything that is bad.

'Judge—Indeed! But as I am to judge between you, I wish to know what they have done, or, what they have endeavoured to do, or, at least, what they profess their wish to do ; because by their deeds they must be judged, unless we would violate the fundamental principles of all righteous law.

'Mr. Canning—Done! Oh, they are cunning dogs: they have done nothing yet; and as to endeavours they have disguised them also; and for professions, they take care not to profess that which they wish to do.

'Judge—Well, then, Sir, what do you think; what do you think, that they wish to do, and that they would do, if they could?

'Mr. Canning—Think! I do not think anything at all about the matter. I know that they wish and intend "to destroy the throne," to "abolish the House of Lords," to "destroy all property," to "obliterate morals and religion from the hearts of mankind," and . . .

'Judge—Stop! stop! Sir. Pray go no further, for, you have

only to prove the first of your allegations, and as the crime is high treason, you will soon be delivered of "the Radicals."

'Mr. Canning—Prove, indeed! Why, I told you, just now, that they were such sly dogs, and disguised their views and intentions so well, that there was no getting at positive evidence of their traitorous and diabolical intentions.

'Judge—Likely enough, Mr. Canning. But if they really have such intentions; and if you know it, you can, surely, produce some circumstantial evidence of an intention, entertained by so many men in such various stations in life?

'Mr. Canning—Oh, yes! Circumstances enough, faith! Why, Sir, their evil intentions are so manifest, that it has been found necessary to pass six acts for the purpose of defeating their intentions. In the first place, they have been forbidden to meet out of doors, except in distinct parishes, and these meetings, were they to take place, are put under the supervision and control of the magistrates, who may disperse the meetings at their pleasure; and to prevent any resistance of the will of the magistrate, fine, imprisonment, transportation, or death, may, according to the degree of the offence, be inflicted on any persons attending the meetings. Then, the same law provides, that there shall be no meeting, even in a room, to debate or discuss matters of church or state, if money be paid for admittance, unless the room be licensed by a magistrate; and then he may attend, and if he please, take away the licence.

'Judge—Did I rightly understand you, Sir? That Englishmen may not now meet even in a room to hear speeches, or lectures, on government or political economy, for instance, and pay for their admission, without offending against the laws? In other words that it is now a crime for an Englishman to take admission money to a lecture on Locke, Montesquieu, or Blackstone.

'Mr. Canning—Yes, you have precisely my meaning and the fact. And this, I say, shows what a nest of rebellious and impious villains these Radicals are. This is, I think, circumstantial proof enough of their wicked designs. But, if you want more, look at the laws for binding printers and publishers, for abolishing cheap publications, for banishing the villains when they put forth anything even tending to bring parliament into contempt. Look at these, and then doubt of their guilt if you can.'

The judge, having heard Canning's indictment, then proposed to hear what the Radicals had to say in their defence, and for this purpose suggested removing the padlocks on their mouths. Such a proceeding, however, drew a strong remonstrance from Canning:

' Mr Canning—What! Take off the padlocks! Suffer them to tell their lies about gentlemen and ladies, who, to uphold a constitution, which is "the envy of surrounding nations and the admiration of the world," condescend to take certain sums, under the names of sinecures and pensions! Suffer them to rail against rotten boroughs and against all that is ancient and venerable! Suffer them to "cut morals and religion from under the feet of future generations!" Suffer them——

' Judge—Gently, sir. You said something about rotten boroughs. Pray, what are those?

' Mr. Canning—Why (what an old fool it is—*aside*), they are the "soundest part of the constitution!"

' Judge—What! Can rotten boroughs be the soundest part of the constitution, which is "the envy of surrounding nations and the admiration of the world?"

' Mr. Canning—(*Aside*—The fellow is a Radical himself) Yes they may and they are and the rottener they are the better I like them; and as to unlocking the jaws of the traitors, who cry out against them, I will consent to no such thing.' [1]

While assailing all classes who upheld the existing order of things, Cobbett was especially severe in his attacks on the clergy. Ever since he had endeavoured to impose Paine on the English people as a national hero he had been pursued incessantly with accusations of irreligion and blasphemy. These cries were raised with great vehemence by the clergy, who especially resented

[1] *Political Register*, 15th April 1820.

his onslaughts on the tithe system. On his part Cobbett
did not spare the clergy, whom he hated on account of
their opposition to reform. He vigorously attacked them
for their worldliness and lack of sympathy with reform.
Commenting on a charge of the Bishop of London, he
wrote :

'You here tell us that the French Revolution was occasioned
by the parsons not having kept sufficiently in advance of the
people of France with regard to *knowledge* ; that is to say, with
regard to knowledge to be acquired from books. This is one of
your assertions. Another is, that a revolution has been prevented in England by the parsons having maintained their
proper place ; that is to say, by their being in advance of the
people in point of *knowledge* of the sort just spoken of.

'These are your two principal positions. They form the
foundation of all that follows ; and I undertake to prove them
both to be *false*. But before I go into this proof, let me ask
how this doctrine of yours agrees with the doctrines of the
Christian religion ; with the doctrines; or, perhaps, maxims, laid
down by Christ Himself. Did He depend on the *erudition* or
cunning, of the teachers, for the success of that doctrine, which He
was teaching ? On the contrary, did He not say that it was from
the mouths of *babes* and *sucklings* ; that is to say, from persons of
the simplest understandings and manners, and most unostentatious dress and appearance, that He expected His gospel to be
spread abroad with success ? Did He choose, for his apostles,
men with immense estates, scores of manors, scores of game-
keepers, and with apparel the most sumptuous that can be conceived ? Did He ever say or ever insinuate, that the success of
His saving word depended upon the teachers of it having palaces
for their places of residence ; having parks well stocked with
deer ; having retinues of servants equal in number to one or more
troops of horse ; having kitchens, the fumes of which give an
odour to the atmosphere, and gardens, coming up to Mahomet's
idea of Elysium ; did He ever say or insinuate, that it was
necessary, in order to make His word successful, that it should
be taught by men, dressed in lawn and lolling in coaches drawn

by six horses? You know well, that He chose for His Apostles twelve men, from amongst the lowest of mankind; from amongst fishermen and labourers and that, when He sent them forth at last, He charged them to take neither staff nor scrip; but to depend for their very subsistence upon what the faithful might choose to bestow upon them. Upon this condition it was that He promised to be with them always, even unto the end of the world.'[1]

In another passage of bitter irony he commented on the character of the clergy of his day:

'In our notions of clergymen, we sublimate and refine too much. We forget, that they *eat* and *drink* like other men. We, in short, forget their *temporalities*, and this is a part of their concerns which we ought never to forget. They have most comfortable livings. They do little, and have good cheer. It is natural, therefore, that they should have great hatred against any body, whose efforts tend to the *disturbing* of this state of things. It is very certain, that some men must undergo bodily labour. Without this the world could not go on. But, there is a desire in every man to live without this bodily labour; to live at ease, while others labour, and, of course, to live on that labour. So that the parsons are by no means singular in their taste. They enjoy a large portion of the good things of this world: perhaps the choicest portion of all. It is, therefore, very natural, that they should dislike anything that might, even by possibility, expose them to the danger of losing these good things. They are born with hearts like other men; but habit gives their hearts qualities different from the general mass. They do not *approve* of the bribery, perjury, drunkenness, and lying at elections; or, at least, many of them do not. But, when they consider that, without these, that system which insures them *ease and plenty*, could not exist, and that they might not find the same security under a better system, they are very apt to console themselves with the observations, that "*nothing is perfect under the sun*"; and that we must wait with *patience* for perfecti-

[1] *Political Register*, 14th September 1822.

bility in *another world*.   In the meanwhile, when times become critical, they become alarmed ; and they do from a feeling of fear that which they would not do from a less powerful motive. In the reformers they imagine they see the besiegers of their temporalities : they get frightened, next angry ; they appeal to the sword instead of the word ; they fear the loss of *tythes*, and they cry out *blasphemy*.'[1]

Irritated by the accusation constantly made against him of blasphemy and want of religious feeling, he resolved to show that he was capable of giving instruction in morals as well as in politics.   On 1st March 1821 he commenced to publish *Cobbett's Monthly Religious Tracts*, known after 1st June as *Cobbett's Monthly Sermons*.   The series was completed on 1st March 1822, no sermon appearing on 1st February, and it was frequently republished under the title of *Twelve Sermons*. The Sermons are among the most notable of Cobbett's writings, and they are characterised by a dignity and self-restraint which are rarely to be found among his productions.   There is, moreover, almost an entire absence of the personal note generally so conspicuous in his treatment of any subject, which, though it is the source of many interesting autobiographical fragments, ends by wearying his readers with its persistent egoism. The Sermons are of course political in their intent, but the political meaning is not forced on the attention, and applications to current events are made with reserve. Nowhere else in Cobbett's writings can be found so moderate or so clear a statement of the moral principles on which his social opinions were based.   Two of the Sermons, those on the 'Sluggard' and the 'Unnatural Mother,' are without political intent.   The eleventh, on

[1] *Political Register*, 26th August 1820.

the 'Sin of Forbidding Marriage,' was directed against Malthus, whose views Cobbett did not understand. The twelfth was entitled 'On the Duties of Parsons, and on the Institution and Object of Tithes,' and was a powerful attack on the ecclesiastical system. Writing at a time when the beneficed clergy were commonly absentees, he says:

'Now . . . I shall suppose it taken for granted, that, if the parson do not live where the flock lives, he can be of no use to them, either in inculcating the faith, or in checking the progress of infidelity; and besides this, when the flock see him set his duties, his obligations, his solemn engagements, and the commands and denunciations of God; when the flock sees the pastor set all these at open defiance, is there not good reason to fear, that the flock will begin to go astray, to wander from the faith, to doubt greatly of the truth of the thing altogether; in short to become unbelievers, or *infidels*; and in the fashionable language of the day, *blasphemers*?

'The Prophet Zechariah, in the words of a part of my text, has, manifestly, such a result in his eye when he cries, "Woe on the shepherd that *leaveth* his flock." And the Prophet *Ezekiel*, in the other parts of my text, clearly means to impress the same thing on the minds of the priests. What, indeed, can be more just, than that *woe* should fall upon those who "*eat the fat* and clothe themselves with the *wool*," but who feed not the flock! Who strengthen not the diseased, who heal not the sick, who bring back not those that have been driven away, who seek not the lost, but who "*rule* the flock with *force* and with *cruelty*"? Must not the flock be *scattered* in such a case? Must they not wander? And, as to the shepherds, "Thus saith the Lord God: behold, I am *against the shepherds*; and I will require my flock at their hand, and cause them to cease feeding the flock; neither shall the shepherds *feed themselves any more*; for I will deliver my flock from their mouth, that they may not be meat for them." Nor are Christ and His Apostles silent upon this great subject. . . .

'What, then! Can we, with all this before us, believe, that a parson does his duty, if he do not even reside in the same place with his flock? And, when we see a man taking the income of two or three livings, and seldom, or never go near either of them, are we still to look upon him as a follower of the Apostles, and entitled to the respect and reverence that is due to their memories and names? I will not say a single word about the *morals* of our parsons; about the way in which the greater part of them spend their time; about the worldly affairs in which they are most frequently busied; about the part which many of them take in political matters, and especially in elections: I confine myself, solely to my text, and I say that he who takes charge of a flock, and does not remain with that flock, subjects himself to the *woes* there denounced against the unfaithful shepherd.'

In the more political sermons although applications to particular persons are avoided, passages are not wanting which must have powerfully affected contemporary readers. With a clear reference to the trials of Carlile, Hone, and others, Cobbett says in his sermon on 'Naboth's Vineyard, or God's Vengeance against Hypocrisy and Cruelty':

'The man who will at once join in the cry of blasphemy against his neighbour, will find it difficult to convince any reasonable person that he would not have joined in the stoning of Naboth to death, and that he would have been the last among those, who cried out for the saving of Barabbas and for the sending of Jesus Himself to the Cross! . . .

'Has such a man forgotten that Jesus Christ Himself was accused of *blasphemy*? Has he forgotten that the hypocrites accused Him of being a blasphemer? How they bellowed out, "Now you have heard His *blasphemy*"? Has such a man forgotten that *blasphemy* was the general charge preferred against Christ and His Apostles? And from what motive? Only because their teaching tended to put a stop to the plunder of the hypocrites of that day. Those whose gainful frauds Christ and His Apostles detected and exposed, took care, like the Nobles and Judges of Samaria, *not to complain of this detection and exposure*. They affected not to have those in their eye, any more than the Judges of Samaria had the Vineyard of Naboth in their eye. It was, however, the exposure in the one case, as it had been the Vineyard in the other, which constituted the real offence. But *blasphemy* was the efficient accusation : that seized hold of popular feeling : that hardened the hearts of the people against the pretended offenders ; and thus hypocrisy indulged its love of plunder under the garb of zeal for religion.'

Again in 'The Sin of Drunkenness in Kings, Priests, and People,' occurs a passage that must have sounded daring to those acquainted with the lives of George IV. and his brothers :

'In the words of my text the reasons are given why Kings should "not drink wine nor Princes strong drink" ; and these reasons are "lest they drink and *forget the law*, and *pervert the judgement* of any of the *afflicted*." And, when was the drunkard mindful of the law ? When was he mindful to discharge his duties ? When did he do justice to any ? When did he ever discover a merciful disposition ? When did he consider the case of the afflicted ? When did he evince that he had one particle of humanity in his bosom ? The sensual man is always unfeeling towards others ; and this imputation more particularly applies to the drunkard and the glutton. Subjects, neighbours, wife, children ; all that ought to occupy a great portion of his affections, all are cast aside to make way for his inordinate and beastly appetites.

. . . .

'Well . . . may the inspired writer exclaim "woe to thee O land, when thy King is a child, and when thy Princes eat, not for strength, but for drunkenness !" Is it not enough to fill the heart with indignation, when we behold Kings or chief Magistrates, under whatever name, answering to the description above given ? Is it not enough to excite rage even in the just mind to hear men addicted to such vices addressed with the appellation of *Majesty*, and to hear them called *most excellent*, and their persons called *sacred*, when it is notorious to the world that they are distinguished from other men more by their vices than by any excellent quality; and that, by their chief characteristic, they are brought to a level with the brute?'

In the sermon on 'the Rights of the Poor' the case of the oppressed labourer is stated with an unsurpassed power of indignant rhetoric:

'The man who wholly disregards every moral and religious consideration; who tells you at once that he regards the labourers as cattle, and that he has a right to treat them in that way which shall be most conducive to his own advantage, is consistent enough; he is a brute in human shape; like a brute he acts, with the additional malignity of human refinement. But what are we to say of the pretended friend of religion; of the circulator of the Bible; of the propagator of the gospel, who, with brotherly love on his lips, sweats down to a skeleton, and sends nightly home to his starving children, the labourer out of whose bones he extracts even the means of his ostentatious display of piety? What are we to say of the bitter persecutor of "infidels," who, while he says grace over his sumptuous meals, can hear, without the smallest emotion, the hectic coughs of the squalid crowds whose half-famished bodies pine away in the pestiferous air of that prison which he calls a factory?

'Can such things be; and can such men know peace of mind? Can avarice and habit have so far obliterated reason, deadened the feelings of humanity, quieted the cries of conscience as to afford tranquillity to such men, on the miserable plea that their conduct squares with the maxims of commerce? So did the conduct of Judas Iscariot; for, to rob men of their blood differs only in degree from robbing them of their sweat; and, in some respects, the former is less cruel than the latter. Deliberately to take away a man's life; coolly to betray him and sell his blood; patiently to lie in wait for the blood of our neighbour seems to admit of no comparison in point of atrocity. But does even the murderous spy much exceed in iniquity the wretch who adopts and steadily pursues a system of fraud on those by whose labour he is enriched? To profit by deceits practised on the community at large; to cheat our neighbours and countrymen by means of short measures, false balances, and extortions; this bespeaks a heart odiously wicked; this bespeaks greediness, dishonesty and cruelty: what, then, must the man be, who can deliberately and systematically act in the same way towards those, who, in his field, or under his very roof, exert their strength and exhaust their ingenuity for his benefit: and who are content if they obtain a mere sufficiency of food and of raiment out of the fruits of that labour, which gives him all the means of indulgence in luxurious enjoyments? What must the man be, who can see his table spread with dainties, with all that nature aided by art can set before him to pamper his appetite; who knows, that he owes no part of this to his own labour; and yet, who can, while he affects to thank God for the blessing, studiously defraud and degrade those whose labour has created all that he possesses, all that fills his heart with pride?'

Probably there will appear to many to be both overstatement and confusion of thought in this fine passage: overstatement in regard to the share of labour in the production of wealth; and confusion of thought, because sometimes Cobbett seems to be rebuking the payment of unduly low wages, while at others he is denouncing deliberate fraud. But it is remarkable for its protest against a purely economic view of the labour question. The theory of *laissez faire* had already begun to take captive the intellect of England, and many years elapsed before the protest against it was renewed in equally powerful tones by the voice of Ruskin. The sermons were hailed with delight by the poor, while many of the rich and better educated appreciated their moderation of language and loftiness of feeling. They were actually read from many pulpits, with the omission, one may conjecture, of the denunciations of parsons and tithes.

Almost at the same time Cobbett was publishing another notable work of an entirely different character, his *Cottage Economy* : 'containing information relative to the brewing of beer, making of bread, keeping of cows, pigs, bees, ewes, goats, poultry, and rabbits, and relative to other matters deemed useful in the conducting of the affairs of a labourer's family.' The Introduction is dated 19th July 1821, and it was originally issued in seven monthly parts between 1st August 1821 and 1st March 1822, there being a two months' interval between the sixth and seventh parts. It was written at Worth Lodge, a farmhouse in Sussex, and at a later time Cobbett cordially acknowledged his obligations to Mrs. Brazier, the farmer's wife, who,

'Though then nearly eighty years of age, had brought up forty children and grand-children, and had it said of her, that she had done more work herself than any woman in Sussex ; and that there was not a working man or woman in the parish who had not, first or last, either resided or been fed under her roof ; and though she could *neither write nor read*, understood well the making of bread, the brewing of beer, the keeping of cows, the rearing of pigs, the salting of meat, the rearing of poultry, the obtaining of honey, the making of rushes to serve instead of candles ; and was able to teach me, practically, all that I myself did not know touching the subjects upon which I was writing.'[1]

The work at once attracted attention. It was praised by many who regarded Cobbett's political opinions with disfavour. Jeffrey, in the *Edinburgh Review* for February 1823, lauded both its intention and its teaching. It has, however, been urged with some justice by one of

[1] *Political Register*, 28th December 1833.

Cobbett's biographers, that much of the book is taken up with politics, that,

> 'When the cottager opens it with a view of being instructed in the art of brewing, he will find a long tirade against taxation, and a violent philippic against excisemen.'[1]

For a practical manual the work is certainly discursive, but for the same reason it contains many very readable passages. As an example may be quoted Cobbett's attack upon tea, which he regarded as very inferior to beer as a household beverage:

> 'I view the tea-drinking as a destroyer of health, an enfeebler of the frame, an engenderer of effeminacy and laziness, a debaucher of youth, and a maker of old age. . . . It is notorious that tea has no useful strength in it; that it contains nothing nutricious; that it, besides being good for nothing, has badness in it, because it is well known to produce want of sleep in many cases, and in all cases, to shake and weaken the nerves. It is, in fact, a weaker kind of laudanum, which enlivens for the moment and deadens afterwards. At any rate it communicates no strength to the body; it does not, in any degree, assist in affording, what labour demands. . . . Then comes the great article of all, the time employed in this tea making affair. It is impossible to make a fire, boil water, make the tea, drink it, wash up the things, sweep up the fire-place and put all to rights again in a less space of time, upon an average, than two hours. . . . Observe, too, that the time thus spent, is one half of it, the best time of the day. By the time that the clattering tea tackle is out of the way, the morning is spoiled; its prime is gone; and any work that is to be done afterwards lags heavily along. If the mother has to go out to work, the tea affair must all first be over. She comes into the field, in Summer time, when the sun has gone a third part of his course. She has the heat of the day to encounter, instead of having her work done and being ready to return home at an early hour. Yet early she must go,

---

[1] Huish, *Memoirs of Cobbett*, ii. 356.

too; for, there is the fire again to be made, the clattering tea tackle again to come forward; and even in the longest day she must have candle light, which never ought to be seen in a cottage (except in case of illness) from March to September.' .

Cobbett's energies were by no means exhausted in teaching morality to the clergy and instructing the labouring classes in household economy. The enlargement of his political influence was continually present to his mind. With this object in view he began in the autumn of 1821 to undertake political tours in various parts of the country. As he no longer possessed the farm at Botley to occupy his leisure, these tours were much more systematic and prolonged than the expeditions which he had undertaken before his flight to America.[1] Those were chiefly rapid journeys to attend county meetings or other assemblies, where he might find an opportunity of publishing his views, while these were leisurely journeys extending over a week, a fortnight, or even a month, and intended perhaps as much to gratify his taste for the country as to spread his opinions. His first journey was commenced on 29th October 1821. Leaving London he rode through Hants, Wiltshire, Gloucester, and Hereford, returning by way of Oxford. The sight of the University produced a characteristic outburst:

'Upon beholding the masses of buildings, at Oxford, devoted to what they call "*learning*," I could not help reflecting on the drones that they contain and the wasps they send forth! However, malignant as some are, the great and prevalent characteristic is *folly*: emptiness of head; want of talent; and one half of the fellows who are what they call *educated* here, are unfit to be clerks in a grocer's or mercer's shop.—As I looked up at what they called *University Hall*, I could not help reflecting that what I had written, even since I left Kensington on the

<hr />

[1] See p. 187.

29th October, would produce more effect, and do more good in the world, than all that had for a hundred years been written by all the members of this University, who devour, perhaps, not less than *a million pounds a year*, arising from property, completely at the disposal of the "Great Council of the nation," and I could not help exclaiming to myself: "Stand forth, ye big-wigged, ye gloriously feeding Doctors! Stand forth, ye *rich* of that church whose *poor* have had given them *a hundred thousand pounds a year*, not out of your riches, but out of the *taxes*, raised, in part, from the *salt* of the labouring man! Stand forth and face me, who have from the pen of my leisure-hours, sent, among your flocks, a hundred thousand sermons in ten months! More than you have all done for the last half-century!,"—I exclaimed in vain. I dare say (for it was at peep of day) that not a man of them had yet endeavoured to unclose his eyes.'[1]

Before the close of the year Cobbett made two more journeys, through Kent, and through Norfolk and Suffolk, while in January 1822 he rode through Sussex. The woods around Battle won his admiration:

'Woodland counties are interesting on many accounts. Not so much on account of their masses of green leaves, as on account of the variety of sights, and sounds, and incidents, that they afford. Even in winter, the coppices are beautiful to the eye, while they comfort the mind, with the idea of shelter and warmth. In spring they change their hue from day to day, during two whole months, which is about the time from the first appearance of the delicate leaves of the birch, to the full expansion of those of the ash; and, even before the leaves come at all to intercept the view, what, in the vegetable creation, is so delightful to behold as the bed of a coppice bespangled with primroses and blue-bells? The opening of the birch leaves, is the signal for the pheasant to crow, for the blackbird to whistle, and the thrush to sing; and, just when the oak-buds begin to look reddish, and not a day before, the whole tribe of finches burst forth in songs from every bough, while the lark, imitating them all, carries the joyous sounds to the sky.'[2]

---

[1] *Rural Rides*, 1885, i. 41-2.   [2] *Ibid.*, i. 80.

In June he traversed Hertfordshire and Buckingham, and in the autumn passed through part of Hampshire, Berkshire, Surrey, and Essex.   The beauty of the scenes through which he passed in no way lessened the terrible intensity of his political hatreds, while the wretched condition of the inhabitants in many districts roused him even to greater animosity towards those who had injured them.   At this time one of his chief opponents came to an unhappy end.   On 12th August 1822 Lord Castlereagh committed suicide at his residence, Foot's Cray, by cutting his throat with a penknife.   Cobbett received the news with sombre pleasure.   In the next number of the *Political Register* appeared a letter to Joseph Swann, a reformer, who had been sentenced by the magistrates of Cheshire to imprisonment for four years and a half in Chester gaol, for selling seditious pamphlets and for being present at a meeting for parliamentary reform.   It commenced :

'CASTLEREAGH HAS CUT HIS OWN THROAT, AND IS DEAD ! Let that sound reach you in the depth of your dungeon; and let it carry consolation to your suffering soul !'

This savage note of satisfaction was sustained throughout this terrible letter.

'As to compassion, as to *sorrow*, upon this occasion, how base a hypocrite I must be to affect it !   Nay, how base a hypocrite to disguise or attempt to disguise my satisfaction ! Can I forget Ireland ?   Can I forget Mr. Finnerty ?[1]   Can I forget Napoleon ?   Marshal Ney ?   Can I forget the Queen, who though she suffered so much, though she suffered to the breaking of her heart, never thought of the dastardly act of cutting her own throat ? . . . The ruffians who continue to praise this man,

---

[1] Peter Finnerty, a friend of Cobbett's, died in 1816, soon after his release from Lincoln gaol, where he had been imprisoned for a political libel.

tell us that the history of his life is found in the measures of the Government for the last twenty-seven years; and that is true enough; . . . it is written in a mass of pauperism, hitherto wholly unknown to England, and it is written in starvation to Ireland amidst overproduction. As to his family and connexions, look at the immense sums which they are now receiving out of the fruit of the people's labour. And as to any compassion that we are to feel for them, we will feel it when an end to the sufferings of the Reformers and their families will leave us a particle of compassion to bestow on anybody else.'[1]

When public wrongs produce such indignation it is the forenote of revolution. Cobbett, however, had private as well as public wrongs to inflame him, for he considered the extreme measures of coercion employed from 1817 onwards as particularly directed against himself, and not only as the cause of his two years of exile, but also of his pecuniary losses. Actuated by this strong sense of injury, he resolved to retaliate by an assault on those principles and beliefs, which were the special pride and glory of the classes which had wronged him. In 1824 he announced his intention of publishing a *History of the Protestant Reformation in England and Ireland*, in order to prove, as a plain matter of fact, 'that the Reformation impoverished and degraded the main body of the people of England.' It was published in sixteen monthly parts, the first appearing on 29th November 1824, and the last in March 1825. According to its author it was chiefly founded on the History of Dr. Lingard,

'Whose laborious work, able and good as I think it (as far as I have read), will never, until the last page shall have been destroyed by the hand of time, produce a thousandth part of the *effect* that mine will produce in the space of three years.'[2]

[1] *Political Register*, 17th August 1822.   [2] *Ibid.*, 30th October 1824.

Cobbett's work was an amazingly vigorous example of historical polemic, of a kind with which every age has been familiar; none more so than the present. But while coarseness, violence, and entire absence of charity are attributes common to all specimens of this kind of literature, Cobbett's daring and originality claim for his work especial recognition. Lingard had too much moderation to paint the evils of the English Reformation in colours startling enough to influence the popular mind. Cobbett, for the first time, supplied the complement to the roseate view which had become the traditional belief of English Protestants. As an essay in history the work is nearly valueless : it contains repeated blunders in fact, and teems with terms of the commonest abuse. He confounds, for instance, the two Ducs d'Anjou, who were successively suitors for the hand of that queen, whom he usually designates as 'bloody Bess.' But by his violence and confident dogmatism he made considerable impression on the public mind. His position was singular. While he wrote with all the bias of a sectarian fanatic, he was not himself a Roman Catholic.

'It is not my object,' he observed, 'to induce one single person to change from the Protestant to the Catholic religion. I wish that the change in the religion of the country had never taken place, and I shall give very solid reasons for that wish. But it has taken place, and I am a Protestant very well contented with the religion of the Church of England by law established. However, since there were a very large portion of my fellow-subjects, who continued to adhere to the religion of their and of my forefathers; and since great numbers of them do still continue to so adhere; since this adherence has been made the ground of grievous suffering to them, and since that grievous suffering manifestly does great injury to us all, and exposes our country to great perils, is it not my duty as their fellow-subject, and as a man faithful to his allegiance to the king; is it not my bounden duty to endeavour to prevail on my brother Protestants to do justice to this oppressed class of my fellow-subjects? In order to attempt this with the best chance of success, it is necessary to go back to the time when we separated ourselves from that Church to which the fathers of us all belonged, and to show what the religion of our fathers was, and what are the calumnies which have been heaped upon it and upon them; to show in their true light the characters, the motives and the means of those who made the change; to trace back to their very source those viperous assertions on the Catholics which have made us a divided people; to reconcile us Protestants to our brethren, descended from one common Catholic stock; to unite us once more, and to insure, if I possibly can, that harmony which is the best defence of nations, and the greatest security for morality and happiness.'[1]

Actuated by this purpose he drew a picture of the Reformation in England, which, though certainly not more accurate or impartial, than that which he opposed, was yet important historically because it presented to the popular mind an aspect of the Reformation which had been ignored by their teachers, and equally important politically because, at that time, the better treatment of Roman Catholics in England and Ireland was a question of the first importance. Though the main purport of the book was controversial, and though much of it consists merely of violent polemic, it is partially redeemed from a literary point of view by some isolated passages. Take for example one, probably inspired, to some extent at least, by his early memories of Waverley Abbey :

' Go to the site of some once opulent convent. Look at the cloister, now become in the hands of some rack-renter the receptacle for dung, fodder, and faggot wood. See the hall

[1] *Political Register*, 11th December 1824.

where for ages the widow, the orphan, the aged, and the stranger found a table ready spread.   See a bit of its wall now helping to make a cattle-shed, the rest having been hauled away to build a warehouse.   Recognise in the side of a barn a part of the once magnificent chapel; and if, chained to the spot by your melancholy musings, you be admonished of the approach of night by the voice of the screech-owl from those arches, which once at the same hour resounded, with the vespers of the monk, and which have for 700 years been assailed by storms and tempests in vain; if thus admonished of the necessity of seeking food, shelter, and a bed, lift up your eyes, and look at the white-washed and dry-rotten shed on the hill called the "Gentleman's House"; and apprised of the "board wages" and "spring guns," which are the signs of his hospitality, turn your head, jog away from the scene of former comfort and grandeur; and with old English welcoming in your mind, reach the nearest inn, and then in a room, half-warmed and half-lighted, with a reception precisely proportioned to the presumed length of your purse, sit down and listen to an account of the hypocritical pretences, the base motives, the tyrannical and bloody means, under which, from which, and by which the ruin you have been witnessing was effected, and the hospitality you have lost was forever banished from the land.'

The popularity of the *History* was very great in England itself, where it commended itself alike to Roman Catholics and to other opponents to the Established Church.   The sale of the first number, according to Cobbett's statement, was nearly forty thousand.[1]   But its fame in America was even more widespread.   John Doyle, a bookseller of New York, said that it had caused the greatest stir there of any book ever offered for sale since he had been in the trade.

'Every person who reads anything on religion, or English history, has read it, and is talking about it.   It is read by all

---

[1] *Political Register*, 1st January 1825.

sects. And such is the demand for it that it is now stereotyping in this city, and, also, two separate translations of it are making into the Spanish language; one by a Mexican, and the other by an Irishman, who has lived with the Spaniards many years in Columbia and the Islands. I have just heard from a bookseller, who has come to-day from Philadelphia, that they are stereotyping it there. This is a thing heretofore unheard of, of any Book, in this country, except the Bible. I am confident from what I see, that millions of them, almost, will be sold on this continent.'[1]

Besides the translations into Spanish just mentioned, translations into French, German, and Italian also appeared at Paris, Geneva, and Rome. On 14th July 1827 a second part was issued consisting of:

'A List of the Abbeys, Priories, Nunneries, Hospitals and other Religious Foundations, in England and Wales, and in Ireland, confiscated, seized on, or alienated, by the "Reformation" sovereigns and parliaments.'

The work was several times reprinted, and a new edition by the Rev. F. A. Gasquet, with historical notes and some excisions, appeared in 1896.

This work of Cobbett's was not entirely unconnected with a new item in his political programme. Hitherto he had taken little interest in Irish affairs since the letters of Juverna had brought him into trouble in 1804. But towards the close of 1824 he began to advocate in the *Political Register* the emancipation and enfranchisement of Irish Catholics. He also showed great attachment to Daniel O'Connell, whom he highly praised in the same periodical. Like all Cobbett's political friendships, however, it did not long remain unruffled. Early in 1825

---

[1] Doyle to Thomas Smith, quoted by Cobbett in *Political Register*, 31st December 1825.

differences arose among the Irish party in regard to the Catholic Relief Bill and especially in regard to the proposal to accompany the measure with two supplementary bills, subsequently known as 'the wings,' for endowing the Catholic clergy and for disfranchising the forty shillings freeholders.   O'Connell tacitly approved of the wings, for which he was fiercely denounced by Cobbett, who regarded the proposal to disfranchise the freeholders with horror and disgust.   Cobbett's quarrel with O'Connell ran the usual course of his enmities.   In July 1825 he still spoke with tenderness of his personal character and professed regret for the political differences between them.   But, stung by some contemptuous, though not ill-natured expressions of O'Connell, in September he made a violent attack on him and Burdett in the *Political Register* under the shape of a comedy entitled, 'Big O and Sir Glory,' in which he advanced charges of corruption and bad faith which, if they could have been established, would have entirely destroyed O'Connell's political reputation.   They gained no credence, however, among the Irish party, and O'Connell's position remained unshaken.

About the same time Cobbett also quarrelled violently with Henry Hunt, whom he had formerly supported against Sir Francis Burdett as a candidate for Westminster.   Hunt like O'Connell was overwhelmed with abuse, designated the 'unny man,' and treated with that vulgar impertinence, which either Cobbett or his readers sometimes mistook for humour.

Having thus emphatically separated himself from most of the Radical leaders, Cobbett again turned his attention to obtaining a seat in Parliament.   In 1825 a young

Norfolk baronet, Sir Thomas Beevor, who had a profound
admiration for Cobbett's principles, issued an address in
which he called on persons of similar opinions to assist
him in promoting Cobbett's return for some popular constituency. Several meetings were held in the early
months of 1826, when a dissolution appeared imminent,
and on 12th May Cobbett presented himself to the
electors of Preston as a candidate. The borough returned two members, and Cobbett's opponents were the
Hon. E. G. Stanley, afterwards better known as the fourteenth Earl of Derby, John Wood, a merchant, and
Captain Barrie, R.N. Parliament was dissolved on 31st
May, and polling commenced on 11th June. In spite of
the popular nature of the constituency, Cobbett was
returned bottom of the poll, with nine hundred and
ninety-five votes, Stanley receiving over three thousand,
Wood nearly two thousand, while Barrie, the other unsuccessful candidate, received between sixteen and seventeen
hundred. The polling terminated in a riot, which obliged
the mayor to call in the assistance of the military. At
the close of the election Cobbett characteristically addressed his followers :

'Gentlemen, I have done much good to you by my coming; I
have sweated your tyrants—I have bled them. I have made the
silly Honourable [E. G. Stanley] throw £15,000 among you, and
that's no joke; for though these lords have too much land, they
have not too much money. I have tickled the captain too; I
have made him dance to some tune; he must have pledged his
half-pay to keep open house for you, and now, like the other
half-pays in London, he must live on plates of beef and goes of
gin for the next seven years. As to Mr. Wood, I could not draw
any money out of him, for the poor devil had none to spend;
but his father, Otty Wood, the miserly old sugar-broker of

Liverpool, I have extracted from his pocket what a hundred horse-power steam-engine could not draw from him—I have made him spend £7000. These are what I have done for you, good gentlemen. But I have done more—I have kept out the Tory Captain Barrie. Not that I like Wood either; I only dislike him least of the two; but you shall not be cursed with either one or other of them, gentlemen. The election is not worth a straw. I'll have it set aside next April, when I'll bleed our opponents again, and you'll elect for your representative the only man who has the wish and the ability, the heart and the head, to serve you and his country—myself, gentlemen, myself.'[1]

On the meeting of the new Parliament, Cobbett presented a petition against the return, but in consequence of his failure to give the requisite securities for the payment of his costs, the petition was discharged.[2]

Cobbett felt severely the failure of this second attempt to enter Parliament. In spite of the fact that the terrible agricultural distress, the disorders in trade, consequent on the resumption of cash payments, and his tremendous denunciations of the game laws had restored much of his former influence among the unfranchised classes, he perceived clearly that he had little chance of election to the House of Commons unless the franchise was considerably extended. His failure postponed indefinitely the accomplishment of what was the immediate, though undoubtedly not the final, object of his ambition. He dreamed of office and power, and he believed that it was only necessary to obtain a parliamentary seat to find these within his reach. But his defeat at Preston dispirited his supporters

---

[1] *Annual Register*, 1826, i. 170-71. This speech has probably been touched by an unfriendly hand.

[2] For Cobbett's account of the circumstances, see *Political Register*, 17th February 1827.

and considerably diminished his personal influence. He further lowered his prestige by occasional conduct of a very undignified character. Thus on 23rd May 1827 he went to the dinner at the 'Crown and Anchor' intended to celebrate the twentieth anniversary of Burdett's election for Westminster, and created a disturbance by attacking Burdett for his complaisance towards Canning. The proceedings became very disorderly. The majority of these present, being ardent supporters of Burdett, declined to give Cobbett a hearing, and he in return not only defied them in speech but insulted them by look and gesture. The episode would hardly be worth commemorating, but for the fact that Heine was present. The incident occurred during his year of residence in England. It was the only time that he saw Cobbett, and the picture was indelibly fixed in his mind. Cobbett seemed to him the incarnation of impetuous and undistinguishing revolt against existing political institutions.

'While I translate Cobbett's words, the man himself comes bodily before my mind's eye, as I saw him at that uproarious dinner at the Crown and Anchor Tavern, with his scolding red face and his radical laugh, in which venomous hate mingles with a mocking exultation at his enemies' surely approaching downfall. He is a chained house-dog who falls with equal fury on every one whom he does not know, often bites the calves of the best friend of the house, barks incessantly, and just because of this incessantness of his barking cannot get listened to, even when he barks at an actual thief. Therefore the distinguished thieves who plunder England do not think it necessary to throw the growling Cobbett a bone to stop his mouth. This makes the dog furiously savage, and he shows all his hungry teeth. Poor old Cobbett! England's watch-dog! I have no love for thee, for every brutish nature revolts me; but I pity thee from my inmost soul, as I see how thou strainest in vain to break loose and to get at those thieves, who make off with their booty before thy very eyes, and mock at thy fruitless springs and thine impotent howling.'[1]

For the years immediately following his unsuccessful candidature at Preston, Cobbett took a less prominent part in politics, and, though he continued to thunder forth his diatribes in the *Register*, he figured less conspicuously than formerly in the general press.   This lull in his political activity was, however, fortunate in reality, for in 1829 and 1830 he produced one of his greatest literary masterpieces.   On 1st June 1829, he began to publish in monthly parts his ' Advice to Young Men, and (incidentally) to young women in the middle and higher ranks of life.'   The Advice was in the form of a series of letters :

' I shall begin,' said Cobbett, ' with the Youth, go to the Young Man or the Bachelor, talk the matter over with him as a Lover, then consider him in the character of a Husband ; then as a Father ; then as a Citizen or Subject ; though if he will be ruled by me he will, if he can, contrive to exist in the former of these two capacities.'[2]

The whole was completed by 1830.   It marks the high-water mark of Cobbett's literary attainment.   In no other of his writings are to be found more perfect examples of his style or more signal instances of his power of narrative. The book is peculiarly rich in autobiographical reminiscences.   It contains pictures of his life as a soldier, an account of his courtship and marriage, and vivid glimpses of his country life amid his family at Botley.   From these personal recollections numerous selections have been

---

[1] The translation is that of Matthew Arnold with one or two slight changes.

[2] *Political Register*, 9th May 1829.

made in the present work. They are full of tenderness and affection towards his family, and bear unmistakable testimony to the essential kindness of Cobbett's character. They could hardly have been written by a very bad or even a very selfish man. The character of Cobbett's counsel to young men is interesting also, for it shows that in spite of the fact that a great number of his countrymen looked on him as a revolutionary and a fire-brand, he was in social morality in accord with the best of his time. His advice is in general grave, restrained, and orthodox, with no trace of undue sympathy for vice or even for weakness of character. Sound common sense is its predominant feature. What can be more admirable in its own way than this advice to a father:

'But there is one fatal error against which every father ought to guard his heart; and the kinder that heart is, the more necessary such guardianship. I mean the fatal error of heaping upon one child, to the prejudice of the rest; or, upon a part of them. This partiality sometimes arises from mere caprice; sometimes from the circumstance of the favourite being more favoured by nature than the rest; sometimes from the nearer resemblance to himself, that the father sees in the favourite, and, sometimes, from the hope of preventing the favoured party from doing that which would disgrace the parent. All these motives are highly censurable, but the last is the most general, and by far the most mischievous in its effects. How many fathers have been ruined, how many mothers and families brought to beggary, how many industrious and virtuous groups have been pulled down from competence to penury, from the desire to prevent one from bringing shame on the parent! So that, contrary to every principle of justice, the bad is rewarded for the badness and the good punished for the goodness. Natural affection, remembrance of infantine endearments, reluctance to abandon long cherished hopes, compassion for the sufferings of your own flesh and blood, the dread of fatal consequences from your

adhering to justice; all these beat at your heart, and call on
you to give way: but, you must resist them all; or, your ruin,
and that of the rest of your family, are decreed.   Suffering is
the natural and just punishment of idleness, drunkenness,
squandering, and an indulgence in the society of prostitutes;
and, never did the world behold an instance of an offender, in
this way, reclaimed but by the infliction of this punishment;
particularly, if the society of prostitutes made part of the offence;
for, here is something that takes the *heart from you*. Nobody
ever yet saw, and nobody ever will see, a young man, linked to
a prostitute, and retain, at the same time, any, even the smallest
degree of affection, for parents or brethren.   You may supplicate,
you may implore, you may leave yourself penniless, and your
virtuous children without bread; the invisible cormorant will
still call for more; and, as we saw, only the other day, a wretch
was convicted of having, at the instigation of his prostitute,
beaten his aged mother, to get from her the small remains of the
means necessary to provide her with food.   In Heron's collection
of God's judgments on wicked acts, it is related of an unnatural
son, who fed his aged father upon orts and offal, lodged him in
a filthy and crazy garret, and clothed him in sackcloth, while he
and his wife and children lived in luxury; that, having bought
sackcloth enough for two dresses for his father, the children took
away the part not made up, and *hid it*, and that, upon asking
them what they *could do this for*, they told him that they meant
to keep it *for him*, when he should become old and walk with a
stick ! This, the author relates, pierced his heart; and, indeed,
if *this* failed, he must have had the heart of a tiger; but even
this would not succeed with the associate of a prostitute.   When
this vice, this love of the society of prostitutes; when this vice
has once got fast hold, vain are all your sacrifices, vain your
prayers, vain your hopes, vain your anxious desire to disguise
the shame from the world; and, if you have acted well your
part, no part of that shame falls on you, unless you *have
administered to the cause of it*.   Your authority has ceased; the
voice of the prostitute, or the charms of the bottle, or the rattle
of the dice, has been more powerful than your advice and
example: you must lament this: but it is not to bow you down;

and, above all things, it is weak, and even criminally selfish, to sacrifice the rest of your family, in order to keep from the world the knowledge of that, which, if known, would, in your view of the matter, bring shame on yourself.

'Let me hope, however, that this is a calamity which will befall very few good fathers; and that, of all such, the sober, industrious, and frugal habits of their children, their dutiful demeanour, their truth and their integrity, will come to smooth the path of their downward days, and be the objects on which their eyes will close. Those children must, in their turn, travel the same path; and they may be assured, that, "Honour thy father and thy mother, that thy days may be long in the land," is a precept, a disregard of which, never yet failed, either first or last, to bring its punishment. And, what can be more just than that signal punishment shall follow such a crime; a crime directly against the voice of nature itself? Youth has its passions, and due allowance justice will make for these; but, are the delusions of the boozer, the gamester, or the harlot, to be pleaded in excuse for a disregard for the source of your existence? Are those to be pleaded in apology for giving pain to the father who has toiled for half a lifetime in order to feed and clothe you, and to the mother whose breast has been to you the fountain of life? Go, you, and shake the hand of the boon-companion; take the greedy harlot to your arms; mock at the tears of your fond and anxious parents; and, when your purse is empty and your complexion faded, receive the poverty and the scorn due to your base ingratitude.'[1]

The essentially puritanical cast of Cobbett's mind is shown strongly in his advice to parents in regard to their children's reading.

'Well, then, having resolved to teach your children, or, to have them taught, at home, let us now see how they ought to proceed as to *books* for learning. It is evident, speaking of boys, that, at last, they must study the art, or science, that you intend them to pursue; if they be to be surgeons, they must

[1] *Advice to Young Men*, 1837, pp. 309-12.

read books on surgery; and the like in other cases.   But, there
are certain *elementary* studies; certain books to be used by *all
persons*, who are destined to acquire any book-learning at all.
Then there are departments, or branches of knowledge, that
every man in the middle rank of life ought, if he can, to acquire,
they being, in some sort, necessary to his reputation as a *well-
informed* man, a character to which the farmer and the shopkeeper ought to aspire as well as the lawyer and the surgeon.
Let me now, then, offer my advice as to the *course* of reading,
and the *manner* of reading, for a boy, arrived at his *fourteenth*
year, that being, in my opinion, early enough for him to
begin.

'And, first of all, whether as to boys or girls, I deprecate
romances of every description.   It is impossible that they can
do any *good*, and they may do a great deal of harm.   They
excite passions that ought to lie dormant; they give the mind a
taste for *highly-seasoned* matter; they make matters of real life
insipid; every girl, addicted to them, sighs to be a Sophia
Western, and every boy, a Tom Jones.   What girl is not in love
with the *wild* youth, and what boy does not find a justification
for his wildness?   What can be more pernicious than the teach-
ings of this celebrated romance?   Here are two young men put
before us, both sons of the same mother; the one a *bastard* (and
by a parson too), the other a *legitimate child*; the former wild,
disobedient, and squandering; the latter, steady, sober, obedient,
and frugal; the former everything that is frank and generous in
his nature, the latter a greedy hypocrite; the former rewarded
with the most beautiful and virtuous of women and a double
estate, the latter punished by being made an outcast.   How is
it possible for young people to read such a book, and to look
upon orderliness, sobriety, obedience, and frugality, as *virtues*?
And this is the tenor of almost every romance, and of almost
every play, in our language.   In the *School for Scandal*, for
instance, we see two brothers; the one a prudent and frugal
man, and, to all appearance, a moral man, the other a hare-
brained squanderer, laughing at the morality of his brother; the
former turns out to be a base hypocrite and seducer, and is
brought to shame and disgrace; while the latter is found to be

full of generous sentiment, and Heaven itself seems to interfere to give him fortune and fame. In short, the direct tendency of the far greater part of these books, is, to cause young people to despise all those virtues, without the practice of which they must be a curse to their parents, a burden to the community, and must, except by mere accident, lead wretched lives. I do not recollect one romance nor one play, in our language, which has not this tendency. How is it possible for young princes to read the historical plays of the punning and smutty Shakspeare, and not think, that to be drunkards, blackguards, the companions of debauchees and robbers, is the suitable beginning of a glorious reign?' [1]

'There is, too, another most abominable principle that runs through them all, namely, that there is in *high birth*, something of *superior nature*, instinctive courage, honour, and talent. Who can look at the two *royal youths* in *Cymbeline*, or at the *noble youth* in *Douglas*, without detesting the base parasites who wrote those plays? Here are youths, brought up by *shepherds*, never told of their origin, believing themselves the sons of these humble parents, but discovering when grown up, the highest notions of valour and honour, and thirsting for military renown, even while tending their reputed fathers' flocks and herds! And why this species of falsehood? To cheat the mass of the people; to keep them in abject subjection; to make them quietly submit to despotic sway. And the infamous authors are guilty of the cheat, because they are, in one shape or another, paid by oppressors out of means squeezed from the people. A *true* picture would give us just the reverse; would show us that '*high birth*' is the enemy of virtue, of valour, and of talent; would show us that with all their incalculable advantages, royal and noble families have, only by mere accident, produced a great man; that, in general, they have been amongst the most effeminate, unprincipled, cowardly, stupid, and, at the very least,

---

[1] This antipathy to Shakespeare was not confined to Cobbett. It was shared by many writers of democratic sympathies, by Swift, Defoe, Goldsmith, and Burns. Burns, however, preferred *Douglas* to Shakespeare's tragedies. See Mr. Thomas Seccombe's article on William Shakespeare in the *Bookman*, October 1903.

amongst the most useless persons, considered as individuals, and not in connection with the prerogatives and powers bestowed on them solely by the law.

'It is impossible for me, by any words that I can use, to express, to the extent of my thoughts, the danger of suffering young people to form their opinions from the writings of poets and romancers. Nine times out of ten, the morality they teach is bad, and must have a bad tendency. Their wit is employed to *ridicule virtue*, as you will almost always find, if you examine the matter to the bottom. The world owes a very large part of its sufferings to tyrants; but what tyrant was there among the ancients whom the poets did not place *amongst the gods*? Can you open an English poet, without, in some part or other of his works, finding the grossest flatteries of royal and noble persons? How are young people not to think that the praises bestowed on these persons are just? Dryden, Parnell, Gay, Thomson, in short, what poet have we had, or have we, Pope only excepted, who was not, or is not, a pensioner, or a sinecure placeman, or the wretched dependant of some part of the Aristocracy? Of the extent of the powers of writers in producing mischief to a nation, we have two most striking instances in the cases of Dr. Johnson and Burke. The former, at a time when it was a question whether war should be made on America to compel her to submit to be taxed by the English parliament, wrote a pamphlet, entitled, *Taxation no Tyranny*, to urge the nation into that war. The latter, when it was a question whether England should wage war against the people of France, to prevent them from reforming their government, wrote a pamphlet to urge the nation into *that* war. The first war lost us America, the last cost us six hundred millions of money, and has loaded us with forty millions a year of taxes. Johnson, however, got a *pension for his life*, and Burke a pension for his life, and for *three lives after his own*! Cumberland and Murphy, the play-writers, were pensioners; and, in short, of the whole mass, where has there been one whom the people were not compelled to pay for labours, having for their principal object the deceiving and enslaving of that same people? It is, therefore, the duty of every father, when he puts a book into the hands of his son or

R

daughter, to give the reader a true account of *who* or *what* the writer of the book was, or is.'[1]

The year 1830 saw the publication of another masterpiece, the *Rural Rides*, which is by far the most familiar of Cobbett's books to the general public. As has been already stated, the series of letters which forms the *Rural Rides* was commenced in the *Political Register* in the autumn of 1821. The tours of 1821 and 1822 have been briefly sketched. In 1823 Cobbett made three journeys, into Surrey, Sussex and Hampshire, into Sussex, and into Kent. After an interval of two years he rode across Surrey and Hampshire in October 1825 and thence into Sussex. In August 1826 he penetrated further westward than hitherto, passing through Somerset, and Gloucester, into Herefordshire and Worcestershire, while in October he visited the New Forest. The first edition of the *Rural Rides* contained the letters written during these excursions. In 1853 a second edition by his son, James Paul Cobbett, included his journeys between 1829 and 1832, among which was a northern tour in the latter year, embracing Newcastle, Hexham, North Shields, and Durham. A third edition in two volumes by Pitt Cobbett, vicar of Crofton, appeared in 1885, with excellent notes. None of these editions, however, comprise the whole of Cobbett's journeys. His northern tour of 1832 extended into Scotland, where he visited, among other places, Glasgow and Edinburgh, but though the whole of the letters referring to it were published in 1833 under the title of *Cobbett's Tour in Scotland and in the Four Northern Counties of England*, in all the editions of the *Rural Rides* those relating to Scotland are omitted. And in 1834

[1] *Advice to Young Men*, pp. 292-96.

Cobbett made a long visit to Ireland, the details of which have never been reprinted, though they appeared at the time in the *Register* in a most interesting series of letters.

Cobbett wrote most of the epistles, which are contained in the *Rural Rides,* at the end of the day's journey and sent them to be inserted in the *Register* without revision or correction. Yet they comprise some of the most effective of his writing, retaining, from their lack of pre-meditation, the freshness and colour of the scenes they describe. The political aspect of the country was of course the predominant interest in his mind, when he wrote, and perhaps politics enter too largely into his letters ; but there are also many passages in which tran-sient controversies are forgotten in his love for country pleasures and people. The *Rural Rides* are so well known that long extracts would be out of place, and several shorter quotations have already been made. An episode in a day's journey on the borders of Hampshire and Surrey, in the month of November, may serve as an illustration of Cobbett's power of narrative :

'We got to Headley, the sign of the Holly-Bush, just at dusk and just as it began to rain. I had neither eaten nor drunk since eight o'clock in the morning ; and as it was a nice little public-house, I at first intended to stay all night, an intention that I afterwards very indiscreetly gave up. I had *laid my plan*, which included the getting to Thursley that night. When, therefore, I had got some cold bacon and bread, and some milk, I began to feel ashamed of stopping short of my *plan*, especially after having so heroically persevered in the "stern path," and so disdainfully scorned to go over Hindhead. I knew that my road lay through a hamlet called *Churt*, where they grow such fine *bennet-grass* seed. There was a moon ; but there was also a hazy rain. I had heaths to go over, and I might go into quags. Wishing to execute my plan, however, I at last brought myself to quit a very comfortable turf-fire, and to set off in the rain, having bargained to give a man three shillings to guide me out to the northern foot of Hindhead. I took care to ascertain, that my guide knew the road perfectly well; that is to say, I took care to ascertain it as far as I could, which was, indeed, no farther than his word would go. Off we set, the guide mounted on his own or master's horse, and with a white smock frock, which enabled us to see him clearly. We trotted on pretty fast for about half an hour; and I perceived, not without some surprise, that the rain, which I knew to be coming from the *south*, met me full in the face, when it ought, according to my reckoning, to have beat upon my right cheek. I called to the guide repeatedly to ask him if he was *sure that he was right*, to which he always answered, "Oh! yes, sir, I know the road." I did not like this "*I know the road.*" At last, after going about six miles in nearly a southerly direction, the guide turned short to the left. That brought the rain upon my right cheek, and though I could not very well account for the long stretch to the south, I thought, that, at any rate, we were *now* in the right track; and, after going about a mile in this new direction, I began to ask the guide *how much further we had to go*; for I had got a pretty good soaking, and was rather impatient to see the foot of Hindhead. Just at this time, in raising my head and looking forward as I spoke to the guide, what should I see, but a long, high, and steep *hanger* arising before us, the trees along the top of which I could easily distinguish! The fact was, we were just getting to the outside of the heath, and were on the brow of a steep hill, which faced this hanging wood. The guide had begun to descend; and I had called to him to stop; for the hill was so steep, that rain as it did and wet as my saddle must be, I got off my horse in order to walk down. But, now behold, the fellow discovered, that he *had lost his way*! Where we were I could not even guess. There was but one remedy, and that was to get back, if we could. I became guide now; and did as Mr. Western is advising the ministers to do, *retraced* my steps. We went back about half the way that we had come, when we saw two men, who showed us the way that we ought to go. At the end of about a mile, we fortunately found the turnpike-road;

not, indeed, at the *foot*, but on the *tip-top* of that very Hindhead, on which I had so repeatedly *vowed* I would not go! We came out on the turnpike some hundred yards on the Liphook side of the buildings called *the Hut*; so that we had the whole of three miles of hill to come down at not much better than a foot pace, with a good pelting rain at our backs.

'It is odd enough how differently one is affected by the same sight, under different circumstances. At the *Holly Bush* at Headley there was a room full of fellows in white smock frocks, drinking and smoking and talking, and I, who was then dry and warm, *moralized* within myself at their *folly* in spending their time in such a way. But, when I got down from Hindhead to the public-house at Road Lane with my skin soaking and my teeth chattering, I thought just such another group, whom I saw through the window sitting round a good fire with pipes in their mouths, the *wisest assembly* I had ever set my eyes on, a real *collective wisdom*, and, I most solemnly declare, that I felt a greater veneration for them than I have ever felt even for the *Privy Council*, notwithstanding the Right Honourable Charles Wynn and the Right Honourable Sir John Sinclair belong to the latter.

'It was now but a step to my friend's house, where a good fire and a change of clothes soon put all to rights, save and except the having come over Hindhead after all my resolutions. This mortifying circumstance; this having been *beaten*, lost the guide the *three shillings* that I had agreed to give him. "Either," said I, "you did not know the way well, or you did: if the former, it was dishonest in you to undertake to guide me: if the latter, you have wilfully led me miles out of my way." He grumbled; but off he went. He certainly deserved nothing, for he did not know the way, and he prevented some other man from earning and receiving the money. But, had he not caused me to *get upon Hindhead*, he would have had the three shillings. I had, at one time, got my hand in my pocket, but the thought of having been *beaten* pulled it out again.'[1]

Here is another short passage in a different style, but more representative of the general character of the

[1] *Rural Rides*, 1885, i. 183-85.

letters, because inspired with a strong feeling of social injustice.

'Standing on the hill at Knighton, you see the three ancient and lofty and beautiful spires rising up at Leicester; you see the river winding down through a broad bed of the most beautiful meadows that man ever set his eyes on; you see the bright verdure covering all the land, even to the tops of the hills, with here and there a little wood, as if made by God to give variety to the beauty of the scene, for the river brings the coal in abundance for fuel, and the earth gives the brick and the tile in abundance. But go down into the villages; invited by the spires rising up among the trees in the dells, at scarcely ever more than a mile or two apart; invited by these spires, go down into these villages, view the large, and once the most beautiful, churches; see the parson's house, large, and in the midst of pleasure-gardens; and then look at the miserable sheds in which the labourers reside! Look at these hovels, made of mud and of straw, bits of glass, or of old off-cast windows, without frames or hinges, but merely stuck in the mud wall. Enter them, and look at the bits of chairs or stools; the wretched boards tacked together, to serve for a table; the floor of pebble, broken brick, or of the bare ground; look at the thing called a bed; and survey the rags on the backs of the wretched inhabitants; and then wonder if you can, that the jails and dungeons and treadmills increase, and that a standing army and barracks are become the favourite establishments of England!'[1]

The passage is intense with feelings which filled Cobbett during the whole course of his rides. There is strong love for the country, admiration for its beauties, and extraordinary sympathy with its habits of life; but these joyous emotions are constantly marred by grief and indignation at the wretched condition of so many of the dwellers in so pleasant a land. It is a common complaint that there is too much political controversy mingled

[1] *Rural Rides*, ii. 348.

with the description of his journeys ; and it is true that many of the gibes and sneers at forgotten politicians might be spared without any great sense of loss. But on the other hand it is impossible to separate the political from the artistic content of the letters. A sense of injustice and wrong colours every part and makes the pictures of natural beauty more vivid by the sombre contrast.

Cobbett's literary activity during the period comprised in this chapter was not exhausted by the great works already noted. He published a number of lesser treatises which have yet to be mentioned. He devoted a great deal of attention to agriculture and forestry, and endeavoured with unequal success to introduce new methods into England. While he was still farming in Long Island he prepared a treatise entitled the *American Gardener*, which was intended to instruct the inhabitants of New England in English methods of laying out gardens. It was published in 1821 after his return to London, and reappeared in August 1828, in an enlarged form as the *English Gardener*. It treated gardens under four divisions : the kitchen garden, the flower garden, the shrubbery, and the orchard, and gave instructions for the management of each. His next agricultural publication was an edition of the *Horse-Hoeing Husbandry*, originally brought out in 1733 by Jethro Tull, of whom he had a high opinion. It appeared in 1822 with an explanatory introduction, and was followed by the *Woodlands*. This work, which was published in complete form in 1825, and afterwards appeared in numbers in 1828, was partly at least the outcome of a seed farm which he had established at Kensington, and gave in a convenient form the practical knowledge which he had acquired in its conduct. In

1828 he wrote a *Treatise on Cobbett's Corn*, a name which he gave to the maize plant, which he endeavoured though unsuccessfully to introduce into England. He was more fortunate in his patronage of the locust-tree or acacia, and realised a considerable sum by the sale of seeds of that plant.

Other works of a miscellaneous character may be briefly mentioned. In 1822 he published *Cobbett's Collective Commentaries*, a series of articles on the proceedings of Parliament between February and August 1822. Most of them were reprinted from the *Statesman* newspaper, to which he was a frequent contributor. In 1824 appeared *Cobbett's French Grammar*, written on the same plan as his *English Grammar* in a series of letters, addressed in this instance to his son Richard. It has frequently been reprinted. Cobbett gives some interesting particulars of the conditions under which it was compiled :

'I wrote the first (and a considerable) part of it, at the house of my friend, Mr. Blount at Uphusband in Hampshire, and all that part was written between three in the morning and breakfast time. It being necessary that I should come to London, and it being impossible that a work requiring so much thought, and in the execution of which reputation was so much involved, should be executed except in a state of abstraction from noise and domestic interference, I went, taking my youngest son with me (for I never went anywhere, if I could avoid it, without some one of them), to the White Hart Inn, at Bagshot in Surrey, kept by Mr. Marlin, whom I had known for a great many years, and there in a tranquil room, looking out on the garden, and having a chop every day for dinner, while the little boy was provided with a pony to ride out at his pleasure with Mr. Marlin's son, I wrote the remainder of this book.' [1]

[1] *Political Register*, 28th December 1833.

In 1826 appeared *Cobbett's Poor Man's Friend,* which he wrote partly at Mr. Blount's at Uphusband, partly at an inn at Everley in Wiltshire, and the rest by the road, while travelling on horseback from Early to Bollitree in Herefordshire.   The book was described as a defence of those who do the work and fight the battles, and consisted chiefly of a criticism of the attitude of English society towards the pauper classes.   In 1829 Cobbett published the *Emigrant's Guide,* in ten letters addressed to the taxpayers of England, intended to instruct those who contemplated settling in North America.   The list may be closed with a school-book, entitled *Elements of Roman History, in English and French, from the Foundation of Rome to the Battle of Actium,* which appeared in 1828. The French was that of Jean Henri Sievrac, and Cobbett only claimed to be a translator.   As in the case of all his translations, his actual share in the labour is extremely doubtful.

CHAPTER IX

COBBETT'S LAST YEARS AND DEATH

ON 26th June 1830 George IV. died. The accession of his brother, William IV., was considered favourable to the cause of reform. Cobbett at once began more active methods of propaganda. On 1st July he commenced to republish in a cheap form extracts from the *Political Register*. Being debarred by the state of the law from issuing them in weekly numbers, he commenced a monthly periodical under the name of *Cobbett's Twopenny Trash*. The name *Twopenny Trash* was originally invented by William Gifford, 'that well-gorged parasite,' and applied to the cheap *Register* of 1816. It was now adopted by Cobbett as a catching title. The new periodical had great success, especially after Cobbett's trial in July 1831 had advertised his publications, and it was continued until July 1832.

Events on the continent of Europe also gave great encouragement to the reformers in England. In August Charles X. was forced to abdicate the French throne and take refuge in Scotland. Immediately afterwards the Belgians rose against the Dutch and succeeded in establishing an independent government. Cobbett declared that he was pleased at these outbreaks, because they made the working classes see their importance and made those who despised them see it also. He made the

French and Belgian revolutions the subject of eleven lectures delivered at the Theatre of the Rotunda, near Blackfriars' Bridge, and afterwards published, both separately as pamphlets, and together in the form of a book. In these lectures he gave a detailed list of the political and social abuses, which in his opinion ought to be redressed by Parliament, and compared them with those which had prevailed in France during the reigns of Louis XVIII. and Charles X. These lectures were supplemented in November by a pamphlet, addressed to the young men of England and entitled, *Cobbett's Plan of Parliamentary Reform*, in which he elaborated his views on that preliminary question also. His proposals were very advanced, including annual parliaments, manhood suffrage, and election by ballot.

Although there was no likelihood of such extreme changes being made, there was no doubt that the reform movement was rapidly gaining strength throughout the country. When Parliament met in November, Wellington, as prime minister, declared himself resolved to maintain the present system of representation. The funds immediately fell four per cent., and within a fortnight the Government was beaten on the civil list and resigned. A Whig administration was formed under Lord Grey, but the new ministers found that they had entered on a difficult heritage. Not only was the cry for parliamentary reform becoming increasingly loud, but the overthrow of the French dynasty had encouraged the more extreme reformers. The ministry was assailed by these men, among whom Cobbett was chief. He did not believe that the Whigs actually desired to redress grievances. On Wellington's resignation he had, in a letter published in the *Political Register*, tendered himself to the King as prime minister, to carry out his own scheme of reform. Upon the formation of Grey's ministry he avowed his disbelief in the Whigs.

'What then,' he asked, 'will the new ministry *do for the people*. That is the question. Not what *speeches* they will make, but what they will *do for us*.' He then detailed a list of twenty-six measures, including, abolition of the property qualification for members, manhood suffrage, vote by ballot, the repeal of high duties on necessaries of life, the reduction of the forces, and the amendment of the laws regulating the liberty of the press, the relief of the poor, and the protection of game, and gave his opinion that Government would decline to deal with any of these matters.[1]

Yet the state of the country was so serious that action of some kind was imperative. The distress of the rural population was very great, and it had begun to show itself in very ugly forms.

A new kind of outrage suddenly became very common. Hitherto the agricultural population, though in great poverty, had been remarkably law-abiding. But about the time of the death of George IV. the practice of burning corn-ricks by night became common in country districts. It had first made its appearance in the north of France a year or two earlier, and thence it spread to England. The farmers found it impossible to protect their property adequately, and in very few cases were they able, after its destruction, to detect and punish the criminals, whose dexterity set at naught the most

[1] *Political Register*, 20th November 1830. For a clever picture of the views of Cobbett and the apprehensions of the old-fashioned Whigs, see Christopher North's *Noctes Ambrosianæ*, No. lxiii., which originally appeared in *Blackwood's Magazine*, October 1832.

elaborate precautions.   The number of the outrages
caused a panic.   They were attributed to a widespread
conspiracy, and were even thought by many to be the
direct work of the devil.   But the most general opinion
was that the labourers were the immediate incendiaries,
but that they were incited by agitators, who, while they
openly advocated parliamentary and social reform, were
at the same time secretly instigating the peasantry to
actual crime.   Among those to be suspected of such
conduct Cobbett was the first, both from the vehemence
of his utterances and from the extent of his influence.
He was closely watched and his speeches during his
political tours were carefully noted.   The Whig ministry,
indignant that the spread of these outrages should mark
their entry to office, resolved to make an example, and,
unfortunately for themselves, chose Cobbett as a leading
culprit, who had not only expressed himself strongly on
the reasons for rural discontent, but had also assailed the
whole conduct of Government.   Nor were they without
some pretexts for their choice.   Among others, a Sussex
labourer, who was convicted as an incendiary, made
several statements, while in danger of death, implying
that he had been perverted by Cobbett's teaching.   On
11th December 1830 Cobbett openly declared in the
Register that, until public distress was relieved, it was
hopeless to attempt to restrain the incendiaries by
coercion.   After some severe reflections on the conduct
of the clergy, he urged that it was useless to try and
persuade the labourers that in burning ricks they were
destroying their own food.

'The working people,' he said, 'have been always told, and
they are told now, and by the very parsons I have quoted above,

that their acts of violence, and particularly the burnings can *do them no good*, but *add to their wants*, by destroying the food that *they would have to eat*. Alas! they know better: they know that one thrashing machine takes wages from ten men; and they also know that *they* should have none of this food; and that *potatoes and salt*[1] do not burn! Therefore this argument is not worth a straw. Besides, they see and feel *that the good comes*, and comes *instantly* too. They see that they *do* get *some* bread, in consequence of the destruction of part of the corn; and while they see this, you attempt in vain to persuade them, that that which they have done is *wrong*. And as to one effect, that of *making the parsons reduce their tithes*, it is hailed as a good by ninety-nine hundredths even of men of considerable property; while there is not a single man in the country who does not clearly trace the reduction to the acts of the labourers, and especially *to the fires*; for it is the terror of these, and not the bodily force, that has prevailed.'

This passage and some others of a similar tendency were considered as direct incentives to the rick-burners, and Cobbett was in consequence indicted on the charge of publishing a libel, with intent to raise discontent in the minds of the labourers in husbandry, and to incite them to acts of violence, and to destroy corn, machinery, and other property. The trial came on on 7th July 1831 at the Guildhall, before the Court of King's Bench. The Attorney-General, Sir Thomas Denman, conducted the prosecution, while Cobbett, according to his usual custom, undertook his own defence. When he entered the Court he was greeted with prolonged applause and turning to his supporters he said, 'Be patient, gentlemen, for if truth prevail we shall beat them.' After the Attorney-General had read the passages alleged as libellous, and contended that their plain intention was to encourage outrage,

[1] Their usual diet.

Cobbett made a long speech in his defence, in which he showed that he had vastly improved as an orator since his trial in 1810.   On this occasion he betrayed no diffidence or hesitation, but attacked his opponents with great power.   He assailed the Government severely ; he alleged that they had carried on more state prosecutions during seven months, than their Tory predecessors in seven years ; he insisted that they were undertaking a systematic campaign against the liberty of the press, while permitting their own supporters the utmost licence ; and he contended that his meaning ought to be judged from the whole of his article and not from a forced con-struction of isolated passages.   He concluded a powerful address with the declaration :

'Whatever may be the verdict of the jury, if I am doomed to spend my last breath in a dungeon, I will pray God to bless my country ; I will curse the Whigs, and leave my revenge to my children and the labourers of England.'

He sat down amid prolonged applause, which was with difficulty suppressed, and proceeded to call Lord Brougham, Lord Melbourne and Lord Radnor as wit-nesses for the defence.   Lord Melbourne was required to state the grounds on which the Sussex labourer, who had testified against Cobbett, had been pardoned, but the Lord Chief-Justice would not allow him to answer. Lord Radnor bore strong testimony to Cobbett's character and writings, stated that he had known him for over thirty years, and that he did not think he was a person likely to excite the working classes to outrage against their masters, but quite the reverse.

The most dramatic part of the trial, however, was Lord Brougham's evidence.

'Denman told me,' says Greville, 'that he expected [the jury] would have acquitted Cobbett without leaving the box, and this principally on account of Brougham's evidence, for Cobbett brought the Chancellor forward and made him prove that *after* these very writings, and while this prosecution was hanging over him, Brougham wrote to his son "Dear Sir," and requesting he would ask his father for some former publications of his, which he thought would be of great use on the present occasion in quieting the labourers. This made a great impression and the Attorney-General never knew one word of the letter till he heard it in evidence, the Chancellor having flourished it off as is his custom, and then quite forgotten it. The Attorney told me that Gurney overheard one juryman say to another, "Don't you think we had better stop the case? It is useless to go on."' [1]

The Lord Chief-Justice, Lord Tenterden, summed up against the defendant, but Greville says he was very timid and favoured and complimented Cobbett through-out; 'very unlike what Ellenborough would have done.' The jury disagreed, and after fifteen hours they were discharged without a verdict having been obtained. The Attorney-General subsequently entered a *nolle prosequi*.

The result of the trial was a severe blow to Government, for nothing is so disastrous to rulers as unsuccessful attempts to coerce opinion. Cobbett in his defence had lashed the party in power.

'I have been writing for thirty years,' he said, 'and only twice out of that long period have I been brought before this court. The first time was by an apostate Whig. What indeed of evil have the Whigs not done? Since then, although there have been six Attorneys-General, all Tories, and although, were I a Crown lawyer, I might pick out plenty of libels from my writings, yet I have never for twenty-one years been prosecuted until this Whig government came in. But the Whigs were always a most tyrannical faction; they always tried to make tyranny double

---

[1] *Greville Memoirs*, 1888, ii. 162.

tyranny; they were always the most severe, the most grasping, the most greedy, the most tyrannical faction whose proceedings are recorded in history. It was they who seized what remained of the Crown lands; it was they who took to themselves the last portion of Church property; it was they who passed the monstrous Riot Act; it was they also who passed the Septennial Bill. The Government are now acquiring great credit for doing away with the rotten boroughs, but if they deserve credit for doing them away, let it be borne in mind that the Whigs created them. They established an interest in the regulation, and gave consistency and value to corruption. Then came the excise laws, which were brought in by the Whigs; and from them, too, emanated that offensive statute by which Irish men and Irish women may be transported without judge or jury. There is, indeed, no faction so severe and cruel; they do everything by force and violence: the Whigs are the Rehoboam of England; the Tories ruled us with rods, but the Whigs scourge us with scorpions.'

Cobbett had made use of his opportunity in the most deadly fashion, and his reputation was greatly heightened by the events of the trial. On the other hand, the Whig Government realised the futility of affording such opportunities to its political opponents. The experience was a salutary one. The prosecution of Cobbett was almost the last occasion on which an English ministry endeavoured to restrain the political utterances of the press by legal proceedings.[1]

The event of the trial not only secured Cobbett personally, but improved his position financially by the advertisement which it gave him. Finding his circumstances easier he resolved to return to a country life and took Normandy farm in the parish of Ash in Surrey, a few miles from

---

[1] For a detailed report of legal proceedings, see *A Full and Accurate Report of Mr. Cobbett's Trial*, 1831; see also Molesworth's *History of England*, 1874, i. 138-42.

Farnham, his birthplace. Normandy continued his residence for the remainder of his life. It was a farm of 160 acres, which in Cobbett's time paid a rental of £160 a year. Alexander Somerville, the social reformer, who visited it in 1844, has described it in *The Whistler at the Plough*:

'It is but a humble-looking place. . . . A wide range of heath variegated with furze, gravel pits, and tracts of absolute sterility, extends for many miles, behind the farm-house; and on either side, right and left, the heath extends for several miles, variegated only with a few clumps of pine-trees, chiefly Scotch firs. In front lies a heathy common, in complete disorder, as commons usually are, and beyond it, to the front, looking eastward, is the farm land, enclosed in small fields, with very badly kept fences. There are trees in the hedgerows; and, in some parts, more of them than should be upon a farm where there is a tenant bound to pay rent.'

Somerville found the farm in a very bad state, and he considered that Cobbett would probably have improved it, if his tenure had not been so short. But even during that brief tenure Cobbett had little time for farming. His last years were almost entirely occupied with politics.

As the year 1831 advanced the nation became more and more absorbed in the struggle for parliamentary reform. The Reform Bill was introduced into the House of Commons on 1st March, and the second reading carried by the bare majority of one on 22nd March. Ministers were defeated in committee on 19th April on a motion of General Gascoyne that the representation of England and Wales should not be diminished, and with some difficulty they prevailed on the king to consent to a dissolution on 22nd April. The general election gave them a much larger majority than they had previously

commanded, and the Bill passed the Commons on 21st
September by a majority of one hundred and nine. On
8th October it was thrown out in the House of Lords by
a majority of forty-one. Cobbett, who had followed the
course of the Bill most minutely in his *Register*, immediately advocated the creation of forty-two new peers
in accordance with the proposal of Mr. Ridgway in a
'Letter to Lord Grey,' which he republished in the
Register. It was widely believed that Earl Grey would
resign, but with great prudence he resolved to reintroduce
the Bill before resorting to any more extreme measure
Cobbett disapproved of this delay because he believed
that it endangered the tranquillity of the country:

'It is impossible,' he wrote to Place on 19th October, 'to
prevent a change, a *great change*; that change *might have been*
not at all injurious to the aristocracy; what it *may be* now, I will
not take upon me even to guess; but of this I am sure, that the
Ministers have, since the Bill was rejected, pursued exactly the
wrong course, if their object be to prevent a *violent* change.'[1]

On 12th December the third Reform Bill, identical
in essentials with the second, was introduced into the
House of Commons by Lord John Russell. It was
warmly welcomed by Cobbett, who considered it better
than its predecessor.[2] On 23rd March it passed the
third reading in the House of Commons, but in its
passage through the House of Lords it again met with
disaster. The ministry was beaten on 7th May on a
motion by Lord Lyndhurst to postpone the disfranchising
clauses of the Bill. Grey then went to Windsor and
advised the king to create sufficient peers to enable

[1] Cobbett to Place, 19th October 1831; Add. MS. 35149, f. 114.
[2] *Political Register*, 17th December 1831.

him to carry the Bill. William IV. refused to do this and in consequence the ministers tendered their resignations on 9th May. The king accepted them, but Wellington after accepting office found it impossible to form a ministry.

'To describe the agitation in London,' says Cobbett,[1] 'and the anger of the people against the Lords, the Bishops, Wellington, and particularly against the King, is a task that no tongue or pen can perform. Every man you met seemed to be convulsed with rage : to refuse to pay taxes was amongst the mildest of the measures that were proposed at the various meetings : the language of the newspapers, especially with regard to the King, Queen, and divers members of the Royal family, was such as to make one doubt the evidence of one's senses, and yet it was a very inadequate representation of what was issuing from people's mouths. A cry for a republic was pretty nearly general ; and an emigration to Hanover formed the subject of a popular and widely-circulated caricature. Resistance in every shape and form was publicly proposed ; and amongst the means intended to defeat the King and the new Minister, was that most effectual of all means, *a run upon the Bank for gold*! which, on Saturday, the 12th of May, was recommended in a placard, posted up all over London in the following words : "To stop the Duke, go for gold !"'[2]

On 17th May William IV. yielded, and gave his written authority to create the necessary peers. The threat was sufficient. On 4th June the Bill passed the House of Lords, and on 7th June it received the royal assent. Cobbett now saw within sight the attainment of his long-sought ambition, a seat in Parliament. For some months he had contemplated presenting himself as a candidate for the borough of Manchester. In August 1831 he

[1] *Political Register*, 19th May 1832.
[2] This placard was the work of Francis Place the Radical breeches-maker. See *Life of Place* by Graham Wallas.

received an invitation to do so, and in September he
issued his first address. In the last week of December
he delivered six lectures in the Minor Theatre in which
he detailed his complete programme of reform. It included many proposals which have never been carried
into effect, such as the repudiation of the greater part of
the National Debt, and others which were only adopted
after many years, such as the disestablishment and dis-
endowment of the Irish Church. The lectures were
published collectively in January 1832. On the passage
of the Reform Bill, Manchester was given two members.
The Whig newspaper, the *Courier*, called upon Government to send down some gentleman, or else Cobbett
would assuredly be elected.

'Yes,' retorted Cobbett, ' "send down some gentleman " by
all means ; but not "a gentleman " that likes *sinecures* ; for no
sinecure will he find in *that job* !'   'To keep me out of Parliament,' he continued exultingly, 'they must *pass an act* to exclude
me by name ; and, again I promise them, that if they have but the
pluck to *do that*, they shall never hear upon the subject, petition
or complaint from William Cobbett.' [1]

A week or two later, however, he determined to present
himself also as a candidate at Oldham, stating frankly
that the electorate at Manchester was too large to enable
him to estimate accurately his chances of election. Oldham returned two members, and Cobbett's colleague was
John Fielden, a Lancashire cotton manufacturer. The
interval before the general election was occupied with a
political tour in the north of England and in Scotland.
At the outset of his journey he held a public debate at
Birmingham with Thomas Attwood on the relative worth

[1] *Political Register*, 7th July 1832.

of paper money and gold. Attwood, although as strenuous a political reformer as Cobbett, was a strong advocate of a paper currency, which he believed would prove an antidote to all the financial distress from which the country suffered. He had distinguished himself before the passage of the Reform Bill by proposing to assemble a million men on Hampstead Heath in support of that measure, and some years later he threatened the opponents of reform that he would march on London from Birmingham at the head of twenty millions of men, an absurd threat which drew from Benjamin Disraeli a bombastic rejoinder in the third of his *Letters of Runnymede*. The discussion, which was originally proposed by Cobbett, seems to have wearied the audience. Both sides claimed the victory, but Cobbett with more justice, for Attwood's speeches were about three times as long, a sure sign of weakness.

His tour in Scotland was a great personal triumph. In Edinburgh, whither he proceeded first, he won admiration by his ability as a lecturer, and especially by the dramatic talent he showed in reproducing on the platform those lively dialogues with political opponents of which he had made so much use in the *Register*.[1] In Glasgow and on the west coast he found many political sympathisers, that part of Scotland being the especial home of reformers. He admired the natural beauty of the country and appreciated the excellence of Lowland agriculture. The seaport of Greenock, near the mouth of the Clyde, especially attracted him.

'The harbour and bay of Greenock are very fine. The town, which consists of thirty thousand people, is built in a little flat,

[1] See p. 226, *supra*.

the high land beginning to rise up immediately behind it to the south; the streets are regular, conveniently wide; the houses built of stone; and everything wearing the appearance of ease, competence, and great solidity. . . . I cannot take leave of Greenock without observing on the contrast which it formed with all the other seaports that I had ever seen in my life. Captain Cobb, with whom I crossed the Atlantic the last time, used to be everlastingly pestering me with his praises of Greenock; about its solidity, cleanliness, and the good manners of the people. As I was going to the church, the sight brought Cobb to my mind. All the people seemed to be in the streets; all going away to their different churches; no noise of any sort; no dirtily-dressed person; and not a soul to be seen who did not seem seriously engaged in the business for which the day was set apart. Cobb used to say, that it was like a Connecticut seaport, and I dare say it is: for the religion is the same, and I dare say that the manners of the people are very much alike.'[1]

On his return, Cobbett was immediately involved in the business of a parliamentary election. Polling at Oldham commenced on Wednesday, 12th December. There were five candidates, but on Thursday evening three of them retired, and Fielden and Cobbett were triumphantly returned. He immediately withdrew from the contest at Manchester, where in a single day he had obtained more than a thousand votes. Parliament met on 29th January 1833, and Cobbett took his seat. He was not much impressed by the aspect of the House of Commons.

'I have taken a hasty measurement of it,' he said, 'and my opinion is, that if the whole of the area were cleared of benches, of the table, of the Speaker's chair, and of everything else, there is not *a foot and a half square* for each of the six hundred and fifty-eight men to stand upon. The length of a bench, does not, I believe, allow to each man fifteen inches. . . . I am satisfied that the six hundred and fifty-eight members cannot be in the

<hr />

[1] *Political Register*, 3rd November 1832.

House without close packing upon all the benches, without fill-ing all the little avenues, and without covering the whole of the floor by persons standing upright. To move from your seat to go out of the House, no matter for what cause, no matter how pressing the necessity, upon an average, a hundred persons must be disturbed. Moving out the pit in the midst of a theatre is nothing compared to it. . . . The *effects* of this want of room are many and most detrimental to the proceedings of this assembly, of which I am now a member. The confusion which arises out of it, beggars all description. The business is retarded by it; the crowds about the Speaker's chair, while the private bills are going on; the everlasting trampling backward and for-ward on the floor; the interruption which men give to one another, in spite of their desire to avoid it; the calls of "order, order" incessantly recurring; all these absolutely distract men's minds, and render it impossible for them to do that which it is their duty to do, and which they wish to do. . . . To take a seat in that House, and to sit as constantly as you ought to do, requires, in the present state of things, not only perfect health, but great bodily strength, and it is not always the wisest heads that are placed upon the shoulders of the strongest bodies. I know pretty well what a regiment of soldiers is : and I never saw one, the private men of which would have been able to undergo a regular and constant attendance in that House, constructed as it now is, and annoying as every man's situation is.'[1]

This description referred of course to the old House of Commons destroyed by fire in October 1834.

Cobbett's parliamentary career has generally been regarded as a failure, and he has been quoted as a con-spicuous example of the insignificance of a demagogue within the House of Commons. But although he did not accomplish those immense results which he had expected to achieve before his entry, he was a sufficiently promi-nent figure during his short period of membership. Lord

[1] *Political Register*, 2nd March 1833.

Dalling and Bulwer, who sat in the same house, and was himself an advanced Radical, has left a vivid picture of the impression produced by Cobbett on his fellow-members:

'To most members of Parliament the elderly, respectable-looking, red-faced gentleman, in a dust-coloured coat and drab breeches with gaiters, was a strange and almost historical curiosity. Tall and strongly-built, but stooping, with sharp eyes, a round and ruddy countenance, smallish features, and a peculiarly cynical mouth, he realised pretty nearly the idea that might have been formed about him. The manner of his speaking might also have been anticipated. His style in writing was sarcastic and easy—such, it was not unnatural to suppose it might also be in addressing an assembly; and this to a certain extent was the case. He was still colloquial, bitter, with a dry, caustic, and rather drawling delivery, and a rare manner of arguing with facts. To say that he spoke as well as he wrote, would be to place him where he was not—among the most effective orators of his time. He had not, as a speaker, the raciness of diction, nor the happiness of illustration, by which he excels as a writer. He wanted also some of the physical qualifications unnecessary to the author, but necessary to the orator, and which he might as a younger man have naturally possessed or easily acquired. In short, he could not be at that time the powerful personage that he might have been had he taken his seat on the benches where he was then sitting, when many surrounding him were unknown—even unborn. Still, I know no other instance of a man entering the House of Commons at his age, and becoming at once an effective debater in it. Looking carelessly round the assembly so new to him, with his usual self-confidence, he spoke on the first occasion that presented itself, proposing an amendment to the Address; but this was not his happiest effort, and consequently created disappointment. He soon, however, obliterated the failure, and became rather a favourite with an audience which is only unforgiving when bored.'[1]

[1] *Historical Characters*, 1876, p. 347.

Cobbett was not the only advanced Radical who found a seat in the first reformed Parliament. ' Some notorious characters have been returned,' wrote Greville.[1] Among them may be mentioned the member for Sheffield, James Silk Buckingham, who in 1823 had been expelled from India for his attacks on the Government; Thomas Attwood, the autocrat of Birmingham, and John Arthur Roebuck, known as ' tear 'em ' from the vehemence of his onslaughts on his political opponents. Cobbett, however, acted entirely independently of any party ties. On taking his seat he established himself on the front bench, usually reserved for ministers, and his maiden speech opened with the words : ' It appears to me, that since I have been sitting here, I have heard a great deal of vain and unprofitable conversation.' He moved the rejection of the address to his Majesty in reply to the king's speech, and the substitution of one of his own composition, but his motion was negatived by a majority of three hundred. This, however, was only a prelude to a more serious attack : on 16th May he made a motion for an address to the king praying him to remove Sir Robert Peel from the Privy Council on account of his legislation in regard to the currency. This attack on Peel was received by the House with extraordinary signs of disapprobation. In the opinion of Gladstone, who was a member, the motion was ' alike wordy and absurd.'[2] Peel on rising to make his defence was received with tremendous applause. He spoke with great effect, and Cobbett was howled down when he attempted to reply. The motion was rejected by 298 votes to 6, the minority consisting of Cobbett, Fielden, Attwood, Roe, Daniel

[1] *Memoirs*, ii. 343.   [2] See Morley's *Life of Gladstone*, 1903, i. 114.

COBBETT ON THE TREASURY BENCH.

"You may know a man by the company he keeps."

O'Connell's son John O'Connell, and Patrick Lalor. In spite of this rebuff, Cobbett continued to speak earnestly and at times with weight, on social and financial topics. He opposed the introduction of the modern poor law system, and the coercion of Ireland, and advocated protective legislation on behalf of factory employees.

After entering Parliament Cobbett found leisure to complete a literary undertaking, which had remained unfinished during the stress of the Reform contest, by publishing in 1834 the second volume of his *History of the Regency and Reign of King George the Fourth.* The first volume had appeared in 1830. This work is perhaps the weakest of all Cobbett's productions, being worthless as history and comparatively tame as a piece of literary invective. After its conclusion Cobbett paid a visit to Ireland in September. He was received on his landing at Kingstown by General Sir George Cockburn, a strong advocate of political reform, and a few days later he made a public entry into Dublin amidst the applause of a large crowd. O'Connell wrote to him expressing his regret at not being present, and filled his letter with enthusiastic eulogy. Cobbett was impressed by the distress of the Irish peasantry. He described his impressions in a series of letters addressed to Charles Marshall, a labourer at Farnham, and published in the *Political Register* :

'There were about a hundred little girls in a *school*, and about as many boys in another, neither had shoes or stockings, and the boys had *no shirts*, their faces were pale, the hundred not having so much red as your little round-faced chap that was set to keep the birds away from the cabbage seed in Dodman's field. Yes, Marshall, that little chap, with his satchel full of bread and cheese or bacon ; he was at the *proper school*! He and Tom Deadman and little Barratt will make strong and able men like their fathers; will live well and be well clothed; and will be respected like their fathers, and be happy in that state of life in which it has pleased God to place them; and will not, I hope, listen to any fanatical man, who would persuade them, that to starve in rags, in this world, has a tendency to give them a crown of glory in the next.

'In another place I saw a great crowd of women sitting and *doing* nothing, each with *a baby* in her arms. They were sitting in rows, waiting, I believe, for their messes. Some of them were young and naturally handsome; but made ugly by starvation, rags, and dirt. It was one mass of rags; and, not what *you* call rags, not rags such as you see on the beggars or gipsies that go to hopping at Farnham; but far worse than any that you ever saw tied round a stake to frighten the birds from our wheat and our peas; far worse than the Kentish people and the South Hampshire people put on a *scare-crow* to keep the birds from their cherries.

' . . . In another place I saw the most painful sight of all: *women*, with heavy hammers, *cracking stones* into very small pieces, to *make walks in gentlemen's gardens*! These women were as ragged as the rest; and the sight of them and their work, and the thoughts accompanying these, would have sunk the heart in your body, as they did mine.'[1]

From Dublin, Cobbett proceeded through the counties of Wicklow, Kildare, Carlow, Kilkenny, and Waterford. Everywhere he found fresh evidence of destitution.

'In coming from Kilkenny to Waterford I and my friend (Mr. O'Higgins), in a post chaise, came through a little town called Mullinavat, where there was a fair for *cattle* and *fat hogs* and *apples*. There might be 4000 people; there were about 7 acres of ground covered with cattle (mostly fat), and all over the street of the town there were about THREE THOUSAND BEAUTIFUL FAT HOGS lying all over the road and the streets; and our chaise was *actually stopped and blocked up by fat hogs;*

[1] *Political Register*, 4th October 1834.

and we were obliged to stop till the civil and kind people could get them out of our way! There was a sight to be seen by me, who had never seen thirty such hogs together in the course of my life, these hogs weighing from *ten* to *thirty score* each! Ah! but there arose out of this fine sight reflections that made my blood boil; that the far greater part of those who had bred and fatted these hogs were never to taste one morsel of them, no not even the offal, and had lived *worse* than the hogs, not daring to taste any *part* of the *meal* used in the fatting of the hogs! The hogs are to be killed, dried or tubbed, and sent out of the country to be sold for money to be *paid to the landowners*, who spend it in London, Bath, Paris, Rome, or some other place of pleasure, while these poor creatures are raising all this food from the land, and are starving themselves. And this is what we shall come to *in England*, unless we call upon our member, Mr. Leech, to protect us.

'I will tell you more about these *landowners* another time; but I will now, before I conclude this letter, give you *one fact* which will enable you to judge of what would be the lot of the working men in England, if there were to be no *poor rates*.[1] There are here, as there are in England, several *sorts* of potatoes; some are called *minions*, others *apple-potatoes*; these are the *best*. Others are called *lumpers*; these are the *worst*. When men or women are employed at 6d. a day and their *board*, to dig *minions* or *apple-potatoes*, they are not suffered to *taste them*, but are sent to another field to dig *lumpers* to eat; and this is called *boarding them*! That fact is enough: it is enough to know that THAT is what the Scotch vagabonds[2] mean when they propose to bring you to "COARSER food": it is enough for you to know THAT to *rouse you all to a sense of your danger*, and to urge you to come to a *county meeting* and to do your duty like men, true to your country and true to the King and to the laws of England.'[3]

After visiting Cork, Limerick, and other places, Cobbett returned to Dublin in the middle of November, and heard

[1] At that time there was no poor rate in Ireland.
[2] Adam Smith and political economists of his school.
[3] *Political Register*, 18th October 1834.

with satisfaction that William had dismissed the Whig ministry.

'I most humbly and heartily thank your Majesty,' he wrote, 'for having dismissed from your councils a set of servants, who, when the House of Commons had resolved upon the repeal of a part of the malt-tax, threatened to quit your service and leave your Majesty without servants, unless that vote were rescinded; a set of servants who sent out the special commissions of 1830 and 1831; a set of servants who have expended twenty millions of money on a project, which has thrown into utter confusion the most valuable of your foreign dominions [1]; a set of servants who have introduced bands of commissioners, and a sort of mongrel government, carried on in detached parcels, by creatures of their own, irresponsible as well to your Majesty, as to the Parliament; a set of servants who have commenced making innovations in everything, giving a shake to every institution of any standing, finishing nothing, tossing all rights and principles of government into the air, till, at last, no man knows what to expect.' [2]

Cobbett looked without apprehension on the formation of a Tory ministry, calling on it to undo the work of the Whigs, and about a month after Peel had accepted the office of prime minister on 9th December, he issued his *Legacy to Labourers*, with a dedication to him occupying almost a third of the entire book, and calling upon him to repeal the new Poor Law. The remainder of the work consisted of a discussion of the nature and extent of the rights of English landlords in regard to their lands. In 1872 the younger William Cobbett, thinking it pertinent to questions then current, reprinted it with an elaborate preface. Cobbett was not ill-disposed towards Peel, in spite of their encounter in the House of Commons, and

---

[1] The emancipation of slaves, which Cobbett strongly opposed.
[2] *Political Register*, 22nd November 1834.

early in 1835 he commenced the series of letters, which
were published in the next year under the title of *A Legacy
to Peel*, calling on him to commence a series of reforms
in Parliament, in Ireland, and with regard to sinecure
offices. It is worthy of remark that in some cases he
anticipated the direction which Peel's reforms subsequently took. He supplemented these two Legacies
in April 1835 by a *Legacy to Parsons*, dedicated to
Charles James Blomfield, the bishop of London. In
this work he urged that dissenters have as much right to
tithes and other Church property as the ministers of the
Established Church, and argued with some vehemence in
favour of disestablishment. The *Legacy to Parsons* was
the last book of Cobbett's published in his lifetime; it
appeared, in fact, very shortly before his death.

In the meantime, on the accession of Peel's administration to power, Cobbett urged Government in the pages
of the *Register* to repeal the Malt-Tax and the new Poor
Law, and warned them of the danger of dissolving
Parliament.

'Notwithstanding the monstrous absurdity that there is in the
belief, that the Ministers would attempt to repeal, or to alter for
the worse, the Reform Bill, or any part of the Reform Bill; or
that they would act upon the principle of not making any
reform whatsoever in the abuses of the several institutions of the
country; notwithstanding the monstrousness of the absurdity of
such a supposition, if they were to go to an election now, the
Whigs would take the name of "Reformers"; would represent
their opponents as Anti-Reformers; and under these names they
would go to the poll. . . . All the deeds of the Whigs would be
cast aside; the mere name of reformer, which would be, and
which already is, adopted instead of that of Whig, would do
wonders.'[1]

[1] *Political Register*, 20th December 1834.

In spite of these considerations Sir Robert Peel, who became prime minister, after the Duke of Wellington had declined the post, dissolved Parliament on 30th December. Cobbett was not altogether so favourably inclined to Peel as he was to Wellington, and he severely criticised his address to his Tamworth constituents promulgated after his accession to office. The Oldham election took place on 7th January 1835, when Cobbett and Fielden were returned unopposed. The general election improved Peel's position, but it still left him to face a Whig majority in the House of Commons. After struggling for some months he resigned office on 8th April and retired with a reputation greatly enhanced by his conduct as prime minister. Cobbett saw his fall almost with regret, although he had not attempted the repeal of the Poor Law and had opposed the abolition of the Malt-Tax.

'I have witnessed the display of your talents with great admiration; though, in the case of the malt-tax, I detested the purpose for which these talents were exercised. You have been more frank and fair than your predecessors were; but your country has to lament that you had the support of those predecessors in opposing one of those measures which would have afforded relief to the country.'[1]

Peel was succeeded by Melbourne, but within three months of the commencement of the new ministry Cobbett's voice ceased to thunder against the Whig party.

In a passage already quoted he referred to the hardships of a member of the House of Commons. Late hours and a crowded assembly were no small tax on

[1] *Political Register*, 11th April 1835.

the constitution of any but the strongest. He added,
however :

'For my own part, I find very little inconvenience, compared
with what others must experience. I live within four hundred
yards of my seat in the House ; I can come away, and return,
with very little inconvenience; my habits are such as to keep
me always in good health: I never dine out: I know nothing of
feasting of any sort; I have nothing to annoy me : I have a great
pleasure in performing my duty: I have sensible constituents:
I have a colleague who is as punctual as the clock ; and, which
is a very great thing, the perfect confidence which our constituents have in us prevents them from making applications
to occupy any part of our time, or demand any part of our
cares.'[1]

But notwithstanding this claim to immunity it is
probable that the change in Cobbett's habits and the
great addition to his labours were far from beneficial.
In the spring of 1834 he was seriously unwell and compelled to absent himself from Parliament for two entire
months. He was distressed by a cough which prevented
him from sleeping and reduced him to a condition of
considerable weakness.[2] During May he gradually
recovered, but in the following year the malady recurred.
On 10th March 1835 he attempted to speak in support
of a motion of the Marquis of Chandos for the repeal
of the Malt-Tax, but was so hoarse as to be almost
inaudible. He insisted, however, on remaining during
the whole of the debate, and probably he never recovered
from his exertions on that evening. During the voting
of supplies on 15th and 18th May he exerted himself so
much and sat so late, that he laid himself up. He deter-

---

[1] *Political Register*, 2nd March 1833.
[2] *Ibid.*, 26th April and 3rd May 1834.

T

mined, nevertheless, to attend the House again on the evening of the Marquis of Chandos's motion on Agricultural Distress on 25th May. He both spoke and voted, but the exertion proved too great for one already seriously unwell. He went down to his farm of Normandy on the next morning, resolved to rest himself thoroughly. On Thursday, 11th June, he felt unusually well and imprudently drank tea in the open air. Early in the night he was taken violently ill, and on Friday and Saturday his life was in danger. On Sunday he revived, and on Monday gave his family hope that he would yet be well. He talked feebly, but in the most collected and sprightly manner, upon politics and farming, and on Wednesday was carried round the farm. That evening he grew feebler and was evidently sinking; but he continued to answer with perfect clearness every question that was put to him. In the last half-hour his eyes became dim; and at ten minutes past one on the morning of Thursday, 18th June 1835, he closed them as if to sleep, and died without a gasp. Thus peacefully passed away a man whose entire life had been spent in conflict.

Cobbett's death removed at once much of the animosity against him. There was, says Lord Dalling and Bulwer, a widespread feeling of loss, not merely of a man but of a habit, ' of a dose of strong drink which all of us had been taking for years. . . . Whatever a man's talents, whatever a man's opinions, he sought the *Register* on the day of its appearance with eagerness and read it with amusement, partly, perhaps, if De la Rochefoucault is right, because whatever his party, he was sure to see his friends abused.'

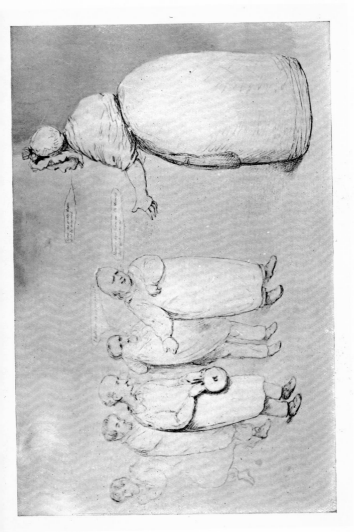

THE NURSERY.

LORD ALTHORP: "Come, my pretty dears. Don't be ashamed."
COBBETT: "Mammy, don't leave us. Oh, mammy, don't, don't leave us."
DR. LUSHINGTON: "I shall lose my pop—pop—pop—o—o—o."

Cobbett's contemporaries were particularly impressed by the force of his writings. James Northcote says in one of those conversations of his reported by William Hazlitt:

'But you have a vast opinion of Cobbett too, haven't you? Oh! he's a giant! He has such prodigious strength; he tears up a subject by the roots. Did you ever read his Grammar? Or see his attack on Mrs. ——? It was like a hawk pouncing on a wren. I should be terribly afraid to get into his hands. And then his homely, familiar way of writing—it is not from necessity or vulgarity, but to show his contempt for aristocratic pride and arrogance. He only has a kitchen-garden; he could have a flower-garden too if he chose. Peter Pindar said his style is like the Horse-Guards, only one story above the ground, while Junius's had all the airy elegance of Whitehall: but he could raise his style just as high as he pleased; though he does not want to sacrifice strength to elegance. He knows better what he is about.'[1]

His love of battle and his prodigious fighting power are features of his character that attract immediate attention. He himself relates how once at Winchester while addressing a meeting of the county freeholders, he was interrupted by an attorney of the opposite faction:

'I fixed my eye upon him, and, pointing my hand downright, and making a sort of chastising motion, said "Peace, babbling slave!" which produced such terror amongst others, that I met with no more interruption.'

This anecdote illustrates vividly his entire self-confidence, which imposed on others even more than on himself. But that confidence was not ill-founded. When engaged in controversy, nothing could exceed

[1] *Mr. Northcote's Conversations*, 1830, p. 224.

the picturesque bitterness of his pen. Here is an example from his earlier writings:

'There's no gallows in Pennsylvania. These glad tidings have rung through all the democratic club-rooms, all the dark assemblies of traitors, all the dungeons and cells of England, Scotland, and Ireland. Hence it is we are overwhelmed with the refuse, the sweepings of these kingdoms, the offal of the jail and the gibbet. Hence it is that we see so many faces that never looked comely but in the pillory, limbs that are awkward out of chains, and necks that are made to be stretched.'

With all his virulence Cobbett never became shrill There was a touch of contemptuous humour in his bitterest passages that doubled their force. Take for instance his description of Madison in *A Summary of Proceedings in Congress*:

'Madison is a little bow-legged man, at once stiff and slender. His countenance has that sour aspect, that conceited screw, which pride would willingly mould into an expression of disdain, if it did not find the features too skinny and too scanty for its purpose. His thin, sleek air, and the niceness of his garments, are indicative of that economical cleanliness which expostulates with the shoeboy and the washerwoman, which flies from the danger of a gutter, and which boasts of wearing a shirt for three days without rumpling the frill. In short, he had, take him altogether, precisely the prim, mean, prig-like look of a corporal mechanic, and were he ushered into your parlour, you would wonder why he came without his measure and his shears. Such (and with a soul which would disgrace any other tenement than that which contains it) is the mortal who stood upon his legs, confidently predicting the overthrow of the British monarchy, and anticipating the pleasure of feeding its illustrious nobles with his oats.'[1]

---

[1] This passage and the preceding one are quoted by Lord Dalling and Bulwer.

But besides possessing an inimitable gift for caricature, Cobbett had a knack of bestowing epithets that clung to their wearers.   For instance, he exasperated Lord Erskine by insisting on his second title of Baron Clackmannan.   Among other familiar examples of his talent are 'Prosperity Robinson,' 'Œolus Canning,' 'The bloody old *Times*,' and 'The pink-nosed Liverpool.'   Nor were his powers less marked in more serious forms of controversy. Though far from a profound thinker, no one excelled him in ability to make the most of a case.   He saw at once the weak points of his opponent's position, and although he was less apt in defence than in attack, he possessed some skill in concealing the deficiencies of his own.   So powerful were his utterances, so keen his perception of the trend of public thought, that on several occasions he effected more by a single effort than others had accomplished by the labour of years.   His 'Letter to the Journeymen and Labourers' first made parliamentary reform a question in practical politics, while his indictment of the Whig party for their persecuting tactics during his last trial for libel gave a deathblow to political prosecutions in England.

But while due prominence must be given to Cobbett's pugnacity, it is not sufficient to dwell on that alone in estimating his character, or to be content with Lord Dalling and Bulwer to style him the Contentious Man. Men in whom the instinct of combat is strong are common enough, and even among Cobbett's contemporaries there were active reformers who, like Thomas Wakley, stood above him in intellect, while others, like the Hunts or Carlile, surpassed him in devotion to a desperate cause.   Cobbett's greatness was due neither to his aggressive temper nor to his love for supporting the weak side in a controversy: it lay rather in his extraordinary capacity for receiving and transmitting emotion. This faculty lay deeper than the warlike energy of his temperament, and it alone explains his greatness as a man of letters. Ability to perceive the supreme emotions which colour the great moments of life, such as the first kindling of strong affection, the realisation of success, or the pang of unexpected separation, is not uncommon. With most people, however, such moments stand by themselves, while the rest of their experience is empty of strong feeling. Cobbett, on the contrary, was one of those to whom nothing is commonplace. His life was intensely emotional, and also intensely happy. Towards its close he said, 'I suppose that no one has ever passed a happier life than I have done.' His capacity for happiness was due to the fact that for him the most ordinary occurrences were clothed with intense feeling. The commonest sights and sounds stirred him as only great crises stir the less gifted, because he was able to realise them so completely. This unusual insight saved him from the narrowness which sometimes besets even men of great intellect, whose affections are restricted to one class of phenomena and who disregard whatever they do not care to investigate. Cobbett's sympathies and antipathies were so wide that they embraced the whole of his world. He might feel either affection or detestation for any object, or he might rapidly change from one feeling to the other, but he could never feel indifference. He made the whole of life his province, and was interested by every human experience. This

catholicity extended to his art, where he was incapable
of the common error of sectarianism.   He did not show
that his Promised Land was only a province by exclud-
ing the Philistines from any part in the heritage.   Men and
women he loved or hated as he found them, but he never
considered them or their opinions unworthy of attention.

While this insight into the emotional value of every
human experience made Cobbett noteworthy, his power
of reproducing what he felt made him a great literary
artist.   He succeeded in accomplishing what Wordsworth
had attempted—in treating the most ordinary topics
from their emotional side.   His vast popularity was due
to this more than to any other cause.   His political
opinions frequently varied.   At one time he was a Tory,
at another almost a Republican, but at either period
he could in a few sentences describe a tramp in the rain,
caricature a prime minister, or picture the delights of a
supper of cold bacon in a manner never to be forgotten.
Born and bred in a rural district, and never wavering
in his preference for a farmer's life, he naturally excelled
in depicting country scenes.   Posterity has recognised
this, and out of all his writings the *Rural Rides* alone
are familiar to the public to-day.   Even at an earlier
time the more keen-sighted of his contemporaries felt
that though his political reputation might pass away,
his pictures of rustic England could hardly be forgotten.
Such a feeling animated Ebenezer Elliott, the corn-
law rhymer, when, at the time of Cobbett's death, he
wrote :

> ' Oh, bear him where the rain can fall,
>   And where the winds can blow,
> And let the sun weep o'er his pall
>   As to the grave ye go !

'And in some little lone churchyard
  Beside the growing corn,
Lay gentle nature's stern prose bard,
  Her mightiest—peasant-born.'[1]

Elliott's wish was also Cobbett's. He desired to be buried in the churchyard at Farnham, whence even at the present day may be seen the green country that he loved so much. He was laid beside his father and grandfather, opposite the great entrance to the church. When his wife died, on 19th July 1848, she was buried in the same tomb. Cobbett's funeral took place on Saturday, 27th June, during pouring rain. Among those present were his four sons, Daniel O'Connell, and Thomas Wakley, the founder of the *Lancet*. His grave was originally covered with a flat stone, which was afterwards replaced by a large altar-tomb, enclosed in iron palings. A marble memorial tablet was placed within the church by his parliamentary colleague, John Fielden. It stands in a recess in the wall on the south side of the nave.

Cobbett's will was dated 14th December 1833, and was proved in the Prerogative Court at Canterbury, when his effects were sworn to be under the value of £1500. He bequeathed the copyright of his works and all his other property to his eldest son, William Cobbett, but his affairs were so embarrassed that William became bankrupt within a few months, perhaps owing to an injudicious attempt to continue the *Political Register*. It was discovered also that the bequest of his literary property was to a great extent nullified by a sale which he had effected of the copyright of twenty-one of his

[1] *Annual Register*, 1835, ii. 346.

books to Jesse Oldfield in return for £1000. This sale
was executed on 18th May 1835, shortly before Cobbett's
death, and was unknown to his family until Oldfield
produced the agreement. The body of the deed was
in the handwriting of Benjamin Tilly, a draughtsman,
and the family unanimously declared that he had also
forged their father's signature, but on the matter being
brought before a Master in Chancery on 27th July 1835,
this theory was refuted in dramatic fashion by Tilly,
who produced the fragments of the original document.
Cobbett had actually torn it in pieces after signing the
fair copy, but Tilly had preserved them in order to
possess a specimen of a famous autograph.[1]

Cobbett was survived by his wife and by seven chil-
dren—four sons, William, John Morgan, James Paul, and
Richard Baverstock Brown, and three daughters, Anne,
Eleanor, and Susan.

The eldest son, William Cobbett, was born in 1798,
while Cobbett was at Philadelphia. He entered Lincoln's
Inn on 30th January 1824, and was subsequently called
to the bar. In his father's lifetime he assisted at various
times in conducting the *Political Register*, and in 1820
took charge of the short-lived *Cobbett's Evening Post*.
In 1824, at a time when his father was much concerned
at the frequent exaction of illegal tolls,[2] he brought out
a treatise on *The Law of Turnpikes*, which consisted of
an analytical arrangement of all the acts dealing with
the turnpike roads of England, accompanied by an
illustrative commentary. After his father's death he
continued to edit the *Political Register*, until his bank-

---

[1] For an account of the transaction, see Brit. Mus. Add. MS. 31125.
[2] See *Political Register*, passim.

ruptcy in September 1835. In January 1836 he revived the periodical, but in September it finally came to an end.

Towards the close of his life he became strongly interested in the case of Arthur Orton, the Tichborne claimant, whom he firmly believed to be Sir Roger Tichborne. After Orton's imprisonment for perjury, he exerted himself to obtain his release by means of the Habeas Corpus Act. He brought an action to recover penalties from Morrish, the governor of Millbank prison, for refusing to produce his warrant for confining Orton, and similar actions against the justices Lindley and Field for refusing writs of Habeas Corpus. He also attempted to recover damages from Lord Beaconsfield, Sir Stafford Northcote, and other ministers of state for conspiring to deceive the judge who tried his action against Morrish. In all these proceedings he was unsuccessful, and finally, while carrying yet another action to the Lords Justices of Appeal, he was suddenly taken ill and died, on 12th January 1878, in the watchman's room at the central hall of the Houses of Parliament. His litigation ruined him, and he left his wife, Blanche, destitute.[1]

The second son, John Morgan Cobbett, was born on 3rd November 1800. He entered Lincoln's Inn on 4th March 1824, was called to the Bar on 26th November 1830, and became a member of the Home Circuit. He represented Oldham, his father's constituency, as an independent member from 1852 till 1865, and again as

---

[1] See *Claim for a Writ of Habeas Corpus on Behalf of Sir R. C. D. Tichborne*, by William Cobbett, 1878, published posthumously; *Annual Register*, 1878, ii. p. 129; Boase's *Modern Biography*; *The Times*, and the *Law Times*, passim.

a Conservative from 1872 till his death, at his sister's house, 20 Brompton Crescent, South Kensington, on 13th February 1877. With his brother, James Paul, he published six volumes of *Selections from Cobbett's Political Writings* (1835), to which were added a number of explanatory notes. He married, on 8th January 1851, Mary, eldest daughter of his father's parliamentary colleague, John Fielden. He was a magistrate for Sussex, and resided, in later life, at Skeynes, near Edenbridge, in Kent. He left a widow and children.

The third son, James Paul Cobbett, was born in 1803, entered at Lincoln's Inn on 9th March 1824, was called to the Bar in the Michaelmas term of 1831, and joined the Northern Circuit. He settled in Manchester and practised until a few years before his death. His father addressed to him the series of letters which constitute *Cobbett's English Grammar*, and in 1823, at his father's request, he made a tour through Northern France with a view of ascertaining the actual state of the farmers and labourers. He published his observations in the *Political Register*, and they were afterwards reprinted in book form as *A Ride of Eight Hundred Miles in France* (London, 1824). Between October 1828 and September 1829 he made a second tour through France, Switzerland, and Italy, and published his *Journal* in 1830 after his return. While a young man he took an active part in politics, and, in 1837, contested Bury unsuccessfully in the Radical interest. Besides assisting his brother, John Morgan, to edit the Selections from the *Political Register*, he furnished the political and historical notes to the edition of the *Rural Rides* that appeared in 1853. He also published several independent works, including *The Law of Pawns and Pledges* (1841). On 17th September 1863 he was married at St. Olave's, York, to Marianne, only daughter of Robert Hudson of York, who died before him without issue. He died on 11th March 1881, at his sister's house, 20 Brompton Crescent, and was buried in Kensal Green Cemetery. Besides the works already mentioned, he published *A Grammar of the Italian Language* (1830), and translated from the French *A Sketch of the Life of General Lafayette* (1830).

The youngest son, Richard Baverstock Brown Cobbett, was born at Botley in 1814, and was articled to a London solicitor, named Faithfull. He was admitted a solicitor in the Hilary term of 1838, and settled at Manchester, where by his unaided efforts he established a large firm, known at the present day as Cobbett, Wheeler, & Cobbett, and containing a member of the family, Mr. Richard Cobbett. From 1837 to 1841 he was a member of the Chartist body, but subsequently he became dissatisfied with the leadership of Feargus O'Connor, and retired from political life. He rendered great services to the Chartists by defending members of their body belonging to the neighbourhood of Manchester, who had been prosecuted for riotous behaviour, and acquired a considerable reputation. In 1841 he was married at Weston-under-Penyard, Herefordshire, to Jane, daughter of William Palmer of Bollitree, near Ross, in the same county, who survived him. He died on 3rd June 1875, at his residence near Wilmslow in Cheshire, leaving two sons and two daughters.

None of the three daughters were married. The eldest, Anne, died at 20 Brompton Crescent, South Kensington, on 22nd October 1877. She was the author of *The*

English Housekeeper (1835), a manual of domestic management, which passed through three editions. Several letters, written by her when a young girl, to her father's assistant, John Wright, are preserved in the Additional Manuscripts, at the British Museum, among her father's correspondence with Wright.[1] The youngest daughter, Susan, who published in 1860 *Henry and Mary*, a translation of a tale by Amalie Schoppe, died on 2nd February 1889, aged eighty-one, at Fulshaw in Cheshire.

[1] In Add. MSS. 22906, 22907.

APPENDIX A

HITHERTO, 19th March 1762 has been accepted as the date of Cobbett's birth, on the authority of his son John M. Cobbett, who wrote in 1835 immediately after William Cobbett's death :

' He was seventy-three years old ; but as he never appeared to us certain of his own age, we . . . procured an extract from the Register of Farnham Parish, in which it appears that the four sons of my grandfather, George, Thomas, *William*, and Anthony, were christened on the 1st of April 1763, and as Anthony was the younger son and William was the third, we infer that he was born one year before he was christened, that is, on the 9th of March 1762. He might therefore have been older, but not much.' [1]

In accordance with this statement, the date, 9th March 1762 has been engraved upon his tomb at Farnham, and has been adopted by former biographers. But an examination of the Farnham Parish Register shows that the statement is inaccurate. Under the date 1st April 1763, the baptism of William, son of George Cobbett, is alone recorded. Under 27th April 1764 occurs the entry of the baptism of two brothers, Thomas, aged two years, and Anthony. The baptism of the eldest son George is not recorded at all.

Now, while the discovery that John M. Cobbett was misinformed in regard to the entries in the Register does away with the only reason for fixing the date in 1762, the actual record of baptisms makes 1763 much more probable. It is certain that William Cobbett was the third son, and there is no ground for questioning his repeated statement that he was born on 9th March. As Thomas was two years old on 27th April 1764, and as he was older than

[1] *Political Register*, 26th June 1835.

William, it is almost certain that William was born on 9th March 1763. If he was born on 9th March 1762, Thomas must have been very nearly three years old at least, when he was baptized. The date 9th March 1762 also would leave only twenty-nine months between the marriage of Cobbett's parents and the birth of their third child, and although this space of time is not impossibly short, a period of forty-one months seems more likely. Finally William himself has stated that he was born in 1766. Although this date is rendered impossible by the testimony of the Register, yet every additional year of difference between his supposed and his actual age makes his mistake more difficult to understand.

APPENDIX B

COBBETT'S PORTRAITS

At least five authentic portraits of Cobbett are in existence. 1. The earliest is a coloured crayon drawing of the bust, full face, by J. R. Smith, executed in 1800. It was engraved by Francesco Bartolozzi. 2. A coloured crayon, by J. R. Smith, full-length, representing Cobbett seated in an arm-chair. This was taken in 1812 while he was in Newgate, and was engraved by William Ward.[1] 3. A print from a water-colour drawing by Adam Buck, taken about 1816, coloured probably by the original artist. 4. A drawing taken on Board the *Importer* on her departure from Liverpool on 27th March 1817. It was drawn and engraved by Edward Smith. 5. An oil-painting, half-length, of William Cobbett, about the age of sixty. The first portrait, taken by J. R. Smith, and also the third and fifth portraits are in the possession of Mr. Cobbett of Woodlands, Wilmslow, Cheshire, a grandson of William Cobbett, while Smith's later protrait is in the possession of another grandson, Mr. J. F. Cobbett of Saddington Manor, Market Harborough.

Much more familiar to the public than any portrait is the figure

---

[1] For a fuller description of these two, see Chaloner Smith's *British Mezzotinto Portraits*, p. 1463.

of William Cobbett at Madame Tussaud's, representing an old gentleman wearing large round spectacles, seated on a bench with a black beaver hat tilted back on his head. He is frequently mistaken for a visitor. The authorities, however, have strangely neglected to clothe him in a *red* waistcoat—Cobbett's most characteristic garment.

Caricatures of Cobbett were of course very numerous. The series on his early life by James Gillray is particularly celebrated, while at a later period he was a favourite character of H. B. (John Doyle), who produced several likenesses of him, more characteristic and memorable, than some of the more serious portraits.

APPENDIX C

SOURCES FOR COBBETT'S BIOGRAPHY

I. The two important biographies of Cobbett in existence have already been referred to in the Preface. They are : *The Memoirs of the Late William Cobbett*, by Robert Huish, 1836, 2 vols. ; and *William Cobbett: a Biography*, by Edward Smith, 1878, 2 vols. Among smaller biographies are an anonymous *Life of William Cobbett*, 1835 ; the article on William Cobbett, by Edward Smith, in the *Dictionary of National Biography*, xi. 142-145 ; Chambers's *Repository of Instructive and Amusing Tracts*, vol. ix. ; C. B. Seymour's *Self Made Men*, New York, 1858 ; Lord Dalling and Bulwer's *Historical Characters*, 1868, vol. ii. ; J. S. Watson's *Biographies of John Wilkes and William Cobbett*, 1870 ; Robert Waters's *Life and Language of William Cobbett*, New York, 1883 ; Preface to *Rural Rides*, ed. 1885, by Pitt Cobbett ; *Chambers's Cyclopedia of English Literature*, 1902, ii. 681-5. Among obituary notices at the time of Cobbett's death may be mentioned those in the *Gentleman's Magazine* ; the *Annual Register* ; *The Times*, 20th June 1835 ; the *Athenæum*, 27th June 1835 ; Tait's *Edinburgh Magazine*, 1835, pp. 493-496 ; and the *Westminster Review*, October 1835.

II. Cobbett's autobiographical contributions are scattered through all parts of his writings. Among the most fruitful sources are :

U

The Life of Peter Porcupine, Advice to Young Men, and of course the *Political Register.* Cobbett's autograph letters to Wright, and other papers chiefly relating to that person, are preserved in the British Museum in Add. MSS. 22906, 22907, 31125, 31126, 31127. Other manuscripts in his handwriting, chiefly letters, are preserved in Add. MSS. 18204 f. 73 ; 22169 ; 22976 f. 212 ; 27937 ff. 51, 117 ; 28104 f. 71 ; 33964 f. 243 ; 34079 f. 90 ; 34455 ff. 393-414; 35149 f. 114.

III. Among works containing references to Cobbett are: *Public Characters,* 1823 ; William Rowley's *Treatise of Putrid, Malignant, Infectious Fevers,* 1804 ; James Grant's *Random Recollections of the House of Commons,* 1836, pp. 184-193 ; Heinrich Heine, *Sämmtliche Werke,* Hamburg, 1861, iii. 77-93 ; Miss Mitford's *Recollections of a Literary Life,* 1852 ; H. C. Lodge's *Studies in History,* Boston, 1884 ; Henry White's *Calm Appeal to the Friends of Freedom,* 1823 ; *The Book of Wonders,* 1821 ; *Report of the Action Wright v. Clement,* 1819 ; *Correspondence between Mr. Cobbett, Mr. Tipper, and Sir Francis Burdett,* 1819 ; *Thomas Dolby's Letter to Friends of Liberty,* 1819 ; *A Defence of Mr. Cobbett,* undated ; *Thomas Cleary's Letter to Major Cartwright,* 1819 ; *Strictures on Cobbett's Unmanly Observations,* 1806 ; *Henry Hunt's Correspondence,* 1820 ; *The Political Death of William Cobbett,* Edinburgh, 1820 ; *Sketches of the Life of Billy Cobb and the Death of Tommy Paine,* undated ; Richard Brash's *General Account of Cobbett's Conspiracy against the Public Confidence,* 1826 ; G. Buckler's *Examination of the Attacks upon Mr. Cobbett,* 1812 ; M. Carey's *Plumb Pudding for Peter Porcupine,* 1799 ; *The Rival Impostors,* by M. G., 1809 ;[1] Howell's *State Trials,* index ; *Edinburgh Review,* July 1807, April 1879 ; *Quarterly Review,* October 1816, January 1819 ; the *Examiner,* 1808-1820, passim ; H. R. Yorke's *Political Review,* 1805-1811, passim ; the *Annual Register,* 1800-1836, passim ; *The Times,* passim (indexed from 1811) ; the *Monthly Magazine,* passim; *Blackwood's Magazine* (indexed); the *Place Papers* in Add. MSS. 27789-27859 (partially indexed) ; the *Anti-Jacobin,* 15th January 1798 ; Jonathan Wooler's *Black Dwarf,* 1817-1824,

---

[1] A large number of controversial pamphlets are enumerated in the Catalogue of the British Museum Library, *s.v.* Cobbett, William.

passim ; H. T. Fearon's *Sketches of America*, 1819, p. 64 ; Christopher North's *Noctes Ambrosianæ*, No. 63 ; Miss Cartwright's *Life and Correspondence of Major Cartwright*, 1826 ;[1] *Samuel Parr's Works*, 1828, viii. 21 ; Robert Huish's *Life of Hunt*, 1836, passim ; Hansard's *Parliamentary Debates*, 1833-1835 ; *Speeches of Lord Brougham*, 1838, i. 4-6; *Memoirs of Sir Samuel Romilly*, 1840, ii. 211, iii. 28; *Bentham's Works*, ed. Bowring, Edinburgh, 1843; *Recollections of John O'Connell*, 1846, pp. 2, 5, 32-34, 39 ; *Life of William Wilberforce*, 1838 ; George Borrow's *Lavengro*, 1851, ch. lxxxviii.; T. Moore's *Memoirs*, 1853-1856 ; Alexander Somerville's *Whistler at the Plough*, 1852 ; H. B. Stanton's *Reform and Reformers*, 1853 ; *Speeches of Sir Robert Peel*, 1853, ii. 694-704 ; J. W. Francis' *Old New York*, 1858, p. 141 ; Samuel Bamford's *Passages in the Life of a Radical*, Manchester, 1859, pp. 6-7 ; *Journal and Correspondence of Lord Auckland*, 1862 ; *Diary of Lord Colchester*, 1861 ; *Miss Berry's Journal and Correspondence*, 1865, ii. 326; *William Windham's Diary*, 1866 ; C. D. Yonge's *Life and Administration of Lord Liverpool*, 1868, ii. 298-299; *Lord Brougham's Life and Times*, 1871, i. 437, 501, iii. 265-267 ; Augustus De Morgan's *Budget of Paradoxes*, 1872, pp. 119-22 ; Frederic Hudson's *Journalism in the United States*, New York, 1873 ; *Lord Minto's Life and Letters*, 1874, iii. 341, 347 ; *Life of Albany Fonblanque*, 1874, p. 63 ; Le Marchant's *Memoirs of Lord Althorp*, 1876, p. 328 ; *William Lovett's Autobiography*, 1876, p. 55 ; W. N. Molesworth's *History of England*, 1874, i. 138-142 ; *Recollections of Samuel Breck*, Philadelphia, 1877 ; *Journal of Thomas Raikes*, 1856, vols. i., ii. ; Miss Martineau's *History of England during the Thirty Years' Peace*, ed. Bohn, 1877-1878 ; Torrens's *Memoirs of Lord Melbourne*, 1878, i. 147 ; Spencer Walpole's *History of England*, 1878-1880 ; Hutton's *Bland Burges Papers*, 1885, p. 314 ; H. R. Fox Bourne's *English Newspapers*, 1887 ; *Greville Memoirs*, 1888 ; Clegg's *Annals of Bolton*, 1888, p. 74 ; C. S. Parker's *Life of Peel*, 1891-1899, i. 356, 407, ii. 213 ; Wemyss Reid's *Life and Letters of Lord Houghton*, 1891, i. 94, 101 ; M. D. Conway's *Life of Paine*, 1892 ; Atlay's *Trial of Lord Cochrane*, 1897 ; Stanley's *Life of Thomas Arnold*, 1898, i. 67, 68, 350 ; *Carlyle's Reminiscences*, ed. Froude ;

---

[1] In this and other cases no exact reference is given, because the work has an adequate index.

Graham Wallas's *Life of Place*, 1898 ; *Hampshire Notes and Queries*, 1898, ix. 79-82 ; Mackail's *Life of W. Morris*, 1899, i. 220 ; *Dictionary of National Biography*, article 'John Wright' (1770?—1844), lxiii. 111-112 ; Home's *Farnham and its Surroundings*, 1900 ; *Macmillan's Magazine*, May 1898, 'A Visit to Cobbett's Grave'; *Journal of the Royal Agricultural Society*, 1902, pp. 1-26; *Creevy Papers*, ed. Sir Herbert Maxwell, 1903 ; Morley's *Life of Gladstone*, 1903, i. 114 ; 'Through Cobbett's Country,' by W. H. Hudson, in the *Saturday Review*, 28th December 1901 ; *Notes and Queries*.

IV. Among literary estimates of Cobbett's life and writings may be mentioned : William Hazlitt's *Conversations of James Northcote*, 1830 ; Hazlitt's *Table Talk*, 1st series, essay vi. ; D. G. Mitchell's *Wet Days at Edgewood*, New York, 1884 ; J. E. Thorold Rogers's *Historical Gleanings*, 1869, series i. ; W. B. Reed's *Among My Books*, New York, 1871 ; George Gilfillan's *Galleries of Literary Portraits*, 1857, vol. ii. ; William Forsyth's *Essays Critical and Narrative*, 1874 ; 'Cobbett's Comedy,' by G. A. Sala in *Belgravia*, February 1875 ; *Cornhill Magazine*, April 1879 ; Mrs. Oliphant's *Literary History of England*, 1882, vol. ii. ; H. E. Egerton on 'Rural Rides' in the *National Review*, May 1885 ; George Dawson's *Biographical Lectures*, 1886 ; 'William Cobbett,' by C. Milnes Gaskell in the *Nineteenth Century*, March 1886 ; William Stebbing's *Verdicts of History Reviewed*, 1887 ; Mabel E. Wotton's *Word Portraits*, 1887 ; *Macmillan's Magazine*, December 1891, 'William Cobbett,' by George Saintsbury, reprinted in Saintsbury's *Essays in English Literature*, 2nd series, 1895 ; *Temple Bar*, October 1891 ; Sir James F. Stephen's *Horae Sabbaticae*, 3rd series, 1892 ; *New Review*, 1893, 'William Cobbett,' by Sir Leslie Stephen ; W. Clark Russell's *Book of Authors*, 1871 ; C. R. B. Kent's *English Radicals*, 1899 ; Sir Leslie Stephen's *English Utilitarians*, 1900, ii. 124-136, and passim ; Herford's *Age of Wordsworth*, 1903, pp. 8-10.

A collection of Cobbett's writings and of editions of his works is being formed at Oldham, his former constituency.

INDEX

[Cobbett's publications are indexed under their titles]

309

Printed by T. and A. Constable, Printers to His Majesty
at the Edinburgh University Press

15